THE
MAIN SOURCE

PEOPLE AND COMMUNICATION

Series Editor: **F. GERALD KLINE** *University of Minnesota*

Volumes in this series:

THE
MAIN SOURCE

Learning from Television News

John P. Robinson
Mark R. Levy

with
Dennis K. Davis
in association with

W. Gill Woodall   **Michael Gurevitch**   **Haluk Sahin**

SAGE PUBLICATIONS
The Publishers of Professional Social Science
Beverly Hills   London   New Delhi

Copyright © 1986 by Sage Publications, Inc.

XE641

For information address:

SAGE Publications, Inc.
275 South Beverly Drive
Beverly Hills, California 90212

SAGE Publications India Pvt. Ltd.
M-32 Market
Greater Kailash I
New Delhi 110 048 India

SAGE Publications Ltd
28 Banner Street
London EC1Y 8QE
England

Printed in the United States of America

Library of Congress Cataloging-in-Publication Data

Main entry under title:

Robinson, John P.
    The main source.

    (People and communication ; v. 17)
    Bibliography: p.
    Includes index.
    1. Television broadcasting of news. I. Levy, Mark R.
II. Title. III. Series.
PN4784.T4R6 1986   070.1'9   85-22195
ISBN 0-8039-2569-7
ISBN 0-8039-2570-0 (pbk.)

FIRST PRINTING

Contents

Preface

This book is about a myth, one of the most pervasive of our myth-dominated age. It is a conventional wisdom so plausible that our most sophisticated media and political institutions take it for granted and plan their actions accordingly. Although this mythical belief is a by-product of an electronic age, its problematics and implications are rooted in centuries-old concerns about the flow of social and political information.

The myth is accepted because it provides a convenient answer to a fundamental question about life in a postindustrial era: In these times of information richness and information overload, how do people learn about the world "out there"? The quick answer, of course, is from the mass media; the mythic answer—from television news.

On the face of it, the logic behind the myth is inescapable. Each of us lives in a narrow circle of family and friends. Each of these "islands," however, is linked to the larger human experience by invisible bonds of mass communication. So, when pollsters ask us, "where do you usually get most of your news about what's going on in the world today?" the answer is immediate. Our thoughts naturally turn to the omnipresent news media that so assiduously act as messengers of the dramatic, the historic, and the nonroutine.

It is not, however, the news media in general that the public considers its main window on the world, but the specific medium of television. Pollsters have been asking us about our main information source for over a quarter of a century. As Burns W. Roper summarized his most recent results:

> Trend questions show that television continues to be regarded by the public as its *main source* of news, and by the widest margin ever. Television continues to be the *number one source* of information on Presidential elections, Congressional elections, and statewide elections, and rivals newspapers as a source of information on local elections [Roper Organization, 1985: 1; emphasis added].

So there it is, with all the cool, pristine certainty of a poll result: Television is the public's "main source" of news. TV has been described that way by the public for more than 20 years, and television's lead over other mass media continues to grow as the public becomes increasingly composed of citizens raised on television. Even the newspaper industry's poll data confirm Roper's TV-sponsored findings (Editor & Publisher, 1983).

There is, however, considerable cause for skepticism over this certainty about the public's main news source. Almost from the beginning, communication scholars have questioned the methodological soundness of the main source question (Carter and Greenberg, 1965; Stone, 1969-1970; Clarke and Ruggels, 1970; Robinson, 1971; Stevenson and White, 1980). Collectively, these researchers have argued that the basic main source question is improperly asked, inappropriate to the subject matter, unable to be answered accurately, and, at best, worded ambiguously. Moreover, several studies have shown it simply does not hold true for local news (Lemert, 1970; Stempel, 1973; Levy, 1978a; Adams, 1981).

Methodological fine points aside, we believe that survey questions in the main source tradition present respondents with a most formidable reporting task: To ask "where do you get most of your news" is to ask about people's self-perceptions of their information sources, that is, where they *think* they find out the news. Such human perceptions, of course, can be notoriously misleading and distorted, particularly when respondents are asked implicitly to sort through all the news to which they have been exposed, to identify the various information sources of all that news, and then to weigh these news stories and information sources to arrive at an unequivocal "Number 1" answer. As the information-processing theory described in Chapter 6 suggests, the question presumes mental gymnastics of a very high order.

Moreover, even if such self-reports about perceived information sources were reasonably accurate, they still would not address more important questions: How much news information is actually acquired? How well is that information understood? How does it affect our subsequent behavior and decisions? In short, by depending on the shortcut device of a single poll question, the main source myth has significantly hindered our ability to understand the complex ways in which the mass media diffuse public awareness and understanding of news events. It has led the public, the media, and elites alike down a blind alley of easy, but fundamentally erroneous, understanding.

In the pages that follow, we present some new and old research into how, what, and where the public learns about the news. Our study is not intended to denigrate television's potential as a news medium, but to question the mythology surrounding its influence on audiences. We have worked with too many talented and dedicated broadcasters to dismiss their efforts with glib disdain. Indeed, even if, as we shall demonstrate, television news is not the public's main source for understanding the news, that does not mean that television could not be the main source, particularly if the medium saw that as an important mission.

This book represents a collective effort over a number of years and in a number of locations. Many hands and minds have contributed to the continually updated and improved chapters of this project, so we must ask forgiveness if the product is not completely tidy or univocal. Consider it rather an evolving state-of-the-art assessment of what we know, and do not know, about public learning from the news media.

Chapters 1, 4, 9, and 10 were written by Robinson and Levy. Chapter 2 was written by Davis and Chapter 3 by Robinson. Chapters 5 and 8 were written by Robinson and Davis, Chapter 6 by Woodall, and Chapter 7 by Gurevitch and Levy. Levy also served as the final overall editor of the book. We are indebted to Haluk Sahin for his many contributions to the operational phases of this research; his understanding, guidance, and journalistic talents were sorely missed when it came time to prepare our manuscript.

We would like to thank the John and Mary Markle Foundation for its support of the 1973 and 1983 surveys reported here. Additional thanks are due to the British Broadcasting Corporation, which had the foresight to support our initial research in this area, and in particular to Brian Emmett, Kenneth Lamb, and Tony Crabb; this research would not have been possible without their early support and encouragement. Peter Meneer also helped. We are also indebted to the many working journalists, both in the United States and Great Britain, who graciously served on our several media advisory panels; to Barrie Gunter of the I.B.A.; and to the hardworking staff of the University of Maryland's Survey Research Center, particularly Marcia Karth, Lisa Alexanderwicz, Sue Dowden, Cynthia Kahn, Tim Triplett, and Jeff Holland. We also benefited greatly from D. Charles Whitney's critique of an early manuscript. Special thanks are also due to Lisa Freeman-Miller.

College Park, Maryland   J.P.R.
                                                           M.R.L.

I Introduction

Chapter 1

INFORMATION FLOW IN SOCIETY

JOHN P. ROBINSON
MARK R. LEVY

I'm afraid that the public is getting brainwashed into a belief that they're getting all that they need to know from television. And this is not so. They need to know a great deal more than we can communicate to them. Somehow or other, we have to teach the American people to seek more information, to be a little more discriminating perhaps. And when they do, they'll get even better news programs on television [Walter Cronkite, quoted in *Time*, 1965].

Cronkite, the most trusted man in America and exemplar of journalistic integrity, was right. But the fears of our country's Dutch Uncle caused little stir 20 years ago—or since. It was a theme Cronkite was to repeat often over the years, though rarely from his anchor desk on the *CBS Evening News*. As broadcast journalism grew in power, and the wider world on which it reported underwent fundamental changes, Cronkite's insight became increasingly apposite: The information needs of a democratic society are poorly served when its citizens rely (or think they rely) so heavily on TV for news and information.

Indeed, every weekday well over 100 million Americans tune in to a network or local television news broadcast, and millions more obtain news information secondhand from those who view those newscasts. The emergence of television as a prominent provider of information has fundamentally altered the organization and flow of public information in modern society.

When television was introduced, some observers felt that the medium might make literacy largely unnecessary. The apparent ease with which important events could be depicted by adding compelling pictures to the already familiar radio format suggested that television might soon render print media obsolete. The television medium, moreover, was thought capable of effectively communicating news images and information to the large "functionally illiterate" segments of society (Barber, 1979).

By some measure, television has realized part of this potential. In survey after survey, Americans report television to be their most important source of information about what is going on in the world (Roper, 1985). It is a trend that has continued over the last two decades and has been found in other Western countries when people are asked to report on their main news source (e.g., Tunstall, 1983).

The reasons for television's perceived predominance as a news information source are not difficult to identify. First, there is simply a great deal of news on American television. Each of the networks has dramatically expanded its regular news programming, and in some major TV markets, three or more hours of local newscasts are not uncommon. Indeed, news stories now intrude on the viewer (regardless of whether or not he or she wants to see the news) in the form of "special" reports or in capsule "updates" sandwiched between entertainment programs. TV news "gatekeepers" take great pains to provide "visuals" to add audience appeal to their stories. They continually seek to maximize television's capacity to bring news to the viewer instantaneously and to make viewers feel they are part of the event itself. Indeed, television's visual qualities do make the news lively and entertaining. TV simultaneously engages both the eye and the ear, the same sense modalities that most people use to learn naturally from their own environment and experiences. Second, broadcast organizations routinely employ news researchers and consultants to keep news producers up-to-date on what audiences like and do not like about the news. But as Nordenstreng (1972: 391) has observed,

> Large audiences and interest or confidence in the news thus do not necessarily testify to successful news activity. The final criterion must be comprehension, i.e., the question whether news programs enable the audience to form a truthful picture of the events described.

Only recently, however, has research begun to document the cognitive impact of this news content on audiences and to provide insights into its shortcomings as an information medium. Those shortcomings and their consequences for society are major concerns of this book.

QUESTIONS ADDRESSED

We are interested in the flow of news in society. Our emphasis will be on television news because TV is so widely presumed to be the main source from which most people in America and other Western countries receive their news. Unlike other studies of the news audience, however, our work attempts to measure the actual news information the public receives, and to do so we use a number of innovative survey research techniques. Our studies and the others we examine cover a 20-year period and a variety of news content areas, research designs, types of audiences, information settings, time frames, and cultural conditions.

Results from our research lead us to challenge the central proposition that the public receives most of its information from television. It also leads us to challenge conclusions from another body of empirical research studies, one that suggests the public learns virtually nothing from the TV news it views. Although we see our research as a useful corrective of both myths, it also raises other important questions about the news. What is it about television news that makes it less effective, and what steps might be taken to increase its effectiveness? How can television news professionals be convinced to take news comprehension seriously?

There are also larger and more fundamental issues about the news audience, not just for television but for all news media. Encouragingly, we find that the public absorbs much more news information than many earlier studies of news comprehension have suggested. Like the journalists who have examined our data, we find that certain news stories are understood remarkably well by the public, indicating that the public is neither as hopelessly ill-informed nor as incapable of learning as many believe. But it is also clear that other important news is ignored or barely sinks into public consciousness. Some of the difficulty in comprehension undoubtedly lies in the nature of these news stories, especially if highly technical or abstract concepts are involved or if complex levels of reasoning are demanded. Some of the problem also inheres in the public's mental inertia, limited interest in, and lack of concern with, political issues and events that seem too remote to affect them personally. But some of the blame must be shared by the way news media tell the news story, particularly when so few news stories take into account the public's limited skills and interests in processing news content.

True, much journalistic practice is already predicated on these audience limitations. Stories and words are often pitched at an elementary level. Sentences are kept short and to the point. Visuals and graphic materials are increasingly used as aids to understanding. These are all generally effective ways of ensuring that news information will reach the people for whom it is presumably prepared. But these packaging devices did not develop as a result of a systematic study of how actual audiences process and comprehend specific news stories. Current news practices have been informed only indirectly by the limited and unique frames of reference that audience members bring to each news story. That is the kind of audience feedback we have tried to introduce into the discussions about the effectiveness of today's (and tomorrow's) journalism.

Broadcast journalism has perennially come under attack from many quarters. Conservative critics continually accuse the news media of an anti-establishment bias, of creating disrespect for, and lack of confidence in, the traditional institutions in society. Marxist and radical scholars, on the other hand, accuse the news media of protecting the status quo. Populist writers choose to criticize the news media for paying too much attention to elites and national issues at the expense of more local and practical matters that directly affect the quality of people's daily lives.

Independent of political content, intellectuals generally criticize the news media for focusing on superficial and trivial stories and of failing to enlighten audiences about truly important developments in society. In this view, the news media's emphasis on facts and information may divert the public from more useful and worthwhile forms of mental work—from knowledge, from insight, from contemplation, or from dialectic. The following passage from Shawcross (1984) provides a recent, cogent summary of this view:

> The flood of information in the world today . . . sometimes seems not to further, but to retard, education; not to excite but to dampen curiosity; not to enlighten, but merely to dismay. . . . Our sense of impotence seems to grow in direct proportion to the spread of our knowledge.

Our grounds for evaluating the performance of the news media are quite different from those of most of its critics. In this book, we generally refrain from criticizing the news media for the types of stories they decide to carry, the conclusions they reach in those stories, or the angle from which they report news. Instead, we ask how well the news media are communicating what they apparently wish to communicate. Do current journalistic practices *work* in terms of reaching the audiences with the messages and information that journalists claim they want to convey? We explicitly suspend judgment, then, about editorial decisions concerning which stories to cover and how to cover them in an unbiased way. We take these decisions as a given, believing they are based on well-intentioned, traditional journalistic norms of newsworthiness, professional judgments of what the public needs or ought to know. In essence then, we are asking how well the news media are doing in terms of what appears to be *their craft's own information goals.*

THE LIMITATIONS OF TELEVISION

Early studies of television news indicated that its effectiveness was very limited. Researchers found that news viewers could recall only one or two of the fifteen to twenty stories then broadcast each night on television (Neuman, 1976; Katz et al., 1977; Gantz, 1978). In the first of these studies, for example, about half of the viewers in San Francisco who watched a network evening news program could not recall a single story that had been shown; the rest of the sample could recall only about two stories (Neuman, 1976).[1] These findings were largely replicated in other survey settings (Robinson and Sahin, 1984) and raised questions about whether anyone "out there" was being reached by television information, or was capable of being reached. They also influenced our research; we first undertook a series of focus-group studies (see Appendix B) to observe firsthand whether or not news audience members were capable of following the news that was being broadcast, and what difficulties audience members had in processing the news. These observational studies proved invaluable in reassuring us that there was a news audience that could be reached.

Our focus-group study results also dovetailed nicely with the information-processing perspective we often take in this book, a perspective that helps to explain why viewers learn less than they might from the newscasts they view. Both highlight the important limitations of television as a news transmitter. Television news stories, for example, are transitory; they cannot be reread. Learning of content must occur quickly. Complex combinations of powerful visual and auditory stimuli must be rapidly decoded. Typical news broadcasts force up to 20 news stories into barely 22 minutes of air time and do so using far fewer words than on the front page of a serious newspaper. Accurate comprehension of such fast-changing, diverse information requires cognitive processing skills of a high order—higher than some audience members may possess. Thus, for many viewers, watching the news may produce an experience of having been informed. But it is a false sense of knowledge, for it is based only on a vaguely understood jumble of visual and auditory stimuli that leave few traces in long-term memory. Indeed, some have charged that the fragmented way television covers the news creates a bias against understanding by disregarding the larger meaning or significance of the stories covered (Birt and Jay, 1975). Thus, television's capacity for presenting the whole picture in a 30-second or 90-second news story is obviously quite limited.

But there are other behavioral reasons to doubt television's predominance as a news medium. One concerns comparative levels of exposure to the news media. First, the three-network ratings for the "flagship" network news programs (i.e., Rather, Brokaw, Jennings) has remained steady, or even declined slightly, at about 40% of television households. Second, in our most recent study of how Americans spend time (Robinson, 1978), the proportion of a national urban sample reading a newspaper on a typical day was 67%, whereas the proportion reached by *any* television newscast (local as well as national) was 52%, or 15 percentage points lower.[2] And about a quarter of these news viewers had seen only a *local* newscast, so that the proportion watching a national newscast was still considerably lower. Moreover, the estimated amounts of time spent viewing newscasts was also (slightly) lower than the time spent reading the newspaper.

Rates of exposure aside, television has other inherent limitations in conveying information, including the following:

(1) the lower number of words and ideas per news story in a newscast in comparison to a front-page article that appears in a quality newspaper;
(2) the considerable amount of distraction and fragmented attention that occurs during watching the newscast compared to reading;
(3) the lack of repetition of information in the television newscast;
(4) the inability of viewers to "turn back," or review, information they do not understand or that they need to know to understand subsequent information;
(5) the clearer delineation of story content in print, with headlines, columns, side-bars, and the like; and
(6) television's limited time in which to tell and develop an entire story, and to develop empathy and human interest in the news.

Such limitations of television news have been obvious to many broadcast news executives. As Charles Curran, former director-general of the BBC, succinctly put it: "It is the nature of pictures to reflect action. It is very difficult for them to reflect thought or policy" (cited in Patterson and McClure, 1976: 55).

THE INFORMATION EXPLOSION

There is, of course, considerable evidence about the "information explosion" taking place in American society. Most important, larger numbers and higher proportions of the American adult population have a college education or have completed high school. And, as Hyman, Wright, and Reed (1975) have documented in their two-decade analysis of survey data, education is the major predictor of being informed on almost any topic.

In addition to this primary demographic expectation of a more informed population, there are also

- the high TV ratings for news magazine programs, such as *60 Minutes* and *20/20*—programs that were not on the air 20 years ago;
- the longer newscasts, cable news channels, all-news broadcast stations, and increased news updates during the evening that should also reach a broader audience with news content;
- the resurgence of national newspapers, such as *USA Today* and the *Wall Street Journal*, which reach new and larger audiences across the country; and
- the emergence or return of national, general-audience news magazines such as *People* and *Life*.

More generally, we have now entered the age of the computer, with its increasingly sophisticated technological capacity for storing and transmitting information on video disks, with laser technology, and in computer networks.

In contrast, however, there is also evidence of stagnant or declining information flow in the public. There is, first, the recent downturn in the proportion of high school students going on to college, or from there on to graduate school. Of more interest was a decline in SAT scores during the 1970s and 1980s that indicated that this generation of college-bound high school students was less intellectually capable than previous generations. Television has been widely cited as one cause of this decline, and this argument is bolstered by the lower achievement and information scores of children who are heavier viewers (Robinson, 1972a, 1972b; Hoffer and Wolf, 1985); the National Center for Educational Statistics has produced charts showing how, at each level of homework assigned, student achievement in mathematics decreases systematically as increased time is spent watching television.

Moreover, there is little evidence that even with the increase in college graduates, the American public is now better able to identify, for example, their representatives in Congress or public figures in general (Kinder and Sears, 1985). Patterson (1980) notes that 37% of 1948 voters were aware of candidates' positions, compared to only 30% in his 1976 election study. In our own national research we have found that the proportion of the population aware of the existence of "two Chinas" is no higher in the mid-1980s than it was two decades earlier.

Further fuel for pessimism comes from discouraging developments in the news media: the demise of big dailies over the last two decades, the stagnant or possibly declining size of the audience for evening network newscasts, and the decreasing number of television news documentaries.

There is additional concern that the media themselves are watering down their news product. Some newspeople have argued that news information is becoming fragmented into isolated and uncoordinated bits of knowledge and that the news media are increasingly in the process of providing "info-tainment," news stories that appear in the guise of regular hard news but in fact are designed more for entertainment value than for the development of a more informed or alert citizenry (Kaiser, 1984). It is a charge made not only about TV news but about newspapers, such as *USA Today* and other print news products that try to emulate its formulaic success.

METHODS OF UNDERSTANDING AUDIENCE RESPONSE

We see considerable merit in all these concerns. Indeed, our research was stimulated by them and by a host of apparent dilemmas. Are Americans, for example, as ill-informed or ill-equipped to pass judgment on the news events and issues the media present as most survey results on public information levels suggest, or is the wisdom of the people sufficient and sensitive enough to keep the political system honest and responsible? If the public remains basically uninformed even about news stories that are presented, what should the media do? Does the public want better news? Does it deserve better news?

On the other hand, we also see how traditional news coverage that has ignored the audience may have precipitated many of these developments. In our firsthand observations of the workings of news organizations, we find an unfortunate lack of concern for, and at times outright disdain for, the mass news audience. Too many news editors treat evidence of the limited information-processing skills of the audience as simply the reflection of the public's lack of concern or incompetence or of the hopelessness of the journalist's mission.

But even newspeople who care about their audiences can find little direct feedback about how the audience is responding to their news stories or news products. Although we have developed in this book one promising mechanism for providing audience feedback, we have often found that audience studies are greeted with less than total enthusiasm in the newsroom. That is in large part because the major target or "reference group" for the stories that most reporters and editors write is usually not readers and viewers, or even the elites about whom they write. It is other journalists and reporters who most carefully scrutinize and evaluate newswork by the standards of "good journalism."

To be sure, newspaper and magazine sales, TV ratings, and market research studies do provide immediate data on the relative size of the audiences or potential profit margin. But they say very little about how news content affects the audience. Has news coverage made the public better informed or more knowledgeable? Are audiences better prepared to cope with life's realities and uncertainties? Will they make better voting decisions or plan their lives more wisely as a result of news exposure?

Although we have very limited answers to these questions, we believe we have made significant progress in developing "micro-behavioral" measures that can address them. These measures were designed as part of[3] "naturalistic" surveys that tap into the flow of information to the American public. The good news from this important methodological development is that the public is far better informed about the news than most previous studies of public information have suggested. Moreover, this research provides direct evidence of how, in their daily activities, the public deals with the news as defined and created by journalists. The bad news is that public information levels are far lower than most news workers may assume as they prepare their stories. But here we think our research suggests some important ways to overcome this problem.

OUTLINE OF THIS BOOK

In this book we have sought to provide a body of new empirical data to address a basic question for communications policymakers: How should a pluralistic, large-scale society use its communications media to serve its citizens better? Of course, we do not provide a detailed master plan of answers to this question. However, we do feel our studies provide a significant starting point for a more informed dialogue. In general, industry research on television news has shown less interest in whether audience members can remember and understand stories than in identifying factors that increase enjoyment or attractiveness of programs. Because such factors are seen as directly linked to ratings, such research has often focused, for example, on the attributes of anchor persons rather than on substantive or presentational forms. Particularly at the local level, news anchors are increasingly chosen for their ability to attract or retain an audience, and not for their reporting skills or insights.

Further, academic research into public comprehension of television news remains quite primitive by social science standards. An outline of previous news comprehension research in this and other countries is shown in Table 1.1. It can be seen that interest in comprehension research has grown in the last few years in a variety of research settings. Table 1.1 identifies some prominent researchers in each country, the dates of their most important publications, their research approaches and questions, and some general conclusions from the research. Some of the best research to which we refer has been done abroad in nations such as Sweden, Finland, and Great Britain. European interest in television news research stems, in part, from the fact that most newscasts are produced by public corporations that are specifically charged with the responsibility of informing their viewers. Indeed, the most advanced statement we have found of the proper role of the news media comes from the statement of Program Activity Regulation of Finnish Broadcasting Company, as described by Nordenstreng (1972: 397):

> The Broadcasting Company should not aim at implanting some particular world view in its audience, but rather at making available the building blocks necessary in the construction of a personal world view. An important part of the Broadcasting Company's activity is the transmission of news and coverage of both cultural and social events.

In Europe, research is being done constantly to ascertain whether this responsibility is being fulfilled, and if it is not, how newscasts might be improved.

The collected chapters in this book are intended to serve as a state-of-the-art guide for future research by highlighting the advantages and limitations of different research perspectives. As is evidenced in the diverse content and questions raised in Table 1.1, and throughout the chapters in this book, news researchers face several cross-disciplinary problems in studying news recall and comprehension. Even the

TABLE 1.1 Selected Examples of News Comprehension Research in Various Countries

Country	Researchers	Approach	Sample Conclusions
England	Trenaman (1967)	Experimental	• Text more important than visuals for comprehension of news content • Concrete information easier to follow than abstract, especially for working-class viewers
	Gunter (1980a, 1980b, 1983)	Experimental	• Confusion in comprehending similar news stories • Time-of-day effects in comprehension
	Robinson and Sahin (1984)	Survey/observational	• Sources of distraction in news viewing • Problems with "meltdown" across similar stories • Prior information more important than education in predicting comprehension
Israel	Katz et al. (1977)	Experimental surveys	• Audio information more important than visual • Pictures do not distract from comprehension
Netherlands	Van Dijk (1983)	Linguistic content analysis	• Need to study news story content at several levels (discourse analysis)
Sweden	Findahl and Höijer (1972, 1981a, 1981b)	Experimental	• Emphasize cause-and-effect information for comprehension
West Germany	Schulz (1976, 1982)	Content analysis surveys	• Dimensions of news content; their relation to comprehension
United States	Robinson (1967, 1972a, 1972b)	Survey data	• Better educated understand more news and become better informed by more media use • Greater daily exposure to newspapers than TV news
	Tichenor et al. (1970, 1980)	Survey	• Formalized increasing knowledge gap hypothesis • Conditions under which gap does not occur
	Edelstein (1973)	Survey	• Newspapers more important source of Vietnam information than televison
	Jacoby and Hoyer (1982) Graber (1984)	Experimental Observation/survey	• Problems in comprehending TV advertising • Factual information in newscast seldom used

authors of the book proceed from different starting assumptions, different levels of analysis, different analytic time frames, different methods, and different definitions of news, information, and meaning. One of the great incentives for future research, however, is the striking convergence of findings across chapters in this book, despite these differences in assumptions and conclusions.

AN ANALYTIC FRAMEWORK

Figure 1.1 presents a process model that attempts to organize our work into a general analytic framework. Starting at the left are the "givens" of the audience: its demographic makeup (age, sex, education, etc.); its psychological predispositions to news information in terms of interest, attentiveness, curiosity, and the like; and the store of prior information primarily resulting from these two factors. This prior information variable plays an important role in our research analyses. The center of the diagram first focuses on the audience's exposure to the news media and what the audience brings to that exposure. These are the major dependent variables in Chapters 3 through 5 of this book. The large box at the top of this middle section refers to the news package itself: the culture and procedures of newswork that create, organize, and present news content. This is the focus of Chapters 8 and 9.

To the right of the center of the diagram is our major dependent variable: the audience's awareness and comprehension of that news product. As noted earlier, we feel that the new measures and approaches for news comprehension that we have developed represent real scientific progress in this area.

Included separately at the far right-hand side of Figure 1.1 is a box for interpersonal networks and discussion. We consider this interpersonal link to mass communication channels to be highly significant. The news as a process of information flow does not end with exposure to mass media messages. News and information have longer-range value and consequences for individual viewers and readers. It can be used as a "coin of social exchange" (Levy and Windahl, 1985) and for understanding where we as individuals fit into society. At a minimum, audiences use news information in their discussions with their friends and acquaintances. It is at this point that we see the real diffusion of information, because it is here that the media accounts are "introspected," discussed, and even challenged. That in turn leads to new

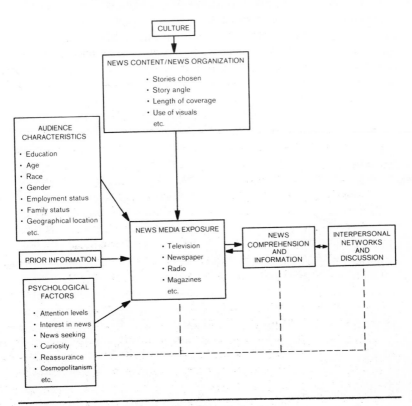

Figure 1.1   Model of Information Flow Process

information, and affects the audience member's subsequent news exposure and interest in the news.

CHAPTER ORGANIZATION

The ten chapters of the book are grouped into four parts. Part I (Chapters 1 and 2) discusses the theoretical background, offers general observations, and airs our assumptions about news audiences and information flow. The theoretical discussion in Chapter 2 attempts to synthesize work from a diversity of disciplines: sociology, communications, history, cognitive psychology, economics, and cultural anthropology, among others.

The chapters in Part II (3 through 7) examine the bottom part of Figure 1.1. It reviews a large body of (largely unpublished) empirical research evidence from the last 20 years dealing with news comprehension and the audience and media exposure variables that affect them. These studies proceed from five specific perspectives: studies of public understanding of "basic," or long-term, political information (Chapter 3); studies of public understanding of specific news stories over the shorter specific period of a week (Chapter 4); surveys focused on yet a shorter time frame, a single day's newscasts (Chapter 5); still shorter-run experimental studies, usually conducted with controlled messages in controlled settings (Chapter 6); and a discussion of the difference between "information" and "meaning," which introduces our concept of "metamessages" (Chapter 7). By metamessages we mean longer-run, more general, and latent meanings, embedded in audience decodings of mass media messages. In these five chapters, we look for common variables and common patterns of findings that cut across different types of research contexts in order to examine which segments of the news audience are more or less able to absorb news information and how they might be better reached. Included among these predictors are the standard survey demographic factors (e.g., education, age); media usage factors (e.g., TV news viewing, newspaper reading); contextual media use factors (levels of distraction/attention, type of newspaper read); and a variety of motivational/psychological factors (need for reassurance, cosmopolitanism, need to be informed).

In Part III (Chapters 8 and 9), our focus shifts exclusively from audiences to the examination of the news content and cultural factors noted at the top of Figure 1.1. It examines the packaging of the news product and the organizational and professional norms that affect it. Chapter 8 builds on Chapter 6 in examining what our research suggests about the value of presenting the news in different ways: with long or short stories, with or without strong visual content, by focusing on foreign or domestic stories, by including or excluding human interest factors, and so on. In Chapter 9, we examine the organizational factors and professional norms among journalists that inhibit increased public understanding of news content and lead journalists to resist even our modest suggestions for making the news more comprehensible. Some of those suggestions are outlined as well.

The concluding section, Part IV (Chapter 10) reviews the various research findings and observations from earlier chapters in light of our original questions and assumptions. We describe the implications of our results for both news practitioners and their audiences and for the more scholarly debates and literature of our academic colleagues.

This book is currently being supplemented and extended by complementary research into news comprehension in other countries. Extensive studies of news comprehension are being conducted in Great Britain, West Germany, and Sweden. We are planning cooperative research with colleagues in other European and Third-World countries. To the extent that our findings are replicated in other societies, they will provide cumulative support of their applicability to improving the news process. It is toward that long-range goal that this work is addressed.

NOTES

1. It should be noted that Neuman did ask his respondents aided recall questions as well and found nearly a 50% recall rate across time. However, it was not clear whether or not his respondents had *comprehended* these stories, a concept of central concern to the present study.

2. However, that gap had been reduced from a 32-point gap found ten years earlier; in that 1965 study, 78% had seen a newspaper and 46% had seen a newscast. There is reason to expect that this gap has further narrowed since 1975 (Editor & Publisher, 1983), particularly given the increase in the national news "updates" that now appear during prime time entertainment viewing hours.

3. Ideally for our research, we should have had a specially devised "information meter" that would have automatically registered when respondents understood a news story and that recorded the source from which the information came. Given the current unavailability of such a device, we simulated the process using a survey approach. Our micro-behavior simulation asked first about the news information that respondents did have and second about the news sources respondents used. If users of news medium A possessed information that users of media B did not, we took that to be reasonable evidence that news medium A was the more important information source. Although this is not causal evidence (if indeed such social science data can be definitively gathered at all), it is the closest field approximation that we believed could be devised.

Chapter 2

THE SOCIAL ROLE OF
TELEVISION NEWS
Theoretical Perspectives

DENNIS K. DAVIS
JOHN P. ROBINSON

Television news has been assessed in many different ways during its evolution as a medium of public information, but with the passage of time early notions have become increasingly inadequate. There are two primary reasons for this. First, our understanding of public communication and its role in the social and political order has undergone fundamental changes. We can no longer confidently make the assertion (based on the libertarian philosophy described in this chapter) that communication freedom alone will produce an informed citizenry and guarantee political and social progress. Second, television has been found to transmit information in qualitatively different ways than earlier print media. Scientific theories developed during the 1940s and 1950s now must be reconstructed to account for the way television communicates.

This chapter describes these developments and traces how our theoretical understanding of public communication generally, and TV news specifically, has changed. Its intent is to introduce conceptions of public communication and TV news that can place our own work in a broader perspective. This work constitutes only a small part of the overall research effort that we believe needs to be undertaken through an empirical assessment of the effectiveness of television news as a source of information for the average person. By tracing the development of past theory and research, and its merits and limitations, we seek to lay the foundations for future research. Our review indicates how much remains to be done if an adequate understanding of TV news is to be developed. Such understanding is necessary if we are to use television effectively to fulfill its promise to make news accessible and understandable to its viewers.

THE DREAM RECONSIDERED

To journalists in the 1950s, television represented an innovative medium for transmitting current events information to vast audiences who needed this information to guide their actions in an increasingly complex postwar society. As practitioners trained in a libertarian tradition, they were both surprised and pleased to discover that television broadened the appeal of their stories, enabling them to earn even larger profits while enjoying high public regard (Westin, 1982). Television offered the opportunity to reach the libertarian goals that print media had failed to attain. It appeared able to interest relatively uninformed persons in politics and to encourage their involvement in social groups. By providing useful information, it might improve the quality of such social and political participation. By increasing the quantity and quality of citizen action, TV news might bring about a revitalization of democracy and allay post-World War II fears concerning the vulnerability of our social order to communist subversion.

By several measures, TV news has proven to be an enormous success. Its audiences have grown steadily in size. In addition, the expansion of network news broadcasts to a half-hour in 1963, with the dramatic coverage of civil rights protests, the Kennedy assassinations, and the Vietnam conflict, established TV news as a forceful information medium. Although a majority of Americans now report dependence on TV for news, and trust it to provide them with news that is more credible than that of print media (Roper, 1984), TV news has come under increasing criticism from both outside and within the journalistic fraternity. Critics have marshaled evidence to support the assertion that it does not fulfill the libertarian and democratic ideals that journalists espouse (Tuchman, 1978). TV news is described as a mere headline service that provides shallow, overdramatized depictions of a narrow range of public events (Powers, 1977a, 1977b). In its efforts to attract the attention of viewers, TV news has neglected to provide background information that would help viewers make sense of the colorful but ambiguous images that often characterize news coverage. Instead of stimulating viewer interest and involvement in social action, TV news may instead spread a political malaise (M. Robinson, 1976) that discourages political participation. During election campaigns, TV news has been found to focus on the horse race, hoopla, and candidate personality, rather than on political issues (Patterson, 1980).

The critics of television have posed important questions about the merits of TV news, but their work has not provided definitive answers to them. Despite its obvious flaws, there is growing evidence that TV news *can* communicate certain types of information regularly to more persons than alternate information sources (Berry, 1983). Still, we need to know much more about the quantity and quality of the information that is, or could be, communicated by television. We need more insight into the purposes this information can serve for viewers. Could it guide democratic, political decision making or is it merely a body of trivia for the parlor games of future generations? Although social researchers since the 1940s have sought to assess the effectiveness of mass media in objectively transmitting information to mass audiences, their work has only recently begun to examine seriously the unique role of TV news.

For social scientists in the 1950s, the appearance of TV news should have raised new questions about the diffusion of certain forms of information to mass audiences. How would the new medium alter the flow and use of information? Theories constructed to explain the flow and use of public information during the 1940s and 1950s should have been rewritten to account for growing evidence of the impact of TV news. But social researchers were slow to recognize the growing popularity of television as a medium for information and to gather data concerning the power of the news medium to diffuse information effectively. Considering that mass media had been found to have relatively unimportant influences on political action during the 1940s (Lazarsfeld et al., 1944), subsequent research tended to exclude media variables from consideration (Kraus and Davis, 1976). Public communication was generally viewed as serving ritualistic or reinforcement functions (Klapper, 1960).

When research on the effects of television news did begin in the early 1970s, some evidence of significant influence was found. The effects of TV news now appear to be quite numerous, but debate has arisen concerning the long-term importance of these effects (Iyengar et al., 1982; Adoni et al., 1984). Graber (1984) found that some TV viewers learned quite a bit from stories that received repeated coverage during a political campaign; however, she also found evidence that this learning did not persist, and thus may not have had much influence on political decisions made months later. Much the same lack of retention of political information was demonstrated in Wade and Schramm's (1969) analysis of information conveyed by media during the aftermath of the Kennedy assassination.

In general, researchers are finding that the precise assessment of the effects of TV news is an elusive goal. As a medium, television is proving to be a very complex information source that can have radically different effects, depending on the orientation and cognitive structure of the viewer, the situation in which viewing occurs, and the format of the programming.

THE CHALLENGE OF TV NEWS FOR THEORY

The gradual evolution of television as a medium for public information in large-scale, industrialized societies has served to challenge most of the early assessments made of it. It is now necessary to move beyond what is currently believed by journalists, audience members, and social scientists about public communication and TV news. What is needed is an integrated perspective on news that has its roots both in the existing normative theories of how public communication ought to function and in *social science* theories about how information diffusion and information processing actually occur. Such a theory should also provide insights to those audience members who desire a more comprehensive and objective understanding about both the strengths and limitations of television as a medium of information.

We begin with a review of how our current understanding of public communication has developed and then suggest how it might develop in the future.

THE EMERGENCE OF NORMATIVE THEORIES
OF PUBLIC COMMUNICATION

Libertarian Theory and American Journalism

During the seventeenth century, libertarian philosophy was developed by various political theorists in an effort to provide a blueprint for the establishment of an ideal political order (Siebert et al., 1956). These political theorists believed that a new era was dawning in which an ideal, underlying natural order would emerge once society overcame the artificial restraints imposed by traditional authority. One of the most unnatural and arbitrary forms of restraint was thought to be official censorship of public communication. Free and open communication would naturally give rise to wide-ranging public debate in which truth could be discovered through the use of reason and falsehood could be rejected. That truth could then be used to guide political action.

Such views won the support of a wide variety of marginal political and societal leaders including religious reformers, radical politicians,

TABLE 2.1   Normative Theories of News

Theory	Theorists	Central Ideas
Libertarian-Free Press theory	John Milton; John Stuart Mill	• Public communication freedom is essential if indivduals are to search for truth. • Discovery of truth will permit evolution of an ideal social order.
Marketplace of Ideas	Penny Press publishers	• Marketplace of ideas is "self-righting." Publishers of the best content will be the most successful.
Social Reform/ Progressivism	Muckraking journalists: —Pulitizer —Scripps	• Press should serve as a watchdog on big business and big government. • Surveillance will initiate and guide useful social reform leading to progress.
Social Responsibility theory	Commission on Press Freedom	• Press exists to serve and advance society. • Press should assist the development and preservation of pluralism.

and ambitious business persons. Among the strongest proponents of libertarianism were journalists and printers. Censorship posed a continuing problem for those who earned a living from the printed word. A license to print official documents guaranteed short-term financial success, but ruin awaited the printer who violated restrictions. Libertarianism emerged as a loosely structured set of ideas that rationalized the utility of decentralizing political and social power and assumed that new, and fundamentally better, social orders could be created. It was supported by those whose power was marginal, and was seen by them as providing the freedom that would permit them to enlarge that power. The freedom to communicate permitted articulate leaders to gain power through appeals for public support. Libertarianism developed in opposition to established, traditional elites and survived best when no single group or social institution could gain the power to dominate competing groups.

Since the American Revolution, U.S. journalists have relied upon libertarian ideas to defend their right to print whatever they have chosen. In order to print the truth, patriot printers such as Benjamin Franklin defied what they considered to be arbitrary and unnatural British laws. Libertarian views enjoyed widespread acceptance in the American colonies because many leaders of radical religious and political groups had sought refuge there. This acceptance was institutionalized with the addition of the Bill of Rights to the U.S. Constitution in 1789. The First Amendment stated that Congress could make no laws restricting freedom of speech, assembly, and the press. With this action, the United States became the first nation to commit itself permanently to the open practice of public communication, even when it posed a direct threat to the power of existing elites. This was done with the expectation that free public communication would result in fair competition between the advocates of political change such that an increasingly better political order might evolve.

Marketplace of Ideas

The most important limitations on freedom of the press in the United States are not externally imposed government restraints, but are self-imposed constraints intended to increase profits in a competitive marketplace. The development and survival of American mass media are dependent on the direct sale of content to consumers and the sale of advertising space. This strategy was originated by Penny Press newspapers during the mid-1800s and has been rationalized by a variant of libertarianism that can be labeled the "marketplace of ideas hypothesis." This hypothesis assumes that ideas can be treated as commodities that are bought and sold in an open marketplace. Good ideas are expected to drive out bad ideas in the same way that the sale of bad manufactured goods should be depressed by the availability of competing superior products. Those who market ideas that survive competition should be those who offer a superior product at a competitive price. Thus, profits alone should serve as a good indicator of the merit of a particular vendor. Newspapers or television stations that lose money can be assumed to be marketing bad ideas that consumers do not want or need.

The marketplace of ideas hypothesis was thoroughly tested during the yellow journalism era from 1870 to 1910. In large, urban areas, newspapers used a variety of questionable tactics to increase their circulations and undermine competitors. Sensational human interest news was found to be much more successful in luring readers than reasoned, political analyses. The success of irresponsible journalists raised basic questions about the practicality of marketplace-governed libertarianism.

The Muckraking Era

Faith in the value of libertarianism was partially restored by the success of muckraking journalists during the late 1800s. In an era of growing capitalist monopolies and political corruption, enterprising journalists found that the public would buy newspapers or magazines that exposed unjust profits, exploitation of workers, shoddy products, or political payoffs. Publishers such as Hearst, Pulitzer, and Scripps built large chains of newspapers by mixing yellow journalism with judicious muckraking.

Muckraking was justified because it provided the public with useful information, even when it threatened the interests of wealthy businessmen or powerful politicians. Muckraking journalists aligned themselves with progressive politicians who advocated reform of both business and politics (Brownell, 1983). Progressives favored reforms that would bring order and efficiency to business and government through the adoption of better bureaucratic practices. They crusaded to reorganize city governments and break the power of ethnically dominated political machines. Although they expressed sympathy for the poor, progressives typically saw poverty as the result of inadequate ambition or weak religious faith. They were skeptical of the ability of average citizens to govern themselves effectively and strongly favored public education, which would enable people to make better political decisions.

Social Responsibility Theory

Progressive themes were widely adopted by journalists and became the basis for a new version of libertarian theory: social responsibility theory. This new theory rejected the marketplace of ideas hypothesis and argued that journalists must exercise social responsibility, if public communication was to succeed in bringing about progress. The economic interests of publishers must not dominate the definition of news to the extent that information that might initiate or guide social reform goes unreported. The advocates of social responsibility theory favored encouraging professionalization of journalism in order to achieve these ideals. Responsible professionals would commit themselves to following certain practices designed to assure that their work would serve the public effectively.

Siebert and others (1956) credit the Commission on the Freedom of the Press with formalizing social responsibility theory in 1947. The report of this commission contained a well-reasoned, but quite fundamental, revision of libertarian theory. The primary justification for this revision was the increased complexity of society and the growing dependence on mass communication for information. Although early libertarian theory was based on the assumption that progress will occur when individuals are free to search for truth through public communication, social responsibility theory argued that all citizens are members of communities in which the quality of life is greatly improved when freedom of expression is permitted. Freedom of expression is defined not as a natural, individual right but as a moral right granted by a community so that individuals can serve the community more effectively. If this right is abused, it can be revoked by the community. Many journalists have found this interpretation of communication freedom quite disturbing. It would appear to justify censorship of any idea that community members or their leaders regard as threatening or controversial.

One important feature of social responsibility theory as articulated by the commission was the role assigned to cultural pluralism. The commission argued that ideal communities have pluralistic cultures. Communities should tolerate the expression of diverse views so that the various cultures can be effectively expressed and maintained. If commercial mass media are unable to provide a platform for the expression of cultural diversity, then the community should provide it. Thus, government intervention may be necessary to promote free expression so that pluralism is advanced. Moreover, social responsibility theory cannot begin to deal with the criticisms now made of journalism, nor does it recognize the strengths and limitations of television as a medium for public communication.

Beginning in the 1920s and 1930s, social researchers began to develop empirically based theories of public communication. Unlike the normative theories we have just reviewed, which describe how public communication should *ideally* be structured, social science theory seeks to provide more or less objective explanations of how public communication actually occurs.

Functionalism

Lasswell (1949), as extended by Wright (1975), identified three general functions of mass communication:

(1) surveillance of the environment;
(2) correlation of the parts of society to interpret interrelationships; and
(3) transmission of the social heritage from one generation to the next.

Functionalist theories often provide cogent descriptions of what media appear to be doing. Most reach optimistic conclusions because the continued existence of a media system implies to them that it is functional.

TABLE 2.2   Scientific Theories of Public Communication

Theory	Theorists	Central Ideas
Functionalism	Lasswell, Wright	• Media evolve to perform various functions for society including transmission of information and correlation of opinion.
Elite Pluralism (a) Conveyor Belt (b) Two-Step Flow	Lazarsfeld, Berelson, Klapper, Katz	• Flow of media influence is not direct but mediated by social and psychological factors. • Information flow to large segments of the public is minimal at best. • Public apathy and ignorance are normal, tolerable conditions as long as pluralistic group leaders guide media use and political action.
Cognitive Effects/ Learning from Media (a) Information Diffusion	DeFleur, Larson, Greenberg, Deutschmann, Danielson, Chaffee	• Information flow is mediated by many factors including message factors as well as social and psychological variables. • The flow of information can be improved through control over mediating variables.
(b) Knowledge Gap	Tichenor, Donohue, Olien Robinson	• Persons already well informed about public affairs will tend to learn more from news coverage. • Over time, the gap in knowledge will widen between those who are well informed and those who are not.
(c) Agenda-Setting	McCombs, Shaw	• The type of news coverage given issues (i.e., prominence, repetition, length) will influence public perception of the salience of issues.
(d) Information Processing of News	Findahl, Höijer, Gunter	• In laboratory experiments news permits rather high levels of learning. • Learning from news is strongly linked to certain message factors.
(e) Uses and Gratifications	Blumler, McQuail, Katz	• Audiences actively seek to acquire information to serve their needs.

One of the most important programs of research to be guided by functionalist theory was initiated by Lazarsfeld et al. (1944). In a classic study of the role of mass media in the 1940 election campaign, Lazarsfeld concluded that campaign propaganda had little direct influence on vote decisions. This was a very reassuring finding in an era when extremist propaganda threatened to undermine American democracy. However, it implied that there was little need to study the specific substance of what people learned from media because it could be assumed that only consistent information would be learned. Therefore, to be parsimonious, research should be focused on the study of attitudes and attitude formation rather than on the learning of information.

The Conveyor Belt Model

Lazarsfeld's findings led to the development of what has been called the "conveyor belt" model of mass communication. This model regarded media as functioning merely as a mechanism that makes information accessible to individuals who are positioned at various levels of the social order and who share certain attitudes or predispositions. These individuals make use of the information conveyed to them in different ways depending on their social position and associated attitudes. Better-educated, higher-status persons make better use of the information made available to them. They learn from it and use it to confirm what they already know and believe. Less-educated, lower-status persons are not influenced because they do not trust media to convey useful information and do not use it routinely. This functional model implies that media practitioners bear no responsibility for such discrepant use of their service and could do little to change it even if they so desired.

This model of mass communication was supported throughout the 1950s and 1960s by an accumulating body of research findings from both surveys, which were interpreted as proving that media rarely have direct effects (Klapper, 1960). However, most of this research examined only short-term influence of media messages. Measures of media exposure and effects were crudely operationalized. Research designs were often inadequate. Perhaps most important, television was not adequately studied because it was just developing (Kraus and Davis, 1976).

Elite Pluralism

The conveyor belt model of mass media was gradually incorporated into a broader conception of the social and political system: elite pluralism. This theory sought to resolve the apparent contradictions between Lazarsfeld's empirical findings and classical democratic theory. Lazarsfeld found that most citizens were apathetic and based their vote decisions on long-standing party preferences. Media messages proved powerless to overcome such strong emotional affiliations. Such vote decisions were hardly the informed rational choices envisioned by democratic theory. How could a democratic political system survive such irresponsible participation?

The answer to this question was found in liberal democratic theory and elite pluralism, two closely related conceptions of U.S. society. According to these theories, a heterogeneous, culturally pluralistic society is more governable and politically stable if it is divided into many well-defined and long-lasting voting blocks. The interests of each rather small voter segment can be advocated by leaders who work within the political party system to negotiate just allocation of resources. Thus, it does not matter if the average group member is ill-informed or apathetic. Allegiance to leaders and to parties serves to stabilize politics and assure that all interests are represented fairly. The system as a whole should be able to function effectively even if ignorance, apathy, and prejudice are widespread. The system will break down only if the representative elites lose control over the political prejudices of their followers or fail to negotiate fairly according to the rules of liberal democracy.

To the extent that elite pluralism gained favor as a useful explanation of the American political system, researchers lost interest in studying the degree to which the American public was informed about various political topics. The survival and development of American politics was seen as being unrelated to public knowledge about politics. Many political scientists turned their attention to the study of the political system (Easton, 1965) or to interest group politics.

The Two-Step Flow Model

During the 1950s, research by Katz and Lazarsfeld (1955) led to the formulation of another related conception of mass communication. Examination of data from a large-scale survey in Decatur, Illinois provided more precise insight into the flow of influence from mass media to audiences. Again, little evidence of direct influence was found. However, leaders of social groups were found to use media more frequently to acquire information relevant to their groups. This information was often passed on to group members. In this way, leaders influenced the opinions held by their followers. They screened out information inconsistent with opinions supported by the group and assisted members in interpreting any conflicting facts that they might inadvertently learn. Thus, the attitudes of the group were protected from external influence.

The two-step flow hypothesis implied that group leaders could keep rather tight control over group attitudes and hence the information acquired from mass media by their followers. Leaders acted as gate-keepers or mediators in the flow of information from media to mass audiences. The media were seen as having limited ability to affect directly the learning of information by average persons.

Subsequent research on the two-step flow, however, has failed to establish its existence conclusively. Even the Katz and Lazarsfeld study noted that the flow of political information differed significantly from the flow of consumer and fashion information. Among the most recent reformulations of the model is J. Robinson's (1976) differentiation of the information flow process into two separate types: (1) opinion-sharing among the most interested and involved segments of the public, and (2) direct influence of the media on individuals not involved in such social networks.

Nevertheless, the hypothesis has been widely accepted and used to support the assertions of elite pluralists (Kraus and Davis, 1976). Acceptance has discouraged research that might have closely examined the flow of specific forms of information to various types of audience members.

News Diffusion Research

Although many social researchers in the 1950s and 1960s did not consider the study of information diffusion to be a very interesting or fruitful topic, some learning research was conducted. Much of this research consisted of small-scale, local surveys done to assess when and what people learned about major news events (Deutschmann and Danielson, 1960; Budd et al., 1966).

Early news diffusion research assessed the sources, speed, and extent of learning about the persons and events reported in news stories. Various factors that impeded or accelerated the flow of news to the public were identified. Variables such as social position (as indexed by demographic measures), group membership and involvement, and psychological attitudes (such as interest in news topics) were studied in relation to learning from news. Education was found to be an important predictor variable (Gaziano, 1983). Mediating variables such as time of day when news events occurred, routine use of media for news, and the structure of event reports were also considered.

Two quite different patterns of news diffusion were identified (Chaffee, 1975). These patterns are graphed in Figure 2.1. In these graphs, time is represented on the horizontal axis and the cumulative number of persons who have heard about a news story is plotted on the vertical axis. The first of these patterns takes the form of an S-curve. It has been found to occur most commonly for highly relevant news items in which there is high public interest as well as extensive news coverage. For such stories, there is a very short initial time period when few people have heard of the event. This is followed by a sudden, exponential rise in public knowledge. After high levels of knowledge are reached, diffusion slows again. When such a pattern of diffusion is found, persons who learn about them have done so from the mass media. On the other hand, persons who learn of the event during the period of rapid diffusion are most likely to have heard about it from another person. The classic example of an event that showed an S-curve of diffusion was the Kennedy assassination (Greenberg and Parker, 1965).

The second diffusion curve is less dramatic but far more typical. Knowledge of most routine news events rises slowly and then tends to level off after a period of several hours (or days). Funkhouser and Mc-Combs (1971) found such diffusion curves for learning about a variety of routine news events including a prison riot, a heart transplant operation, and a Supreme Court nomination. With the passage of time, public knowledge of events was found to decline. For such events, media were found to serve as the predominant source of information.

The extent to which information about such events diffuses has been found to be a function of four factors: (a) the amount of coverage, (b) the frequency with which a story is repeated, (c) the level of public interest in the story topic, and (d) the level of existing public knowledge about the topic. Research by DeFleur and Larsen (1958) found that public awareness of material contained in civil defense leaflets was strictly a function of the number of leaflets dropped over a given area. They determined that public interest was not high enough to provoke conversations about the leaflets with others.

News diffusion studies have isolated several factors that are consistently linked to learning about news content. These include preexisting knowledge, level of interest in story topic, level of education, level of communication with members of social groups, and position in social groups. Persons who are most likely to find out about news events soon after they occur are those who are interested in the events, already know something about the events, are well educated, are active in groups, and occupy central positions in group communications networks.

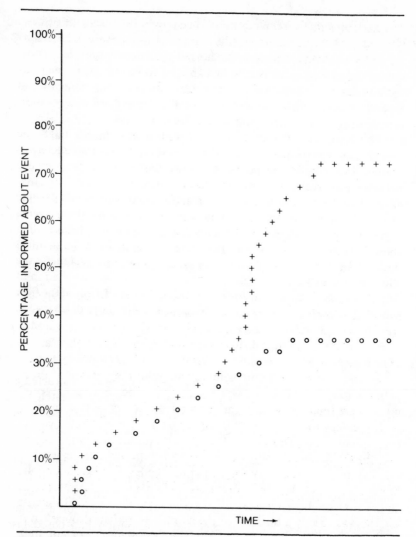

Figure 2.1 Information Diffusion Curves

More recently, Chaffee (1975) has attempted to build upon such empirical generalizations to construct a model of the diffusion process for political information. He draws upon Easton's (1965) model of the political system, which identifies demands and supports as key factors affecting the operation of the system. During periods when large segments of the public, or important social groups, became actively involved in making demands upon the system, the relevance of news related to such demands should rise for those persons whose self-interests might be served or threatened if demands are met. Thus, social security recipients could be expected to follow closely news of congressional debates over eliminating cost-of-living increases in social security benefit payments, especially if there are widely publicized demonstrations by groups of retired persons.

The relevance of various issues for different groups might be gauged by measuring the type of diffusion curve that characterizes each group as well as the public as a whole. For example, the presence of an S-curve would indicate that an issue is highly relevant. Fluctuations in the extent and rate of diffusion of various issues could provide a useful index of change in political systems. If news about events relating to a specific topic suddenly begins to rapidly diffuse, then important changes can be assumed to be taking place in the political system. Chaffee's model assumes that it is useful to study directly the flow of information rather than merely to examine the distribution of opinion about a topic, as is done by pollsters. Measurement of the flow of information should reveal much about the dynamics of change in the political system.

The Knowledge Gap Model

Tichenor and his colleagues (1970, 1980) have also constructed a useful model based upon news diffusion work. Their research has focused on three variables: level of education, level of preexisting knowledge, and level of interest. They find that persons who are better educated, with high levels of interest in and knowledge of topic areas, tend to learn more correct information from reading news stories and also to become aware of events sooner. Tichenor et al. (1970) formalized the knowledge gap hypothesis, which served to summarize both their work and an earlier "Newtonian inertia model" of information flow proposed by Robinson (1967). Robinson had based his model on his survey findings that better-educated and informed persons "kept in motion" by routinely attending to more about events and issues in the news media; this suggested that a gap in knowledge would normally widen between such persons and those who are poorly educated and ill-informed. This hypothesis has since been supported by a series of studies (see Tichenor et al., 1980) and has been replicated in Sweden (Nowak, 1977). Knowledge gaps have been found to be greatest for complex, abstract topics that are of interest to only a few persons.

Earlier theories, such as elite pluralism, which gave low priority to a consideration of information flow failed to allow for the possibility of such learning or minimized its importance. Tichenor and Chaffee have demonstrated the need for further research that can assess information flow and use.

In a series of recent studies, Tichenor and others (1980) found that knowledge gaps may be narrowed when social conflicts arise that stimulate widespread public discussion of specific topics. Gaps narrowed the most when conflict levels were high and the communities in which the conflicts occurred were homogeneous. This research appears to be consistent with Chaffee's argument that prominently articulated demands can raise the relevance of news topics and thus encourage learning as well as social change.

Both suggest that widespread ignorance or apathy are not permanent social conditions but that they can fluctuate rapidly in response to events. If prominent and dramatic news stories articulate demands for resources or services, even normally apathetic segments of the public may be stirred to pay attention and learn about issues.

Agenda-Setting Research

Since the early 1970s, McCombs and Shaw (1972) have published a series of studies that investigate the power of media to influence audience members directly. They have argued that media may not have the power to change "what people think" but that they can influence "what people think about." Media can call public attention to (and confer status on) specific people, events, and issues. By extending coverage over days or weeks, media can imply that these people, events, and issues are more important than those that are not covered. McCombs and Shaw (1976) report stronger statistical correlations between the amount of coverage that issues received during political campaigns in newspapers and the ranking of those issues by voters, than were found for television news.

Agenda-setting research looks at cognitive effects of media rather than feelings or attitudes (Becker et al., 1975). Media suggest when subjects are important enough for people to form attitudes. Media then serve as a crucial source of information on these subjects. Although the resulting attitudes may not be directly controlled by media, substantial influence has occurred. For example, in the case of Watergate, media coverage coupled with the action of elites may have ultimately induced most Americans to form a whole set of opinions that had disastrous consequences for the Nixon administration.

Other Cognitive Effects

It is our view that previous research has concentrated on only one aspect of agenda setting: the degree to which media influence what people think about. But a broad range of similar cognitive effects are plausible. News stories do far more than tell us what is important; they tell us *who* is important, *where* important things happen, *when* to expect specific things, and *why* to think about these things. Thus, we see the news media as also likely affecting the four other "W's" of journalism:

(1) Who to think about? To the extent that specific individuals or groups are identified in a news story, their importance will also be inflated, much as Lazarsfeld and Merton (1947) note in describing the "status conferral" effect of the media; that is, the media confer status on individuals (and stories) they cover frequently.

(2) Where to think about? The location in which a story occurs also may affect its perceived importance as a locale. If it is an area where much conflict, famine, or disaster occurs, viewers may feel better about not being there themselves. The most direct audience effect of this type would be on whether the public sees domestic events or foreign events as deserving more attention, depending on media coverage of the two types of stories.

(3) When to think about a story? Here again, the public pays attention to the news stories at the time that they receive attention in the media. Many stories reported in the news media have a strong seasonal (e.g., holidays, anniversaries or major events) or cyclical (e.g., release of government statistics, elections, earnings reports) element in them that affect when the public thinks about issues.

(4) Why to think about (the story)? To the extent that this element is communicated in news stories, this should also be plausibly linked to public thinking about the story. Is the story covered because of some important larger change that is taking place in society, or because it violates common assumptions or values about life?[1]

The existence of such wide-ranging cognitive effects assumes that media can influence our orientation to the social environment in quite subtle ways, without directly conveying specific information or promoting specific opinions or attitudes. Thus, the mere fact of coverage conveys an important message: It asserts that something is worthy of attention and it implies why the attention is necessary—a variant of the familiar McLuhan aphorism, "The existence of the message is the message." Thus, recent news coverage has focused heavily on new medical technology and surgical techniques. Coverage of high-tech medicine implies that it is an important development and that the practice of medicine is constantly improving. It may lead members of the audience to expect medicine to be able to cure many problems that it formerly could not.

In Chapter 7, we refer to such subtle, implicit messages as "metamessages." No single news story contains these messages. Rather, they are conveyed by the recurrent use of familiar story lines and themes and by audience decodings of them. In addition to the five W's of journalism, metamessages also call attention to the *how* component of news coverage. *How* the story is covered, we suggest, may have even more important consequences for audience comprehension of news stories than the five W's, as we discuss further in Chapters 7 and 10.

Uses and Gratifications Research

Another body of recent research that has probed learning from television news has linked such learning to the conscious intentions that media users have when they make use of certain forms of media content. The approach in its current form was pioneered by Katz and Blumler in a series of studies (Blumler and McQuail, 1969; Blumler and Katz, 1974). They consistently found modest correlations between the uses of media that audience members reported and the type of learning that took place. Thus, voters who reported that they followed political campaign coverage to ascertain candidates' stand on issues tended to learn more about issues than those who followed coverage to ascertain who was winning. In general, those who followed politics in the media to be entertained learned less than those who were seeking certain forms of information.

The uses and gratifications approach has sought to revive the notion that people are active in their use of media rather than passive collectors of whatever comes down the conveyor belt (Levy and Windahl, 1985). The findings that it has produced have generally been encouraging. At least some audience members appear to be able to make media do things that they desire. However, most findings have had very modest statistical significance (Neuman, 1976; Gantz, 1978). In Chapter 5, few consistent links are found between reports of information-seeking objectives and subsequent learning from TV news.

Information-Processing Theories

Another area of empirical news research that has developed recently is based on information-processing theories as originated by cognitive psychologists. These theories provide insights into the cognitive processes that underlie learning of information from news stories. They permit many different predictions to be made about such learning. News stories structured in particular ways or containing specific types of content can be predicted to be more or less successful in inducing learning. Chapter 6 reviews this research in considerable detail.

Cultural Studies

The empirical studies of public communication reviewed above have provided useful insight into the flow of news to audiences. But as we have noted, this research does not provide a broad explanation of the role of news for average citizens. The most macroscopic explanation that has been derived from empirical research is elite pluralism. The assumptions of this theory have been called into question by the growing evidence of the cognitive effects of news. Opinion leaders may do little to mediate the flow of information about routine news events. Average citizens may be more able and willing to learn about societal events than was assumed by elite pluralism.

As an alternative to elite pluralism, we have considered some of the broader implications of the role of news for society by reviewing recent theory and research in the area of cultural studies. This review provides additional perspectives that have influenced our interpretation of our own research and the guidelines that we have developed for further research and theory construction.

The cultural studies approach to the analysis of mass media has its origin in phenomenological theory (Tuchman, 1978), in linguistics (Bernstein, 1971), and in literary studies. In Britain, neo-Marxist researchers led by Williams and Hall (for a discussion, see Curran et al., 1982) have pioneered the application of such theories to the study of mass communication. Researchers under the direction of Halloran (1970) at the University of Leicester have also been instrumental in shaping the cultural studies approach. This approach has been most successfully applied in the United States by Carey (1977) and Newcomb (1984).

The heart of recent cultural studies theories is an important reconceptualization of the nature of culture and its role in society. For the functionalists, culture amounted to a socially created consciousness that the individual had to internalize if he or she was to control action effectively. Once socialized, the individual was little more than a social automaton incapable of violating social norms.

TABLE 2.3   Culturalist Theories of News

Theory	Theorists	Central Ideas
Neo-Marxist	Williams, Hall	• Media propagate a form of consensual culture that serves the interests of a small elite class. • Elites maintain power through domination of "politics of signification."
Status quo culture	Tuchman, Fishman	• News legitimates the status quo.
Public culture	Shibutani, Gusfield, Gans	• News orients public to remote, heterogeneous, ambiguous social environment. • News propagates consensual definitions of events and persons through dramatization and ritual presentation. News provides functional alternative to rumor.

Only poorly socialized individuals would become deviants. The threat of mass media was that it might promote an inferior form of culture that would interfere with proper socialization. As we have seen, the early empirical research on media effects suggested that there was little to fear from media as a transmitter of culture. Social groups and their leaders could be expected to keep the power of media in check.

Recent culturalist theory assumes that culture does not exercise such a direct and dominating influence. Rather, culture is conceptualized as a constantly changing social resource that individuals routinely, but only incompletely, internalize. Once culture is learned, it serves to orient individuals to the social environment and provides a basis for planning and controlling action. Shibutani (1966: 171) defines culture as

> an ordered view of one's world, what is taken for granted about the attributes of various objects, sequences of events, and traits of human nature. It is an organized conception of what is possible and what is plausible; it constitutes the matrix through which one perceives his environment.

Although the world view that a specific individual develops may be highly ordered, the culture from which it is derived may be quite pluralistic and heterogeneous.

This view has given rise to the conceptualization of new roles for mass communication. Media may provide messages that disorient individuals who have developed narrow world views on the one hand or that assist individuals in sorting out and coping with cultural diversity on the other. In the past, such messages were provided by churches, political groups, and families. But in a pluralistic mass society, these agents of culture tend to provide only limited information about the total range of what is possible and plausible. Media can come to be regarded as the most current, broadest, and most useful sources of information about culture.

Culturalist theories of mass communication have predicted a variety of consequences if mass media become primary agents of culture. Neo-Marxists argue that media will propagate quite a restricted culture that serves the interests of a small governing elite (Hall, 1982). Media are said to compete to identify and reflect a cultural consensus to audiences. But they rely upon elite sources to assist them in defining such a consensus and in communicating it. Politics comes to center on control over the manner in which cultural consensus is defined. Given that elite sources are relied on by media, they have a dominant position in such politics. Hall (1982) has coined the term "politics of signification" to refer to the debate among elites that determines cultural consensus.

Golding and Elliott (1979) provide evidence to support Hall's arguments. They studied news production practices in three nations: Sweden, Ireland, and Nigeria. They report that these practices benefited elites in rather direct ways. Researchers of the Glasgow University Media Group (1977, 1980, 1982) have found that TV coverage of industrial disputes in Britain routinely presented strikes as dangerous threats to the national economy and as serving only the narrow interests of the strikers. Such studies suggest how TV news might be providing a systematically biased view of cultural consensus. However, no audience research has been conducted that demonstrates that people do in fact learn or accept the hegemonic world views contained in this news content. Our own efforts to probe the audience reception and reproduction of such hegemonic meanings, what we call "metamessages," is reported in Chapter 7.

News as Culture

U.S. researchers who have adopted the culturalist perspective have differed from their British counterparts in one important respect: They have been reluctant to view media as necessarily giving consistent support to a narrow elite class. Instead, they have argued that media tend to limit the potential for social change by promoting status quo perspectives. Tuchman (1978) has articulated this argument:

News, I have argued, is a social resource whose construction limits an analytic understanding of contemporary life. Through its dispersion of the news net, its typifications, the claimed professionalism of news workers, the mutual constitution of act and source, the representational forms of the news narrative . . . news legitimates the status quo. I do not mean to accuse newsworkers of bias. . . . But I do claim that it is valuable to identify news as an artful accomplishment attuned to specific understandings of social reality.

Gans (1979) reached similar conclusions after extensive field observations of network news and national news magazines. Although much news was structured with reformist values, the reforms implied or suggested were minor. Typical stories dealing with social disorder were devoted to the reestablishment of order by leaders or officials. The causes of disorder were rarely explained.

Fishman (1980) described how New York officials were able to induce journalists to perceive and cover a "crime wave." Leads from officials guided reporters to stories that were then explained by official statements. Fishman concludes,

Whether or not anyone consciously promotes it, routine news advances a definite interest: it legitimates the existing political order by disseminating bureaucratic idealizations of the work and by filtering out troublesome perceptions of events.

Shibutani (1966) presents a view of news similar to that of Fishman and Tuchman, but it focuses on the virtues of "filtering out troublesome perceptions." He has argued that during major social or political crises, people seek reassurance and will turn to rumor for explanations if news is not available. News can quickly and broadly disseminate plausible, credible explanations of troublesome events. The advantage of news over rumor is that it is likely to promote widespread acceptance of similar event explanations. Rumor may result in propagation of several contradictory and potentially divisive explanations. Highly contradictory explanations can be created in such a context because groups can arouse emotions and induce moods that facilitate acceptance of quite novel perspectives that are alien to established (consensual) beliefs.

Thus, news may play a central role in pluralistic societies as a vehicle for development of a form of public culture that links diverse groups and assures some uniformity in the world views that these groups use to guide their participation in public events. News may compete with rumor to supply such world views. When news proves inadequate, group subculture will permit the production of rumor. In our society, we have come to expect that news will be widely accepted by most persons as providing a consensual view of important events.

Gusfield (1981) discusses how news might provide another form of public culture, one that explains social problems rather than disasters or crises. He argues that public officials have promoted the drunk driver "myth" as a consensus view of the drinking-driving problem.[1] This myth suggests that drunk drivers are the sole cause of drinking-driving and therefore the problem is best attacked by punishing them. He argues that the myth persists despite the consistent failure of the solutions that it implies. It persists because it has been so effectively communicated to the public.

TOWARD A PARTICIPATORY PLURALISTIC THEORY OF THE NEWS MEDIA

The theories and research reviewed in this chapter hold many implications for future news research. Some—especially the conveyor belt and the two-step flow models—provide explanations or expectations of minimal direct effects of media news content, but other models emphasize those audience factors that are more predictive of news reception (e.g., uses and gratifications research, news diffusion models, knowledge gap models). Other perspectives lead us to expect either quite broad-ranging effects of news messages (e.g., the culturalist models, especially from the status quo school; the normative theories), or more narrow or clearly defined effects (e.g., agenda setting, other cognitive effect models, knowledge gap models). These models, then, serve to broaden and put into perspective our present understanding of what people are routinely learning from news and how they use what they learn.

In particular, we need to know whether and how news has the capacity to serve as a source of public culture such that it supplies the themes and the categories that people routinely use to make sense of their social world. We may find that news serves as nothing more than a source of amusement and diversion, or we may find its influence to be far more subtle and pervasive. Culturalist theorists have developed very plausible arguments for their views, but the empirical research needed to verify them requires extremely sophisticated research designs. Nonetheless, more research should be designed to examine these important predictions about news functions and social implications.

Although the most immediate and practical goal of future news comprehension research will be to provide some guidelines for news story construction, our review of the history of press theories (see also

Chapter 9) demonstrates a need for a new normative theory of the press. Libertarian ideals have proved too general and vague to guide the practice of journalism in complex, pluralistic societies. Social responsibility notions guided a very useful reform of the press during the early part of this century and continue to inspire reporters to render service, but these notions are also quite abstract and vague. The Commission on Press Freedom's goals to some extent have already been implemented through the development of public television and the evolution of news programming, such as the *MacNeil/Lehrer News Hour*.

We live in an era in which there is ample survey and experimental evidence to allow one to be more cynical about the average citizen's capacity for observing reality or truth. As we note in Chapters 3 through 5, the level of public ignorance on important topics is often high, and the public's recurrent fascination with professional wrestling, soap operas, and simplistic patriotism (e.g., Rambo movies) serves to confirm elitist suspicions that the masses cannot be trusted to govern themselves.

In this chapter, we have found that social scientists' first confrontation with such pessimistic findings in the late 1940s and early 1950s resulted in the formulation of elite pluralism (or liberal democratic) theory. This theory argues that apathy and ignorance are tolerable if the society is structured to encourage and permit leaders to be drawn from all levels and all important social groups in society. Pateman (1980) had summarized the key limitations of elite pluralism as follows:

> That the orientations of the civic culture are found mostly among these individuals who are likely to belong to voluntary associations and to be politically active, is not a finding that empirical theorists of democracy can take for granted. Such findings suggest that political apathy is not, as one writer dismissively claimed, "nobody's fault."

Pateman went on to describe how democratic theorists, perhaps especially empirical democratic theorists, could not regard political expertise as unproblematic:

> The ancient and radical idea was that in a democracy all citizens were experts about their own political life, no matter what their special knowledge and skills in other areas. This idea has now been cast aside. "Democracy" is now held to be a system where citizens alienate their right to decide about their own political lives to nonpolitical experts (usually, today, lawyers and other professionally qualified men). It is hardly surprising that, in view of this conception of the political and

citizenship, working-class individuals and women feel it is not worth-while to be active; their skills and knowledge are not seen as politically relevant, either in the politics of the state or in the workplace.

The challenge voiced by Pateman and a growing number of political theorists is to dare to believe once again in the quite radical tenets of classical democratic theory. We have chosen the term "participatory pluralism" to emphasize two essential features of such theory. Citizens representing all groups of a complex social order can and should be expected to participate in the political decision-making that affects their lives and shapes their social worlds. Is such participation possible? Can significantly more citizens be expected to become sufficiently informed and motivated to participate in politics? What will be the consequences of such a transformation?

Pateman's argument makes it apparent that this transformation will not be simple. Current patterns of knowledge and participation are rooted in an existing political structure that unevenly rewards participation. How can this structure be changed without changes in the patterns of knowledge and participation?

To some extent we have already observed the potential for such changes during the past three decades. Media coverage of civil rights and the women's movement undoubtedly stimulated learning about events, persons, and politics that would not otherwise have occurred. This learning in turn guided and stimulated more widespread participation. Tuchman (1978) has documented how traditional formulas for covering events produced distorted, misleading accounts of the women's movement. Largely mythical accounts of bra-burning took precedence over straightforward coverage of the movement's objectives. Dramatic coverage of idiosyncratic leaders and of staged confrontations created highly misleading impressions of the movement's members and their typical actions. The result of such stylized and routinized coverage was a journalism inadvertently biased toward the status quo.

The various measures of political knowledge that we review in Chapters 1 and 3, together with data on the public's meager political participation, suggest that our political system has been essentially stagnant for several decades. The small gains that have been made in these areas can be accounted for by rising levels of public education and by the strong social movements that have flourished from time to time. Can a reoriented press take advantage of rising education and rising incomes? Even lower social status persons now have higher incomes, more available free time, and better education than their counterparts in the 1930s or 1940s. As long as news limits itself to covering politics as usual, there are few alternatives to inspire involvement, learning, and, ultimately, action.

A participatory pluralistic theory of the press would recognize that the press now operates as a relatively centralized bureaucracy in a complex, large-scale social order. National news cannot be expected to provide a totally independent or comprehensive account of all important events. Although the press must successfully market a commodity to mass audiences, its long-term survival is dependent upon effective service to pluralistic groups.

A participatory pluralistic press theory would seek to identify the way in which news assists or retards intergroup politics. Pluralists have argued that the foundation of pluralistic social orders lies in successful negotiation of complex political arrangements between groups. Groups are always in competition for resources, but news that heightens conflict or intensifies misunderstanding will contribute to a breakdown in group negotiations.

New technologies can serve intergroup politics by decentralizing media bureaucracies such as evidenced by the proliferation of cable channels serving specialized audiences. To the extent that such channels come under the control of specific groups, they permit the growth of alternative media that will complement rather than completely replace existing media.

New media could motivate and inform group members more effectively by reaching them with messages in which they are interested and possess the background to interpret, a kind of news that Gans (1979) has labeled "multiperspectival." Participation in groups would serve to reinforce what is learned from media and permit action upon this learning. As the gap between learning and action is reduced, public learning should become enhanced and, at the same time, motivated by higher levels of political interest.

NOTE

1. Gusfield discusses numerous news story themes that serve to perpetuate the myth. These range from themes dealing with stereotypes of drunk drivers as irresponsible, antisocial hedonists to stories that imply that police crackdowns on drunks are necessary and effective. Such stories continue to be created despite research evidence that suggests that drunk drivers differ little from other persons and that harsh punishment produces only temporary decreases in the level of drunk driving.

II   *Audience Studies*

Chapter 3

LONG-TERM INFORMATION
AND MEDIA USAGE

JOHN P. ROBINSON

Empirical evidence of the public's ignorance of basic political and social information goes back almost to the advent of the social survey itself. Many survey questions through the years have inquired into the public's general information about such "long-run" information as awareness of one's local representatives in Congress, the names of vice-presidential candidates, the locations or political alignments of various foreign countries, and the existence or intention of various pieces of domestic legislation (Hyman, Wright, and Reed, 1975). As noted in Chapter 1, the results of such survey questions invariably highlight the public as poorly informed and often gain prominent media coverage—even though the presumed audience for such messages is the same public that was unable to answer the survey questions in the first place. Collections of data on poor public performance on such questions have now become standard passages in essays and in textbook summaries of the role of public opinion in the policy process.

A recent example of such research can be found in Robinson and Clancey's (1984) study of public information levels. Robinson and Clancey found only minorities of their national respondents who could explain why two prominent and controversial members of the Reagan administration (Edwin Meese and Charles Wick) had been in the news; barely higher than chance proportions knew of clear improvements in inflation and unemployment; and in addition, less than half of their respondents seemed aware of Ronald Reagan's infrequent church attendance (which Democrats and media accounts had unfavorably contrasted to the president's religious stances on many issues). Yet each of these had been the subject of considerable and continuing news media attention in the months prior to the survey.

Such findings are not without important political implications. They can reinforce and justify elitist political orientations among decision makers who treat public opinion as an incompetent or irrelevant guide on policy matters (Robinson and Meadow, 1982). Thus, although the Robinson-Clancey study was done more carefully and was more media relevant than many studies of public information flow, its findings are in line with previous information poll data that portray the public as basically out of touch with political realities.

However, there are several problems with both the methodology and assumptions of most public information studies. First, the information questions asked often focus on isolated, detailed, or technical knowledge that is beyond the political interests or capabilities of most members of the public. Second, such issues are also of limited practical importance to most people. Third, the questions are usually asked in closed-ended format, giving respondents little opportunity to respond with partial or incomplete information, or to convey their understandings and frames of reference in approaching the news. Even the open-ended survey information questions that are usually asked require respondents to recall the names of political actors (e.g., members of Congress) who are not exactly household names available from memory at a moment's recall.

These flaws in survey methodology often lead to serious misreadings of public opinion and knowledge. For example, in the late 1970s, much was made of the survey finding that only one-quarter of the survey respondents could name the two countries involved in the SALT II Treaty; yet, we found in our 1979 national study (see Chapter 5) that nearly two-thirds of our respondents knew that the treaty was concerned with nuclear weapons. Similarly, although less than half of the population of the United States may be able to recall the name of their member of Congress, that is not to say they do not know whether that representative is a Democrat or a Republican or that they cannot offer an evaluation of the member's performance in office (Mann, 1978). Few survey respondents may be able to give sophisticated explanations about the ideological terms "liberal" or "conservative," but most of them can identify the Republican party as the more conservative. Voters in 1980 may not have known many details about the leaders in Iran or what their long-run political-historical aims were, but most of the public seemed aware that Iran had moved to a religion-based form of government—and that the leaders of that government were making the leaders of the American government appear helpless and foolish.

Additional evidence that the public sometimes is well informed and pays attention to the news can be found in the rapid public opinion shifts that occur in line with stories in the news media—such as with the surge and decline of Gary Hart in the Democratic primary elections in 1984 or in the sales drops of products (such as Tylenol and caffeinated beverages)—that receive unfavorable news coverage. Moreover, to the extent that research evidence now suggests that media coverage can be linked to meaningful shifts in public opinion (Page et al., 1985), some elements of public comprehension obviously must be at work in such a process. In short, it seems premature and elitist simply to dismiss the public as hopelessly out of touch with politically relevant information, even if public information levels are lower than those of the elites or lower than hoped for by America's Founding Fathers.

When we raise these objections to previous information studies, we speak somewhat from our own (salutary) experience. In the late 1960s, we undertook some comprehension research in the area of popular music, particularly into audience understanding of the lyrics of new songs that conveyed messages of broad social significance as opposed to the familiar themes of courtship and romance (Robinson and Hirsch, 1969). Our initial research focused on particular songs (e.g., "Eve of Destruction," "Mr. Businessman," "Heavy Music") that we as researchers saw as important, and we found that relatively few teenagers were able to identify the "messages" of these songs. However, as we continued our research into the 1970s, we found our teenage audience to be increasingly aware of what song lyrics really meant. Moreover, when we finally turned our attention to audience-centered responses to *its* favorite forms of music, we discovered a robust relationship between attachment to "underground rock" music and participation in underground behavior and attitudes (Robinson and Hirsch, 1980). Our research (and perhaps the audience) had come full circle—from minimal association between content and comprehension of this music to it acting as an integral expression of the life-styles of those who were attached to it. It was a discovery that would not have been possible had we not been asking the survey questions from the respondent's perspective, rather than imposing our own "top-down" view.

This chapter will present our analyses of data (much of it previously unreported) from surveys that, unlike most public information studies, have asked both information (or information-related) questions *and* media use questions. The analyses in this chapter make it less possible to tie information levels specifically to news media use than those in Chapters 4 and 5; however, because the information covered is rather broad and long term and has been diffused by multiple media sources, it is almost impossible to pinpoint exactly how much information came from which source.

However, we can use the data to note whether certain patterns of media use are related to information levels in a consistent and representative way. Are heavy TV news viewers, for example, more likely to be consistently better or worse informed than users of other media? Alternatively, we can use such studies to infer something about the limits or capacities of audience members to absorb various types of information from different media. We turn first to an example that illustrates the general research approach employed in this chapter.

MEDIA USE AND WORD FAMILIARITY: AN EXAMPLE

Our first analysis involves information from a national-level sample from which minimal or no media effects may be expected, but that does, however, illustrate some general information-processing capabilities of the mass audience. We will also use this example to illustrate our general analytic approach in relating information levels to news media usage. Our analysis is based on a series of questions on the public's basic vocabulary skills that the General Social Survey (GSS) of the University of Chicago has included in its annual national assessments of public opinion since 1972.

In the ensuing years, the GSS asked nearly 8000 respondents whether they understood the meaning of ten standard vocabulary words.[1] On average, respondents have consistently identified almost six of the ten items correctly through the years. Like the test score data in Chapter 1, then, this suggests that public information levels have not significantly improved in recent decades.[2]

As shown in Table 3.1, there are some substantial differences in vocabulary scores across groups, depending on media use. Those who report that they read a newspaper every day have an average score of 6.2 words—that is, 1.8 words higher than those who say they never read the paper, who average 4.4 words on this test. (This difference is noted by the + 1.8 entry in the "high-low" figure in Table 3.1.) Those who claim to watch 6 or more hours of television are generally familiar with only 4.9 words (which is 1.5 words lower than the 6.4

figure for those who watch no television). Of course, it is not clear whether these differences for television viewers may apply to TV *news* viewers, who are not identified by the media questions on GSS; nonetheless, one would expect a certain degree of overlap between viewing TV generally and being exposed to TV *newscasts*. Respondents who listened to the radio more, however, scored higher than average, but not monotonically so—those who listened 1-2 hours scored higher (6.1) than those who watched three hours or more (5.6).

Table 3.1 also indicates that more socially isolated people (i.e., people who "never" get together to talk with friends or with neighbors) are also below average in vocabulary skills. However, the differences with higher levels of socializing are not large enough to describe these factors as very important differentiators of word familiarity, given that those who socialize most (i.e., the "almost every day" groups) are also below average in vocabulary scores.

The data in Table 3.1, then, suggest some important differences in the language skills of the audiences of certain media. Newspaper readers and radio listeners are above average, whereas heavier TV viewers are below average. People who socialize least often, and most often, are below average—but those who socialize with friends more often do tend to score slightly higher than those who never socialize.

Are these differences due to usage of these communications media? Or do they reflect the fact that people who use various media are different on other factors that are related to vocabulary scores, such as age or education? The answers to these questions can be inferred from a statistical analysis program called multiple classification analysis (MCA). MCA was developed by Andrews and others (1973) to allow researchers to examine the extent to which group averages such as those in Table 3.1 are true independent differences, or whether they disappear or are severely affected when other factors are statistically taken into account. An MCA, for example, would allow us to examine whether daily newspaper readers score higher in Table 3.3 because they are more likely to be better educated or have higher income, or because they have less time for television or socialize more with friends? Or do newspaper readers simply have higher vocabulary scores under all these conditions?[3] In brief, MCA addresses the perpetual question: "Other things being equal, does this result still hold?"

The MCA entries in Table 3.1 show the average scores for each of these media use groups, after adjustment for that group's usage of the other four media and for that group's level of education, gender, age,

TABLE 3.1   Differences in Vocabulary Word Score
by Media Use and Demographics

	Communication Factors	
	Before Adjustment	*After Adjustment*
Average Score	5.8	5.8
Read newspapers		
every day	6.2	5.9
few times/week	5.7	5.8
once/week	5.5	5.8
less than weekly	5.2	5.7
never	4.4	5.5
High-Low*	+1.8	+.4
Watch TV per day		
0-1 hrs/day	6.4	6.0
2 hrs	6.1	5.9
3 hrs	5.7	5.7
4-5 hrs	5.5	5.7
6+ hrs	4.9	5.7
High-Low	+1.5	+.3
Listen to radio per day		
0 hrs/day	5.3	5.5
1-2 hrs	6.1	6.0
3+ hrs	5.6	5.7
High-Low	+.3	+.2
Socialize with friends		
almost every day	5.6	5.9
1-2/week	5.8	5.8
several/month	6.1	5.9
once a month	6.0	5.9
several/year	6.3	6.1
once a year	5.1	5.4
never	4.7	5.4
High-Low	+.9	+.5
Socialize with neighbors		
almost every day	5.1	5.7
1-2/week	5.6	5.7
several/month	6.1	5.8
once a month	6.1	5.9
several/year	6.4	6.1+
once a year	6.1	6.0
never	5.5	5.8
High-Low	−.4	−.1

TABLE 3.1 Continued

	After Adjustment
Demographic Factors	
Average Score	5.8
Age	
18-25	5.4
26-35	5.6
36-45	5.9
46-55	5.9
56-65	6.1
66-75	6.3
75+	6.0
Education	
grade school	4.1
some high school	4.9
high school graduate	5.8
some college	6.5
college graduate	7.5
graduate school	8.0
Gender	
male	5.6
female	6.0
Race	
white	6.1
black	5.0
other	4.7
Income (in thousands)	
Under $5	5.6
$5-9	5.7
$10-14	5.8
$15-19	6.0
$20-24	6.1
$25	5.8

SOURCE: Data from General Social Survey 1972-1983.

race, and income. First it can be seen that the initial high-low difference of 1.8 points among readers and nonreaders of newspapers drops to a difference of only 0.4 after the other media and demographic factors are taken into account. The differences for each of the other four communication variables are similarly constricted: from -1.5 to -0.3 for TV viewing, from $+0.3$ to $+0.2$ for radio listening, from $+0.9$ to $+0.5$ for socializing with friends, and from -0.4 to -0.1 for socializing with neighbors.

Education is found to account for most of these differences, as shown at the right side of Table 3.1. Vocabulary level scores rise systematically and monotonically with education, so that every increase in education is related to an increase in vocabulary scores. The high-group minus low-group difference, after adjustment of 3.9 points, is more than double the differences found for newspaper reading *before* adjustment. The relation between education and this information measure is so strong that it also affects the initial *unadjusted* relation (not shown) with three of the other background factors in Table 3.1. The initial negative relation with *age* is reversed, so that after controlling for their lower educational level, older respondents are more familiar than average with these words (perhaps due to their longer experience with the language or to their more frequent exposure to these words when in school). The relation with *gender* is slightly enhanced, with women emerging as more familiar with the ten words than men. The initial relation with *income* is decreased significantly, so that people with higher incomes do not score much higher than people with lower incomes, which is the case prior to MCA adjustment. The racial differences betweeen whites and blacks in Table 3.1 are also considerably lower than they are prior to adjustment.

This strong and persistent difference in information by educational levels has been amply documented elsewhere, particularly in Hyman, Wright and Reed (1975) who found the effect in nearly all of the results of 250 survey information questions they examined over a 20-year period. Thus it is clear that the factor of educational level needs to be taken into account before any firm conclusions can be drawn about the differential impact of media use on information levels. That is the case particularly given that Hyman and his colleagues repeatedly found educational level to be a major predictor of mass media usage as well. Unfortunately, they were unable to conduct any analyses that linked the three variables of media use, educational level, and information. It is to such studies that *do* attempt to link media use and information that we now turn, with knowledge from Table 3.1 that we should not be surprised to find that prior to adjusting for respondent education, newspaper users will be above average in comprehension or information levels and TV users (but not necessarily TV *news* viewers) will be below average.

STUDIES OF MEDIA USE AND INFORMATION

The data examined in this section differ from those in our example in that the examination is of information questions that are focused more on topics actually covered in the news media. The studies cover a broad range of topics, from politics to entertainment, and from science to culture. Most of the studies cover national-level information, but some cover local and international topics as well. Many of the studies were conducted by the present authors, and because these analyses are not published elsewhere, we will provide more statistical documentation for them. Both national studies and studies of more limited, localized areas are included. The local studies, however, were usually designed to be representative of these local populations and can be expected to reflect the spectrum of information of concern to the population of these areas.

(1) 1964 Detroit Area Study (Robinson, 1967). In this study of international attitudes, three sets of straightforward, factual questions about various foreign countries were asked. The first questions concerned whether five countries had communist governments, the second set whether five (other) countries were located in Africa, and the third set whether six (other) countries had developed their own atomic weapons. Although these questions tended to concern somewhat "textbook" knowledge, there was a certain functional element to the communism and atomic weapon questions in that each related to major factors of political activity and strategy within other countries of the world.

Respondents scored an average of seven out of sixteen items correct on this foreign affairs quiz, with scores varying between twelve for college graduates and three for those who were in low-income occupations and had not completed high school. Unlike the results in Table 3.1, men here scored higher than women after adjustment for other factors; as in that earlier table, blacks scored lower than whites after adjustment.

Of the eleven indices of news media usage examined (three for TV, three for newspaper, three for types of newsmagazines, and one each for books and radio), information use related mainly to usage of the print media of newspaper (Pearson's $r = .30$) and magazines ($r = .28$). Viewing of TV newscasts was not strongly related to information, although viewing news documentaries *was* related ($r = .26$). Analysis within subgroups of this sample revealed information-media relationships that were larger in less-educated groups than in college-educated groups, which indicates that news media might play a more important informational role for those with less formal education. (We shall return to this point at the end of this chapter.) One further communication factor, equal in significance to print media usage, was the extent of interpersonal conversation about foreign affairs with family, friends, and neighbors (r = .33). Moreover, this factor continued to predict information levels after control for demographic and media use variables.

This study produced two findings, then, that will become familiar in our review of subsequent studies: (1) Information levels are more strongly related to print than to broadcast media use, and (2) the interpersonal communication variable emerges as an important predictor of information levels.

(2) Knowledge and the public mind (Wade and Schramm, 1969). As part of their large literature review of mass media use and knowledge of public affairs, science, and health, Schramm and Wade conducted several secondary analyses on national surveys. Their analysis concentrated more on the main source question than on actual extent of media exposure. In their reanalysis of six information items from the University of Michigan's 1964 election study, for example, they found that respondents who claimed to depend more on print media scored higher on public affairs information questions than those who depended more on broadcast media.

These media differences held up across educational levels, although more so for less-educated than better-educated respondents. Our recalculation of their data shows that, on average, among respondents with a high school education or less, the average percentage correct figures per item were 84% for print-oriented respondents versus 71% for broadcast-oriented respondents. For those with at least some college exposure, the figures were 92% for the print-oriented respondents and 90% for broadcast-oriented respondents. Thus, the average gap among the less educated was thirteen percentage points compared to only two percentage points among the college educated.

Wade and Schramm cautioned against interpreting these differences in terms of the greater power of the print media among the less educated, because of a "ceiling effect" resulting from the practically universal knowledge among the better educated (regardless of their media dependence). In fact, they found the opposite pattern for knowledge about science—that is, larger print-broadcast media gaps existed among the college educated than among those with only a high school education. Nonetheless, the higher science knowledge scores were also found among print users rather than broadcast media users in all four of the education categories examined. Even controlling for education, then, print media devotees were better informed than those depending more on the broadcast media.

(3) 1970 National Inventory of Television Viewing Behavior (Robinson 1972a). In this national study of 512 adults, conducted as part of the U.S. Surgeon General's investigation of Television and Social Behavior (Rubinstein et al., 1972), five information questions were included concerning recognition of names that were prominent in the news at the time: Ralph Nader, Martha Mitchell, Robert Finch, Bob Dylan, and Tom Hayden. Respondents in the survey were able to identify about one-third of these names, the average being 1.5 out of 5.

Variations around this average for five types of media exposure are shown in Table 3.2 before and after control for various demographic factors and usage of these other media. These controls did reduce some initially large differences in information levels associated with use of each medium. For example, prior to adjustment for other factors, newsmagazine readers scored over three times as high (3.0) as people who reported not reading any magazines (.8). After control, that difference was still the largest in Table 3.2, but it dropped to less than a two-to-one differential (an average of 2.1 vs. 1.3 items correct). Similarly, the low information scores before adjustment of heavy viewers of TV in general and of nonviewers of national newscasts moved upward after adjustment for these other factors. The one exception was for newspaper reading, for which the differences between high and low usage were as strong after control as before control.

Thus, differences in print media usage again emerge as larger than for use of television or radio. The high-low print media use differences are .9 for news magazines, .7 for newspapers, .3 for national TV newscasts, and − .3 for TV viewing in general; it is .1 for overall listening to the radio, which, given the regularity of radio newscasts on most stations, is probably reflective of listening to radio newscasts (there is, however, a below-average dip for the 4- to 5-hour listening group).

Interestingly, virtually the same pattern of results was obtained when the same information and media use questions were asked of a more restricted sample surveyed at about the same time. In this sample of 949 teenagers (in Prince George's County, Maryland), the education factor—years of education—was, of course, a virtual constant. The same media use patterns predicted higher information scores as in the national adult sample. That is, after control for several factors, print media differences were more than twice as large as for watching TV news. These print media use variables predicted almost as much difference in information scores as the two leading predictors of information scores in these teenage samples: year in school or grades in

TABLE 3.2   Average Number of News Personalities Recognized
According to Media Usage (1970 National Sample)

	Deviation from	
	Before Controls	After Controls*
Total Sample (512)	1.5	1.5
Hours of TV on an average day		
less than two hours (64)	1.9	1.6
two-three hours (172)	1.8	1.6
four-five hours (127)	1.3	1.4
six or more hours (67)	0.6	1.3
High-Low	−1.3	−0.3
Frequency of national news viewing		
at least twice a week (270)	1.6	1.6
about once a week (81)	1.8	1.6
never (82)	0.7	1.3
High-Low	+0.9	+0.3
Reads a newsmagazine		
yes (60)	3.0	2.2
no, but reads other magazines (214)	1.5	1.5
does not read any magazines (159)	0.8	1.3
High-Low	+2.2	+0.9
Reads a newspaper		
every day (293)	1.8	1.7
at least once a week (99)	1.9	1.2
less often (41)	1.1	1.0
High-Low	+0.7	+0.7
Hours of radio on an average day		
less than two hours (235)	1.5	1.5
two-three hours (113)	1.6	1.5
four-five hours (34)	1.2	1.2
six or more hours (51)	1.5	1.6
High-Low	0.0	+0.1

*After adjustment for use of other media, sex, race, and education.

school; although parents' education and occupational status were related to higher scores, those were at lower levels than for the print media use or school achievement variables. Moreover, the same pattern of results was found for a second set of information questions (knowledge of the characteristics of various foreign countries) asked of these teenagers. In this sample, the factor—years of education—was, again, a virtual constant.

(4) Communication in decision making (Edelstein, 1974). In his pioneering 1970 study of media use for decision-making problems, Edelstein examined local and world problems that his respondents themselves identified as highly important. These open-ended questions were followed up first with probes about the information sources from which the respondents had learned about this specific situationally defined problem and, second, with questions concerning from which of these sources the respondents had learned the most useful information.

Among his sample of 700 Seattle residents, Edelstein found that 61% identified newspapers as the most useful source of information for the local problem of most interest to them, in comparison to the 32% who named television; the remaining 7% naming radio. For world problems, the proportion citing newspapers was slightly lower (57%) but still well above that for television (40%) or for radio (3%). Edelstein found the same pattern of results among residents in two cities in Yugoslavia interviewed at about the same time with the Yugoslavian press being slightly higher for local problems (65% in the first city and 71% in the second) and slightly lower for world problems (49% and 54%).

In general, then, Edelstein's respondents cited the newspapers and one-half to two times as often as television as the most useful source of information. In a separate analysis, Edelstein (1973) also found newspapers to be used slightly more than television as an information source about the Vietnam war. More recently, Edelstein (1985) has been able to update and replicate his results with student samples in four countries.

(5) Election issue awareness (Patterson and McClure, 1976). As part of their intensive study of the role of the mass media during the 1972 election, Patterson and McClure asked their sample of Syracuse, New York respondents to identify the issue stands of candidates Richard Nixon and George McGovern on 18 separate issues. Patterson and McClure compared the percentage increases in issue awareness among newspaper readers and network news viewers at the beginning of the election and again at the end.

Across their entire sample, they found about a 26% increase in issue awareness across the election campaign. The increase for regular viewers of network news was only 28%, or not much higher than for nonregular viewers. The figure for regular newspaper readers, on the other hand, was 35%, almost double the 18% gain registered for nonreaders. In attempting to explain the much lower difference for TV news viewers, Patterson and McClure noted how "network coverage of campaign issues had none of the virtues that might make it informative." Not only did their content analysis show there to be few newscast references to these issues, but those issue references that were broadcast were either of very short duration (ten seconds of coverage or less) or were accompanied by distracting or unrelated visual material (e.g., candidates stepping off airplanes or wading through crowds).

From this study, Patterson and McClure concluded that network television newscasts presented "an impossible learning situation." Four years later, Patterson (1980) replicated his earlier findings with a new panel study based on more than 1200 voters in the 1976 election.

(6) 1973-1974 social context of media effects study (Robinson, 1974). This was another local study, this time conducted in the two smaller Midwestern cities of Flint, Michigan and Toledo, Ohio (both roughly equidistant from the major metropolitan center of Detroit). Unlike the previous studies, this was a panel study in which respondents were interviewed three times subsequent to their initial interview; this provided the opportunity to observe the dynamics of information flow across time. A second feature of this study was that it included a rich variety of psychological, social context, and media use variables as independent control factors. It also examined a diverse body of information measures: information about not only personalities in the news but also people in the entertainment side of television, people involved in Watergate (the initial round of interviewing took place in January 1973, before Watergate broke as a major scandal), and certain terms in popular use at the time (e.g., *Future Shock, Peter Principle*). The variety of background variables and their straightforward correlations with these four information measures are shown in Table 3.3.

The first column in Table 3.3 shows the correlates of straightforward recognition of four names in the news (Ralph Nader, Martha Mitchell, Sargent Shriver, and Henry Kissinger). On average, respondents in the first wave of the study were able to identify about two. The major media correlates of average identification scores, as shown in the first column of Table 3.3, are daily newspaper reading (Pearson's $r = .32$) and readership of more magazines ($r = .31$); reading of books was also related to higher information levels ($r = .31$). Although viewing of national TV news was also associated with

TABLE 3.3 Pearson Correlations Between Information Measures and Media Use, and Psychological and Demographic Factors (1973-1974 Flint-Toledo Study)

	News Personalities Winter 1983	Entertainment Personalities Winter 1983	Popular Culture Terms Winter 1974	Watergate Information Winter 1974
Media Use Factors				
TV hours	-.20	.12	-.23	-.05
national newscasts	.15	.10	-.11	.05
local newscasts	.04	.11	-.15	.02
radio hours	-.01	.03	-.09	-.03
read newspaper	.32	-.05	.02	.14
national news in paper	.25	.05	.06	.12
number of magazines read	.31	.16	.23	.21
read newsmagazines	.24	.06	.27	.11
read community magazines	.02	.06	.01	.04
read books	.31	.25	.38	.21
number of friends	.16	.13	.03	.10
news conversations	.22	.15	.17	.07
"network"	.17	.07	.13	.14
Psychological Factors				
news seeking	.26	.20	.26	.18
freedom from distraction	.24	.04	.07	.04
realistic entertainment	.22	.16	.18	.15
cosmopolitanism	.30	.12	.04	.13
news complaint	.22	.10	.08	.17
assertiveness	-.06	.07	-.01	.00
Demographic Factors				
education	.45	.31	.47	.31
sex	-.14	.02	-.13	-.10
race	-.25	-.08	-.13	-.14
age	.02	-.38	-.41	-.14
occupation	.24	.05	.25	.05
News Information—TIME 1	x	.45	.42	.37

higher information levels (r = .15), it was again at a much lower level than for print media. Viewing of more television in general was associated with significantly *lower* news information (r = -.20). Listening to the radio, watching local newscasts, and reading community newsmagazines were all unrelated to this news information measure (as well for the other information measures in Table 3.3).

Frequency of interpersonal conversation about the news was also associated with higher information levels (r = .22), as was having a wider circle of friends that one visited regularly (r = .16) and being part of a "network" of news-oriented individuals. However, the correlations for these variables were not as high as for more frequent print media use.

Relationships of equivalent strength were found for scales of five psychological variables constructed to describe internal processes and orientation by which different individuals might become better informed. These five scales, which are described in detail in Appendix A, correlated between .22 and .30 with news information.[4] They are

—*News Seeking:* feelings of being "left out" or "anxious" if not up-to-date on the news, or wanting to try to learn or to talk with other people about things that were happening
—*(Lack of) News Distraction:* the following indicators of distraction were examined: not feeling that personal matters take up most time, engaging in daydreaming, or finding that interests in life are closer to home than outside the home
—*Preference for Realistic Entertainment:* preferring less predictable endings, wanting to figure out how dramas will end, or liking TV entertainment that simulates real-life situations
—*Cosmopolitanism:* relatively greater interest in events in the larger national and international environment rather than state or local news
—*News Complaints:* being able to offer and articulate criticisms of the performance of print and broadcast news media

Information about the news personalities showed the familiar relations with demographic factors as did those in earlier studies. The most important correlate was education (r = .45). Men scored slightly higher than women (all the news personalities were male) and whites scored higher than blacks (all the news personalities also were white). Older people tended to score higher than younger; but given that the highest scores were obtained by the 40-59 age group, the linear correlation in Table 3.3 is small. The education-related factor of occupational status also was related positively to news information.

With regard to the other information items in Table 3.3, this pattern of results was most similar to that for the information about Watergate (obtained in the third interview in the winter of 1974). Information about events surrounding the Watergate affair was strongly related to education (r = .31), as expected. But it was more strongly related to the news information score at Time 1 (r = .37) and to the amount that people engaged in more extensive personal *conversations about Watergate* (r = .33, a variable not shown in Table 3.3). It also was related significantly (r = .21) with general book and magazine reading, with the reading of national news in the newspaper, and with four of the five psychological factors. Watergate information was also higher among whites, among men, and among younger people. Much the same pattern of correlations found for Watergate information was found for a single information item on the figure of King Faisal who had gained prominent media attention in the Arab oil crisis by the time of this third wave of the study. The major differences are the stronger negative correlations with daily hours of TV viewing and viewing of TV newscasts. As with Watergate information, this information was again related more to newspaper reading than to viewing national TV newscasts.

These patterns change considerably, however, for the other two information measures in Table 3.3. Thus, information about entertainment personalities (Sandy Duncan, Barbara McNair, Howard Cosell) again showed the strong relation with level of education, but at a lower level (r = .31) than for news information.[5] However, the major turnaround from news information (which *was* correlated .45 with entertainment information) occurred for media factors. Entertainment information was *positively* related to hours of TV viewed. Although it was also positively related to TV news viewing and to general book and magazine reading, entertainment information was not related to other print media use factors. This positive relation with amount of TV viewing continued to hold after MCA adjustment for other factors, providing clear evidence, then, of certain information gain among people who watch more television and evidence that some information transfer from heavier TV viewing does occur.

The second information measure, information about popular culture terms, was also significantly higher among the younger adults; education, news seeking, and news personalities information were also strong predictors. The distinctive media correlates here are book and magazine reading, which perhaps is not surprising given that the cultural information items were taken mainly from book titles that had been widely published and cited in magazines. This cultural information was not only negatively correlated with viewing of TV, but with viewing of TV news programs and listening to the radio. Although newspaper reading was unrelated to cultural information, it was not negatively related as were the TV exposure variables.

Most of the larger correlations (i.e., those above .20) in Table 3.3 persisted after MCA control for other factors in that table, although, as in Tables 3.1 and 3.2, most are also at a lower level after control. In particular, these multivariate MCA analyses reinforce the impressions from Table 3.3 that

(1) Education is the most important background predictor, although the initial (Wave 1) news information score itself is often as powerful a predictor. However, educational differences tend to be lower for entertainment personalities than for knowledge of news personalities and cultural terms.

(2) More extensive use of the print media sources in newspapers, magazines, and books is associated with higher information levels across all topics; this holds true after the effects of education and other demographic factors are controlled.

(3) More frequent viewing of TV newscasts is associated with at best marginally higher information scores and, in some cases, below-average scores, after other factors are controlled.

(4) People who watch more general television than average have lower news information scores (found also in a cross-lag analysis that provides some causal implications about the negative impact of viewing) but higher than average information about entertainment personalities.

(5) Extensiveness of interpersonal conversations and friendship networks is generally related to higher information scores, but generally not as high as those for print media exposure.

We have also found that information scores tend to be higher for males (entertainment personalities again being an exception), for whites, and for young people (especially on information about entertainment personalities and cultural terms). Also of some interest is the finding that scores on five psychological "knowledge process" variables that were developed for this study correlated significantly with news information and continued to do so after controls for other factors—even if they did not explain much of the effect of the education variable for which they were intended as a surrogate. What seemed to work better as a surrogate for education—and did serve to reduce the statistical relationship with education—was information itself.

(7) Newspapers, television, and political reasoning (Clarke and Fredin, 1978). In this secondary analysis of data from the University of Michigan's 1974 election study, Clarke and Fredin used respondents' ability to offer any reasons for liking or disliking the candidates for their state's U.S. Senate seat as their information variables. The number of such reasons that respondents gave to these open-ended questions was correlated with several media exposure variables, education, and political interest. Correlations were considerably higher for newspaper exposure ($r = .45$) than for television news exposure ($r = .10$). After multivariate control for the other factors, however, exposure to newspapers and to television were reduced to insignificance; more important, so was the factor of education.

What did emerge from this analysis, however, was a related print media variable: exposure to the discrimination of messages in the newspaper. The counterpart discriminator variable for television, on the other hand, was *negatively* related to number of reasons, which indicated to Clarke and Fredin that "television may actually exert an inhibiting effect on knowing about politics." Given that reasoning about political choice depended primarily on an area's newspapers, Clarke and Fredin examined specific newspaper markets that seemed to have more politically articulate readers. These markets turned out to be either those served by the "higher-quality" papers (e.g., *New York Times, Baltimore Sun, San Francisco Examiner*) or those areas marked by higher newspaper competition and less monopoly. Not only were the print media again more important generally than television, but differences were also found for qualitative newspaper factors as well.

(8) Citizen assessment of government (Becker and Whitney, 1980). In this 1977 telephone study of 548 adult respondents in Columbus, Ohio, Becker and Whitney related news media use to political knowledge. Four items about local affairs were included (the name and party affiliation of the mayor, the date of a court-ordered busing plan, and a solution to a local waste disposal problem) and four parallel national items (the name and party affiliation of the local member of Congress, the effective date for the Panama Canal Treaty, and offering a solution to the national problem of the oil shortage). Average scores were about 2.7 for the local items and 1.9 for the national problems.

After a multivariate path analysis, the coefficient relating newspaper exposure and the local knowledge measure was .20; for TV exposure the path coefficient was −.03. The same pattern was found for the national knowledge measure: .25 for newspaper versus .10 for television. Becker and Whitney also related the most used source to both measures with similar results. Respondents who claimed to get most of their news from newspapers scored 2.8 on the local knowledge items and 2.2 on the national items, compared to 2.4 and 1.5, respectively, for those who were dependent mainly on television. The same pattern was found within all age and education breakouts of the sample. This study is important because it suggests that similar processes may operate for the flow and comprehension of both local news information and national news.

(9) 1980 national election study. The series of national election studies conducted by the University of Michigan's Center for Political Studies (CPS) has included several information questions over the past two decades, as we have already seen. The 1980 CPS election study asked its national sample of about 1300 respondents if they knew (1) the names of the congressional candidates running for election in their district and their respective political parties (a two-point scale running from 0.0 to 2.0), (2) whether Democrats or Republicans had more members in the House of Representatives before the 1980 election, and (3) which party had more House seats after the 1980 election. Respondents in this national probability sample of the population were also asked several questions about their mass media use during the campaign, allowing us once again to relate media exposure to political information.

The results of separate analyses of each of the four questions are shown in Table 3.4, before and after adjustment by education, degree of political interest, other media use, and other demographic or background factors. The pattern of unadjusted results is strikingly similar across the three items. Heavier users of all four media are better informed than nonusers, and the trends tend to be monotonic for intermediate use groups. The media are ranked in terms of their overall magnitude of high-low differences, with newspapers at the top, followed by magazines, television, and radio. The differences by newspaper use are fairly large, actually being greater than for the factor of education and for knowledge of candidates and their parties.

However, this impression of notable "media effects" changes drastically after adjustment for other predictors (particularly, it

TABLE 3.4 Variations in Political Information by Media Exposure and Education (1980 National Election Study of the University of Michigan's Center for Political Studies)

		Knowledge of Names and Parties*		Party with Most House Members		Party Elected Most Members	
		Before Control	After Control	% Before Control	% After Control	% Before Control	% After Control
Total (1253)		0.61	0.61	73	73	15	15
Newspapers stories read							
good many	(321)	.98	.76	88	78	26	22
several	(383)	.66	.62	80	76	16	15
just 1 or 2	(189)	.46	.54	75	78	09	10
none	(361)	.31	.49	52	64	07	12
High-Low		+.67	+27	+36	+14	+19	+10
Magazine stories read							
good many	(86)	1.11	.68	92	75	28	15
several	(204)	.75	.52	89	75	23	16
just 1 or 2	(153)	.55	.46	79	71	15	11
none	(811)	.53	.65	67	73	12	16
High-Low		+.58	+.03	+25	+02	+16	-01
TV programs seen							
good many	(307)	.82	.56	79	70	22	17
several	(463)	.68	.64	81	77	15	15
just 1 or 2	(313)	.43	.61	63	70	12	15
none	(171)	.37	.61	58	71	07	12
High-Low		+.55	-.05	+21	-.01	+15	+05

TABLE 3.4 Continued

		Knowledge of Names and Parties		Party with Most House Members		Party Elected Most Members	
		Before Control	After Control	% Before Control	% After Control	% Before Control	% After Control
Radio stories heard							
good many	(321)	.95	.75	84	77	20	14
several	(383)	.70	.58	82	74	20	17
just 1 or 2	(189)	.47	.51	74	74	15	16
none	(361)	.55	.63	67	67	12	14
High-Low		+.40	+.12	+17	+05	+8	+00
Education							
grade school only	(139)	.48	.39	51	55	07	08
some high school	(152)	.37	.39	57	63	10	12
high school graduate	(459)	.48	.52	70	73	10	11
some college	(258)	.72	.75	84	82	19	19
college graduate	(125)	.88	.83	90	83	20	17
graduate school	(121)	1.04	.94	89	79	34	30
High-Low		+.56	+.55	+48	+24	+27	+22

*One point given for name and one point for party, making a possible score of 2.0

seems, for professed personal interest in the campaign). Differences by TV and magazine usage virtually disappear, and the differences by radio and newspaper use are more than halved. Newspaper use continued to play a role in predicting levels of political information, and much more than radio, but its effects were now less than half those attributed to levels of education. Nonetheless, newspaper use was the only media variable that remained a significant predictor of information for all four questions beyond the 99% level of statistical confidence. Exposure to political television programs was related to slighty *lower than average scores* for the first two items in Table 3.4 after MCA adjustment.

(10) Economic knowledge (Kennamer, 1983). This was a telephone study of 389 individuals in the Madison, Wisconsin area conducted in 1982, focusing on public information about Reaganomics. The interviews were conducted by undergraduate students with no information given on response rates or weighting to offset any sample imbalance. Some 12 questions were asked in the survey, some questions requiring the matching of names of persons in the news with their positions, others concerning how specific spending areas had been affected by Reaganomics, and other general (open-ended) questions on inflation rates, budget deficits, and unemployment rates. Respondents averaged 6.8 items correct.

At the bivariate level of analysis, Kennamer found newspaper exposure measures to be more highly correlated with economic knowledge. Thus, those who said they relied primarily on newspapers for economic news correctly answered 7.8 questions compared to only 6.0 for those who relied primarily on television; the same result held true for those relying on newspapers for public affairs information generally. Frequency of newspaper reading correlated significantly ($r = .17$) with economic knowledge, whereas frequency of television news exposure did not. More significant predictions were found for the *attention* paid to economic news in each medium, with the newspaper attention measure again being a stronger correlation ($r = .30$) than the television attention measure ($r = .23$).

However, after multivariate control, the predictive power of all of these media variables was reduced to insignificance, with differences by respondent's education and gender predominating as predictors. One other media exposure variable remained highly significant: Frequency of interpersonal discussion had a better coefficient of .25 after control (and a correlation of .40 with economic knowledge at the bivariate level).

(11) Processing the news (Graber, 1984). Undoubtedly the most unique study reviewed in this chapter in terms of its sample design and field procedures, this project had a sample that was too small (n = 21) to be considered representative even of the local area (Evanston, Illinois) from which it was drawn. What the study lacked in breadth, however, it more than made up for in depth.

Graber got to know her respondents far better than most researchers usually do. Her respondents composed a panel who were interviewed individually ten times through the year 1976. Each interview lasted about two hours and focused on the kinds of information the panelists had extracted from the news stories to which they had been exposed. In addition, 18 of the panelists kept running news diaries of the stories to which they had been exposed during the study, with an average of over 500 stories recorded per panelist.

In examining a sample of 275 of the news stories covered through the year, Graber asked her panel to name the source from which they remembered seeing that story. From the total of 1,568 stories about which the 21 respondents were considered to have ample knowledge, the news source for nearly half (48%) was the newspaper. Television was cited for only 27% of the stories listed (with 9% for radio, 6% for magazines, and 10% for other sources). Much the same ratio was found for the more than 10,000 stories that panelists had noted in their news diaries: 57% came from newspapers versus 30% for television. Graber (1984: 85) concluded that these data "provide strong support for the view that newspapers, even in the age of television, remain the chief source of remembered information . . . especially for the better educated."

(12) 1983 news awareness project. The final study in this section is one examined in more detail in the following chapter. It is based on another small, national probability sample of 544 respondents interviewed by telephone in the month of June 1983 by the Survey Research Center of the University of Maryland. Like the 1970 study reported earlier, this survey included several questions on mass media use, along with five questions involving identification of various news personalities (e.g., Federal Reserve Board Chairman Paul Volcker, consumer advocate Ralph Nader), which were similar to those analyzed in Table 3.2. These questions were scored in terms of the respondent's ability to describe the long-term role and position in society of these figures, and not on the specific short-run stories in the news, if any, that might have brought them into prominence during the previous week. (This short-term news information is considered in Chapter 4.)

It can be seen in Table 3.5 that respondents in our 1983 survey identified fewer than half of these news figures correctly (with an average score of 2.2 out of 5). Education was again the major predictor, being at least twice as predictive as any of the individual media use variables. Prior to adjustment for education and other media usage, newspaper and magazine use were the major predictors of ability to identify these news personalities. Radio and television use in this survey were associated with *lower* than average scores. After adjustment, moreover, newspaper and magazine use were only slightly less effective predictors, with the effect of radio newscasts listening being reversed. Watching television newscasts also continued to show a negative relation to news information.

One further interesting corroboration of this latter finding is provided by the final question listed in Table 3.5—the familiar survey item on the source of most news. Once again, respondents indicating more TV dependence scored slightly lower than average in information, and this was also true after control for the other media use and demographic factors.

(13) Other studies. In addition to the studies cited above, we may briefly note the following results from studies that have less generalizable samples or that have been reported in less detail than those summarized above. In the most recent of these, Turner and Paz (1984) reported that California residents claimed to rely more on newspapers than on television for their main source of information about earthquakes, and increasingly so through the duration of the study. Tan and Vaughn (1976) found newspaper reading to be more highly correlated with public affairs knowledge ($r = .34$) than television viewing ($r = .05$) among a local sample of 257 black high school students, and remained so after control (partial $r = .27$). Atkin and others (1976) found political knowledge to be (slightly) more related to newspaper use than television use in the 1972 University of Michigan election study after multivariate control, much as we found in Table 3.5 with the 1980 election data.

Certain research in the agenda-setting literature also indicates stronger relations between the media's agendas and the public's agendas for newspapers than for television (McClure and Patterson, 1976; McCombs and Shaw, 1976).

SUMMARY

In this chapter we have reviewed the findings of 15 different studies relating mass media use to a variety of measures of news information

TABLE 3.5 Average Score Differences in Identification by Various Factors (1983 News Awareness Project)

		Before MCA Adjustments	After MCA Adjustments
Total Sample (544)		2.2	2.2
Read newspaper/week			
no days	(85)	1.5	1.8
1-2 days	(91)	1.9	2.0
3-4 days	(74)	1.6	1.7
5-6 days	(42)	2.8	2.9
7 days	(246)	2.8	2.7
High-Low		+1.3	+.9
Read newsmagazines			
no	(375)	2.1	2.2
yes	(165)	3.1	2.7
High-Low		+1.0	+.5
National TV news watched			
no	(70)	2.4	2.4
yes	(472)	2.2	2.2
High-Low		−.2	−.2
Radio newscasts heard			
no	(142)	1.8	2.4
yes	(398)	2.4	2.2
High-Low		+.6	−.2
Educational level			
grade school	(88)	1.4	1.5
high school graduate	(168)	2.2	2.2
some college	(157)	2.8	2.7
college graduate	(81)	3.5	3.4
graduate school	(47)	4.2	3.8
High-Low		+2.8	+2.3
Most used source			
newspaper	(149)	2.5	2.3
television	(248)	1.9	2.0
radio	(64)	2.7	2.7
magazine	(7)	3.1	3.1
other	(9)	1.2	1.7
Newspaper-TV		+.6	+.3
TV-Average		−.3	−.2

across a 20-year period. These studies involve a wide range of informational content, study designs, age groups, geographical locations, and information settings. In *not one* of these studies do we find viewers of TV newscasts in general emerging as much more informed than nonviewers after other factors are controlled; that is especially true for people who claim that television is their main information source. Further, hours of television viewed is correlated with lower information of all kinds except one: knowledge of entertainers on television. Obviously these results call into serious question the meaning and validity of the main source question. They also raise the possibility that TV itself may be almost inimical to the successful learning of news information.

In general, the largest gains in news information are associated with newspaper usage. In some of the studies in this chapter, we have also found newsmagazine readers to be as informed as or more informed than newspaper readers, which is not unexpected given the more specialized and intensive news coverage in magazines. The results in this chapter also indicate that the channel of interpersonal communication may have been overlooked as a news source, and that conclusion is examined in more detail in the following chapter. Radio use was generally not found to be related to information gain, although general or prior information may be of considerable importance.

Before leaving the material in this chapter, it is important to note that we have been examining the role of these media for the entire mass audience and not for its subsegments. In that context, it is important to note that the patterns of greater information differences by newspaper usage (or usage of magazines or radio) rather than television may not be an across-the-board result, as Graber and other analysts have suggested. Table 3.6 contains some evidence from two of our studies of differential media patterns within certain education groups, again after adjustment for other media use and education. In particular, differences associated with TV news viewing in both parts of Table 3.6 appear greater for people with less than a high school education than for those with more education.

In the case of the University of Michigan's political information questions, for example, regular news viewers with less than a high school education scored .19 points *higher* than nonviewers, but of those with a college education, heavy news viewers scored .10 *lower* than average. In the case of our 1983 News Awareness Project questions, TV news viewers among the less educated scored .33 points *above* average, but among college graduates, TV news viewers again scored *below* average (− .31 points); in the case of the Washington regional part of our study (not shown in Table 3.6 but discussed in Chapter 4) these differences were both positive but were +2.4 for television viewing among the less educated and only + .9 for the college educated. All these findings suggest that television does play a

TABLE 3.6   High Group Minus Low Group Differences in Information
Levels by Media Use (After Adjustment by MCA)

	Low Education	Middle Education	High Education
(a) University of Michigan (1980 CPS Election Study)			
Radio	+.34	−.20	+.29
Magazines	−.65	−.31	+.36
Television	+.19	+.04	−.10
Newspapers	+.80	+.49	+.51
	(290)	(459)	(503)
(b) News Personalities (1983 News Awareness Project)			
Radio	−.03	+.48	−.25
Magazines	+.03	+.89	+.88
Television	+.33	−.47	−.31
Newspapers	+.77	+.91	+.79
	(101)	(257)	(161)

more positive informational role for less-educated people, consistent
with early expectations of television's greater ability to reach the less-
literate members of society. Parallel results are reported for television
use in the 1972 election study by Atkin and others (1976), although, as
seen in Table 3.6, the effects for newspaper exposure are also stronger
among the less educated.

We shall review further evidence to this effect in the following
chapter. Evidence from both chapters thus suggests that TV and to a
lesser extent other media may act as something of an information
leveler for the less-educated segments of society, raising them closer to
the overall average—but at the same time depressing the scores of the
college educated closer to the average. Nonetheless, the weight of the
evidence in both chapters predominantly shows the television medium
to have a rather dismal record as a medium of information.

NOTES

1. The exact words have not been identified in order to prevent contaminating later
survey responses.

2. Separate cohort analyses of the 1974 and 1984 sample data indicate little
monotonic shift in scores by age groups, with younger age cohorts (i.e., those under 35)
showing about a 0.3 point decline between 1974 and 1984, those aged 36-44 a 0.4 increase, those aged 45-64 a 0.2 decrease, and those over age 65 a 0.4 point increase;
cohort effects are virtually nonexistent, with only one cohort (those aged 18-25 in 1974)
showing more than a 0.2 difference. Interestingly, however, the average score for each

equivalent educational level in 1984 was slightly lower (about 0.3 points) than in 1974, which would be consistent with the failure of the overall score of correct answers to rise despite population increases in level of education—the main factor related to vocabulary scores in the static sense. (It would be necessary for the above unadjusted differences to be 0.7 or above to be considered statistically significant at the customary 95% confidence level.)

3. The advantage of the MCA program over other multiple regression programs, then, is that it provides such straightforward adjusted averages for specific categorical groups in the sample (e.g., for men and for women; or for blacks, whites, and other racial groups). An MCA is also useful for ordered groups, for example, high versus middle versus low income (or age or education) because one can see whether relationships are linear and monotonic or have "peaks" or "valleys" in the middle categories. The principle drawback of an MCA is that it does not provide error estimates that are necessary to conduct standard statistical tests on average difference scores between groups.

4. A sixth psychological factor that did not work well as a predictor was "Assertiveness," which asked people whether they preferred giving rather than receiving opinions from others, or defending their own point of view rather than listening to another's point of view, or generally talking more, rather than listening, during conversations. Further information about all of the above scales, their question wordings (which were generally presented in forced-choice format rather than agree-disagree format to reduce "response-set" effects), and the distribution of responses to them is given in Appendix A. The scales were also correlated with certain attitude dimensions (e.g., anticommunism, nostalgia) in the Flint-Toledo study.

5. Racial differences were also less pronounced, and the patterns with age and sex were opposite to what they were with news personalities: Younger adults scored significantly higher than older people and women scored slightly higher than men. Scores were also higher among people who scored higher on our psychological measures of news seeking, preference for realistic entertainment, and cosmopolitanism. People who said they took part in more conversations and who were involved in wider friendship networks were better informed about entertainment personalities, and at about the same level as for news information.

Chapter 4

COMPREHENSION OF A WEEK'S NEWS

JOHN P. ROBINSON
MARK R. LEVY

The preceding chapter examined audience recall and comprehension of long-run news information. This chapter reports on research that reduces that unrestricted time frame to focus on a week's worth of news. Although there is nothing magical about a seven-day period, there are several reasons why assessing audience awareness and comprehension of news presented over the course of a week may provide more valuable insights into the public's responses to mass communicated news.

First, asking about news at the end of a week more realistically reflects actual patterns of audience exposure. The chances, for instance, that an individual will watch a given network newscast on any evening (discussed in the following chapter) may be as small as one in twenty. However, over the course of a week, the likelihood of *any* TV news exposure and its associated opportunity for information gain and comprehension may increase up to three-quarters or more of the population.

Second, over the course of a week, there is an accumulation of exposure to the news as individuals see or hear multiple newscasts and read subsequent days' editions of the newspaper. To the extent that coverage of "important" news within and across news channels is complementary or redundant, audiences are more likely to receive several accounts of the same news item, and that should further aid awareness and comprehension. The news media themselves often provide weekly news summaries in the Sunday newspapers or on TV programs such as CBS News's *Sunday Morning*.

Third, gauging news comprehension after roughly a week allows some time for interpersonal discussion of the news to take place. News stories often serve as a topic of conversation, and it is possible that the interpersonal utility of the news enhances recall and comprehension.

Fourth, unlike the study of a single night's news, taking a week of news stories virtually assures that a greater substantive variety of news will have had time to unfold and develop. Greater variety may provide a larger number of stories, any one of which could attract audience attention. Increased story "maturity" may aid individuals seeking to integrate the news into short-term or long-term memory, and thus make it less likely that events will be forgotten.

This chapter reports findings about news awareness and comprehension drawn from two different national surveys, one in England and the other in the United States. The British survey was based on an in-person quota sample of 507 adults and was conducted on Saturday, June 24, 1978, by interviewers from the Audience Research Department of the BBC. Although the survey was carried out using a nonprobability method of respondent selection, it used a sampling technique that has been used on a regular basis to produce nationally projectable figures (it was the BBC's "Daily Survey"); quota controls for age, sex, and social class to match national population characteristics assured some representative spread of respondent characteristics.

The American study, on the other hand, was a national probability survey. A total of 544 adults were interviewed by telephone from the Survey Research Center at the University of Maryland, phone numbers being selected by the random-digit-dialing method. The U.S. national interviews were "in the field" through the month of June 1983, with most interviewing done on weekends. Fieldwork was split into four separate weeks' news in order to cover a broader variety of news stories and to reduce the possibility that an atypical news week would be chosen. In addition to this national sample, public understanding of weekly news stories had also been examined across four weeks in the prior month (May 1983) to add to the generalizability of the news stories under investigation and further ensure that one unusual news week would not skew the results. That study interviewed a random sample of 407 residents of the general Washington, D.C. area, also by telephone from the Maryland Survey Research Center.

In both the British and American surveys, respondents were asked about their exposure to the news during the preceding week, as well as questions that attempted to measure respondent awareness and comprehension of the 8 to 15 "most important" news stories of the previous week.

As in the research to be reported in Chapter 5, the selection of "most important" news stories represented a collective judgment by news media professionals. Stories were chosen after discussions with panels of high-ranking TV *and* print journalists. Panel members in England included news editors from the BBC and ITN, the London *Times,* the Manchester *Guardian,* and other news media; panelists in the United States worked for the *Washington Post, USA Today,* Associated Press, CBS News, and ABC News.

We asked our working journalists the following questions: (1) What have been the "big" stories during the past week? (2) What were the one or two most important things (i.e., the "main points") that the audience should have learned from those stories? We made a conscious effort to include only news stories that had received extensive coverage in *all* news media, and the wording of the survey questions was checked with the panel to ensure appropriateness and accuracy.

Respondent comprehension was measured by the adequacy of responses to questions about the central piece of information in the news item, as had been established by the panel of journalists. (See Table 4.1 for U.S. examples.) Responses were coded using the 0 to 8 comprehension scale described in more detail in Chapter 5. Coding was by "consensus" between two separate coders, with initial intercoder agreement being in excess of 90% of all codings. A response that provided the main point of the story but gave no additional important details was coded 5 and the respondent was said to have comprehended the item. Scores were allowed to range up to 8, a value indicating that the respondent knew the main point of the story plus three additional important details.

In addition, a summary measure representing total news comprehension was constructed for each respondent. For each answer scored 5 or higher, the respondent received 1 point. These points were then summed and (for the U.S. survey) normalized to equalize the total number of weekly news items, which did vary slightly from week to week. Scores on this summary measure for the U.S. national survey ranged from 0 (indicating no items comprehended) to 14, indicating comprehension of all items for a given week; in the Washington sample, scores ranged from 0 to 9.

NEWS AWARENESS: SOME EXAMPLES

In order to receive a comprehension score under our scoring scheme, a respondent first had to be aware of the story. Audience awareness in

TABLE 4.1   Examples of U.S. News Items and Their Main Point

News Story	Main Point
(1) Reagan's problems in passing his defense budget	GOP senators giving him more trouble than democrats
(2) Catholic bishops pastoral letter on nuclear war	Letter opposes Reagan policies
(3) Large earthquake in California	No fatalities
(4) John Glenn in news	Announces presidential candidacy
(5) American killed in El Salvador	First U.S. military advisor to be killed
(6) AIDS	Groups most susceptible
(7) Reagan, Mondale statements on education reform	Specifics of proposed policies
(8) Pope's visit to Poland	Pope critical of Polish government
(9) Space shuttle	Weather problems at Florida landing site
(10) Supreme Court rules on abortion	Ruling made it easier to get abortion

the American study, for example, was measured by a "yes-no" response to a question that took the generic form, "Did you hear or read anything last week about _____?"

Through the course of each four-week field period, we asked respondents in the U.S. regional sample about 23 different persons, events, or phenomena that had been in the news, and respondents in the U.S. national sample about 31 distinct persons, events, or phenomena. (See Appendix C for text of questions used.) The mean single "awareness" score was 68% in the regional sample and 62% in the national sample. That means roughly two-thirds of respondents in each sample said they had heard or read about the story. However, awareness varied considerably among the news items, as the examples in Table 4.2 demonstrate.

Stories detailing government actions, in both domestic and foreign policy, tended to rank near the bottom in terms of public awareness. Almost three-quarters of respondents, for example, did not remember hearing or reading that Paul Volcker had been reappointed to head the Federal Reserve Board. And despite a presidential address to a joint session of Congress, roughly the same proportion of respondents could not recall anything about Reagan administration policy in Central America in general or about a major shake-up in State Department personnel dealing with the area in particular. Further, roughly half or fewer of the respondents could recall being exposed to

TABLE 4.2   Selected U.S. News Items and Proportions
             of Respondents Aware of Each

		% Aware
(1)	Paul Volcker (reappointed)	28
(2)	Change in State Department officials	30
(3)	Supreme Court ruling on legislative veto	40
(4)	Developments at Geneva arms talks	42
(5)	"Stolen" debate briefing books	53
(6)	Western economic summit	67
(7)	Elections in Great Britain	67
(8)	Pope's trip to Poland	73
(9)	Disease called AIDS	80
(10)	American killed in El Salvador	85
(11)	Floods in Utah	89
(12)	Space shuttle flight	94

news about a Supreme Court ruling regarding legislative vetoes, the latest developments in the strategic arms talks between the United States and the Soviet Union, or the so-called Debategate briefing book scandal.

By contrast, two-thirds or more of the American public was aware of the economic summit of Western industrial nations at Williamsburg, elections in Great Britain, and the Papal visit to Poland. Among the news stories of which our respondents were *most* aware were "human interest" items (e.g., the victims of AIDS, floods in Utah) or especially dramatic news of real or potential danger (e.g., the space shuttle flight) or violence (e.g., the murder of an American military advisor in El Salvador). As we shall see shortly, human interest or dramatic stories often, but not always, tended to be the items that also received the highest comprehension scores.

NEWS COMPREHENSION

The 8 comprehension questions asked of the British sample are shown in Table 4.3. Items included both domestic and international news and varied in terms of personal relevance (e.g., gas prices) and human interest (e.g., the items on Margaret Jones described below, an Ulster kidnapping and ambush, and the arrest of British citizens in Arabia). All of these stories had been given extensive coverage in the week prior to the interview.

The average British respondent received a score of 5 or better on 2.3 of the survey's 8 comprehension questions. Not one respondent in

TABLE 4.3   Survey Questions and Percentage of British Respondents
Giving "Correct" Answer

		%
(1)	Did the OPEC countries this week decide to raise the price of oil, lower the price of oil, keep it roughly the same, or what?	66
(2)	What have the Americans been arguing with the Russians and Cubans about over the last few years?	40
(3)	Who were the people kidnapped in Ulster and what happened to them?	35
(4)	What have the Britons been arrested and punished for in Saudi Arabia?	30
(5)	What reason did the British army give for ambushing the three men in Ulster?	23
(6)	A rise was reported in the government's pay policy figures on earnings. Why is this seen as important?	16
(7)	Can you briefly describe who Margaret Jones is and why she is in the news?	15
(8)	Can you briefly describe who Egyptian General Shazli is and why he is in the news?	2

the sample got all questions correct, and only 2% of English respondents got 6 or 7 items correct. As with awareness, however, news stories with high personal relevance or those that were high in "human interest" were often comprehended by larger numbers of people.

Some examples of comprehension items from the American surveys are shown in Table 4.4. In the U.S. national sample, fewer than 4% of respondents comprehended 10 or more of the week's average of 14 major news stories. Results were quite consistent with the British results: On average, American respondents understood the main point of 4.6 out of the average 14 news stories per week. In the regional sample (Washington area) the average score was 2.7 across the average of 9 items asked per week; not one of these respondents successfully understood the main point of more than 5 of the week's major stories.

Comprehension levels by story type showed substantial cross-national similarities. Thus, in England, two-thirds of respondents understood that OPEC was again raising the price of oil. About the same proportion of American respondents gave answers indicating that they understood news stories about the kinds of people most susceptible to AIDS. Dramatic events with a human-interest angle (e.g., the unsuccessful attempt of Sirhan Sirhan to win parole, the

TABLE 4.4   Selected Questions and Percentage of U.S. Respondents
Giving "Correct" Answer

		%
(1)	Why was Sirhan Sirhan in the news?	64
(2)	What groups are most affected by AIDS?	61
(3)	What was the American who was killed in El Salvador doing there?	61
(4)	Why was Dan Rather in the news?	53
(5)	Why was Lech Walesa in the news?	45
(6)	Why was Margaret Thatcher in the news?	42
(7)	Why were the Nicaraguan diplomats expelled from the U.S.?	34
(8)	Why was Jesse Jackson in the news?	29
(9)	What did the Supreme Court decide in its recent ruling on abortion?	22
(10)	Why did Congress want to limit the July 1st tax cut?	19
(11)	What is the Nicaraguan government doing that the Reagan administration wants stopped?	11
(12)	What did Walter Mondale say about education in America?	8

murder of an American advisor in El Salvador, the kidnapping in Ulster) also scored comparatively higher in comprehension.

However, in both nations, there were some notable exceptions to these general patterns. In the British study, for example, the name and situation of Margaret Jones (an unmarried school headmistress who had just resigned her prestigious position because she was pregnant) was not widely comprehended, despite its apparent human drama. Similarly, only one U.S. respondent in five understood that the Supreme Court had made it easier to get an abortion. Even more striking, despite a presumed universal interest in taxes, fewer than one American respondent in five understood the wrangle over the tax "cap" (Democrats in Congress claimed a cap would affect only "the rich"; Republicans said the middle class would be hurt).

News reports about personalities and foreign events, particularly when the events were personified, were sometimes comprehended at above-average levels. More than half of the American respondents, for example, knew that CBS newsman Dan Rather was involved in a libel trial. A larger than average percentage of the British respondents knew the main point that the continuing U.S.-Soviet-Cuban dispute was over Angola; above-average percentages of our American respondents understood that Margaret Thatcher had just won a stunning reelection victory, or that Lech Walesa was again in trouble with the Polish authorities.

On the other hand, only one American respondent in nine seemed to understand the Reagan administration's "beef" with the Sandanista government of Nicaragua; only 2% of the U.K. sample knew that Egyptian General Shazli had had a falling out with the Egyptian government (he was later to be accused of leading the assassination of Anwar Sadat). News about more complex and detailed governmental actions or policies (e.g., the British government's pay policy figures on earnings, proposals for educational reform by Walter Mondale) were comprehended at below-average levels.

BACKGROUND FACTORS AND NEWS COMPREHENSION

An examination of the average comprehension scores of four main background factors is shown in Table 4.5 and indicates considerable consistency between the three samples in the two countries with regard to predictors of news comprehension.

In both England and the United States, for example, there were fairly large differences in comprehension scores between men and women, with men tending to have higher scores. Comprehension also increased with respondent age, although the differences were somewhat less pronounced in the U.K. sample, and showed some tendencies for curvilinearity in the U.S. studies, in which somewhat lower scores were found among older than among middle-aged groups. For all respondents, level of formal education was a major predictor, especially in the two American samples, in which the mean comprehension score for respondents with some postcollege education was more than double that of respondents who had only a high school education.

Similarly, "prior news knowledge" (an independent measure related to formal education and interest in the news) showed the strongest positive relationship to news comprehension. Similar results will be found and discussed in more detail in Chapter 5. In the British sample, respondents who scored highest in *prior* knowledge had average comprehension scores for the week's news that were more than twice as high as those of respondents who had the lowest scores on the "prior knowledge" measure; in the U.S. samples, such differences were more than six times as high. It also can be seen that self-professed interest in the news was also strongly correlated with news comprehension in the national U.S. sample; for example, respondents who followed the news "very closely" had comprehensive scores that

TABLE 4.5 Variations in Comprehension Score by Demographic and Other Variables

British Sample			U.S. Samples	National		Regional	
Total Sample		2.3	Total Sample		4.6		2.7
Sex			**Sex**				
male	(242)	2.8	male	(258)	5.7	(174)	3.2
female	(265)	1.8	female	(286)	3.8	(217)	2.3
High-Low		+1.0	High-Low		+1.9		+.9
Age			**Age**				
18-34	(133)	2.1	18-29	(128)	3.7	(104)	2.1
35-49	(167)	2.3	30-39	(129)	4.9	(85)	3.3
50+	(207)	2.3	40-49	(83)	5.0	(61)	3.1
			50-59	(63)	5.1	(65)	2.6
			60-69	(70)	5.6	(47)	2.5
			70+	(61)	4.3	(27)	2.9
High-Low		+.2	High-Low		+.6		+.8
Education			**Education**				
14-16 years	(171)	2.0	high school	(88)	3.1	(75)	1.7
17-18 years	(196)	2.1	high school graduate	(168)	4.2	(117)	2.1
19-20 years	(98)	2.2	some college	(157)	5.4	(70)	2.6
21+ years	(42)	3.4	college graduate	(81)	6.7	(129)	3.9
			graduate education	(47)	8.6		
High-Low		+1.4	High-Low		+5.5		+2.2
Prior news knowledge			**Prior news knowledge**				
none	(283)	1.7	none	(117)	1.4	(72)	.5
one	(121)	2.6	one-two	(165)	3.1	(58)	1.6
two	(75)	3.3	three-four	(163)	6.5	(102)	2.5
three	(28)	4.0	four-five	(67)	9.5	(54)	3.7
High-Low		+2.3	High-Low		+8.1		+4.1
			How closely follow news				
			very	(97)	6.4	not asked	
			somewhat	(250)	5.4	not asked	
			not very	(165)	2.4	not asked	
			High-Low		+4.0		

95

on average were two and one-half times higher than respondents who followed the news "not very closely."

MEDIA USE AND
NEWS COMPREHENSION

Patterns of news media usage were also generally related to news comprehension, but at a much lower level than for the background factors. In the case of the British sample (Table 4.6), the "quality" of media exposure was often as significant as its quantity. Thus, although no direct relationship between amount of radio news exposure and comprehension was found in the British data, they did show that *which* radio station respondents listened to made a difference. Listeners to Radio 4, which provides a heavy concentration of news and public affairs programming, scored significantly higher.

Similarly, greater frequency of exposure to newspapers produced relatively little difference among British respondents. However, readers of the "quality" press in England (e.g., the *Guardian* or the *Times*) did score higher than respondents exposed to the tabloids. Further, news comprehension increased modestly, but monotonically, with exposure to BBC-TV news; but comprehension was slightly negatively related to greater exposure to ITN-TV news programs.

In the American data, shown in Table 4.7, exposure to national TV newscasts was also likely to be associated with increased comprehension of the week's news. But the TV usage differences shown in Table 4.7 were again not as large as for print media or radio usage. In contrast to the .3 and .5 gains for TV usage (in the national and regional data, respectively), the gain for radio usage, newspaper usage, and magazine usage were two to three times as high. Moreover, in the U.S. national sample, respondents who claimed to get most of their news from newspapers or from radio were also more likely to outscore "television-dependent" respondents. In fact, those who claimed to use TV most for information were below average in their information levels; and the same was found in the regional sample among respondents who clearly claimed TV to be their main information source. (In the regional sample, however, most respondents were not forced to make a single medium choice as in the national survey.) These findings echo earlier studies of TV news dependency and political knowledge (e.g., M. Robinson, 1976; Clarke and Fredin, 1978; Becker and Whitney, 1980; Kennamer, 1983).

TABLE 4.6   British Respondents' Comprehension Scores by Media Use

		Score
Total Sample	(507)	2.3
Radio news hears		
0-1 days	(215)	2.1
2-7 days	(292)	2.4
High-Low		+.3
Radio station listened to		
none	(139)	2.0
Radio 1	(133)	1.9
Radio 2	(58)	2.6
local	(90)	2.3
Radio 4	(87)	3.1
High-Low		+1.1
Newspaper reading		
0-1 days	(120)	1.9
2-7 days	(387)	2.4
High-Low		+.5
Which newspaper read		
none	(53)	1.7
popular, tabloid	(362)	2.2
"serious"	(92)	3.0
High-Low		+1.3
BBC-TV news watched		
0-1 days	(158)	2.0
2-3 days	(212)	2.2
4-7 days	(145)	2.7
High-Low		+.7
ITN-TV news watched		
0-1 days	(158)	2.3
2-3 days	(172)	2.5
4-7 days	(177)	2.0
High-Low		−.3

However, the largest consistent differences in the Table 4.7 data are not for the mass communication variables but for the interpersonal communication measure. Talking about the week's news with other people was related to considerably higher comprehension levels. As the number of conversations about the news increased from none to twenty or more for the week, the average comprehension score almost doubled in both U.S. samples.

TABLE 4.7   U.S. Respondents' Comprehension Scores by Media Use
            and Communication Behaviors

	National Score		Regional Score	
Total Sample	(544)	4.6	(405)	2.7
Radio newscasts heard				
none	(142)	3.7	(74)	2.0
1-2	(23)	3.1	(24)	2.6
3-5	(78)	3.8	(58)	2.8
6-9	(121)	5.5	(69)	2.6
10-19	(82)	5.2	(66)	3.0
20+	(93)	5.0	(99)	3.4
High-Low		+1.3		+1.4
Watch any TV news				
yes	(471)	4.6	(335)	2.8
no	(70)	4.3	(55)	2.3
High-Low		+.3		+.5
Read newspaper				
none	(85)	2.9	(67)	1.2
1-2 week	(91)	3.9	(58)	2.6
3-4 week	(74)	3.9	(54)	2.9
5-6 week	(42)	5.2	(31)	3.1
7 week	(246)	5.6	(180)	3.2
High-Low		+2.7		+2.2
Read newsmagazines				
yes	(165)	6.3	(145)	3.5
no	(375)	3.7	(245)	2.4
High-Low		+2.6		+1.1
Main source of news information				
newspapers	(149)	5.0	not asked	
television	(248)	4.2	not asked	
radio	(64)	4.8	not asked	
other	(80)	4.2	not asked	
High-Low (TV-Newspapers)		−.8		
Talk about news				
none	(190)	2.9	(132)	1.8
1-2	(71)	4.2	(38)	2.3
3-5	(133)	5.5	(100)	2.7
6-9	(65)	5.7	(63)	3.8
10-19	(35)	6.8	(37)	3.7
20+	(31)	6.4	(20)	3.9
High-Low		+3.5		+2.1

NOTE: Sample sizes for individual categories are smaller than for total because of missing data.

This striking relationship between news comprehension and talking about the news reinforces the familiar findings in the communication literature about interpersonal channels playing a crucial role in communication effectiveness. In the multivariate analyses that follow, we examine this result in greater detail and ask whether it occurred because people who engaged in large numbers of news-related conversations were more attentive to other news media, or whether these conversations raised comprehension scores for those with relatively inattentive low and high media exposure.

MULTIVARIATE ANALYSES

Up to this point, weekly news comprehension scores have been linked to possible predictor variables, with those predictors considered individually. Subjecting the data to the same multiple classification analysis (MCA) procedures we have used in Chapter 3, it is possible to examine these findings adjusted for several predictor variables simultaneously. The results of such analyses are presented in Table 4.8 for the British study and Table 4.9 for the two phases of the American study. They show that even after extensive controls, most of the differences by media factors in Tables 4.6 and 4.7 are diminished, but that these media factors still provide some predictive power. Moreover, they show that some similarities remain in both the British and American results.

In the British sample, for example, controls for age, education, and sex—but particularly prior knowledge—explain several of the apparent differences between the respondent groups, noted earlier. As shown in Table 4.8, there are, for instance, no longer any meaningful distinctions between the scores of men and women or among respondents of different ages. Even the differences by education level are all but eliminated.

Among British respondents, the MCA also reduced to insignificance most relationships between the quantity and quality of exposure and news comprehension scores. The one exception is with regard to listeners of Radio 4, who continue to outscore those exposed to other stations. Watching TV news is also associated with higher scores, again more so for BBC than for ITN; but no one of the differences by TV exposure is very large. The same is true for exposure to newspapers, with very minor increases found for those who read newspapers more frequently and those who read higher-quality newspapers.

TABLE 4.8   MCA of Comprehension Scores with Controls for
Background and Media Use Variables
(U.K. Sample)

		Score			*Score*
Total Sample	(507)	2.2			
Sex			Radio news heard		
male	(242)	2.3	0-1 days	(215)	2.2
female	(265)	2.2	2-7 days	(292)	2.3
High-Low		+.1	High-Low		+.1
Age			Radio station listened to		
18-34	(133)	2.3	none	(139)	2.2
35-49	(167)	2.4	Radio 1	(133)	2.1
50+	(207)	2.2	Radio 2	(58)	2.4
High-Low		−.1	local	(90)	2.0
			Radio 4	(87)	2.8
Educaion			High-Low		+.6
14-16 years	(171)	2.4			
17-18 years	(196)	2.3	Newspaper reading		
19-20 years	(98)	1.9	0-1 days	(120)	2.1
21+ years	(42)	2.6	2-7 days	(387)	2.3
High-Low		+.2	High-Low		+.2
Previous information			Newspaper read		
none	(283)	1.8	none	(53)	2.2
one	(121)	2.6	popular, tabloid	(362)	2.3
two	(75)	3.0	"serious"	(92)	2.4
three	(28)	3.2	High-Low		+.2
High-Low		+1.4			
			BBC-TV News		
			0-1 days	(150)	2.1
			2-3 days	(212)	2.2
			4-7 days	(145)	2.6
			High-Low		+.5
			ITN-TV News		
			0-1 days	(158)	2.1
			2-3 days	(172)	2.4
			4-7 days	(177)	2.3
			High-Low		+.2

In the American data, on the other hand, the differences by TV
usage are among the smallest in Table 4.9. Radio differences continue
to be larger, as was true in Table 4.8. In the national sample, differences by magazine usage are even larger, and the differences by
newspaper exposure are far larger than in the British data.

TABLE 4.9 MCA of Comprehension Scores by Background and Media Use
Variables (U.S. Samples)

	National		Regional	
Total Sample	(544)	4.6	(407)	2.7
Sex				
male	(258)	5.2	(174)	2.9
female	(286)	4.0	(271)	2.5
High-Low		+1.2		+.4
Age				
18-29	(128)	3.9	(104)	2.2
30-39	(129)	4.5	(85)	2.8
40-49	(83)	4.6	(61)	2.8
50-59	(63)	5.0	(65)	2.7
60-69	(70)	5.5	(47)	2.9
70+	(61)	4.6	(27)	3.6
High-Low		+.7		+1.6
Education				
high school	(88)	3.3	(75)	1.9
high school graduate	(168)	4.3	(117)	2.2
some college	(157)	5.0	(70)	2.7
college graduate	(81)	6.1	(129)	3.6
graduate education	(47)	7.5	(129)	3.6
High-Low		+4.2		+1.7
Watch any TV news				
yes	(471)	4.7	(335)	2.7
no	(70)	4.4	(55)	2.7
High-Low		+.3		0
Talk about news				
none	(190)	3.5	(132)	2.2
1-2	(71)	4.3	(38)	2.3
3-5	(133)	5.2	(100)	2.6
6-9	(65)	5.2	(63)	3.6
10-19	(35)	6.2	(37)	3.2
20+	(31)	5.4	(20)	3.3
High-Low		+1.9		+1.1
Read newsmagazines				
yes	(165)	5.4	(150)	2.8
no	(375)	4.2	(245)	2.6
High-Low		+1.2		+.2
Reading newspaper				
none	(85)	3.4	(67)	1.6
1-2 week	(91)	4.3	(58)	2.8
3-4 week	(74)	4.2	(55)	2.8
5-6 week	(42)	4.9	(31)	2.7
7 week	(246)	5.2	(180)	3.0
High-Low		+1.8		+1.4

TABLE 4.9   Continued

	National		Regional	
Radio newscasts heard				
none	(90)	4.1	(74)	2.3
1-2	(23)	3.7	(24)	2.8
3-5	(78)	4.0	(58)	2.8
6-9	(121)	5.3	(69)	2.9
10-19	(82)	4.9	(66)	2.7
20+	(93)	4.8	(99)	3.0
High-Low		+.7		+.7
News dependence				
newspaper	(149)	4.7	not asked	
TV	(248)	4.4	not asked	
radio	(64)	5.0	not asked	
other	(16)	4.2	not asked	
TV-newspaper		−.3		

NOTE: Sample sizes do not reach total for individual questions due to missing data.

Moreover, among American respondents the multivariate analysis tends to narrow, but not completely eliminate, variations in comprehension scores between men and women. Some of the curvilinear relationships between comprehension and respondent age continue but are "straightened out" in the regional data, with the most elderly best informed. Differences by education level remain relatively strong with education remaining the major predictor in Table 4.9.[1]

Thus, after the MCA, American respondents who claim to have paid most attention to newspapers for their news in the preceding week emerged with higher comprehension scores than those who read less. Most interesting, however, is that interpersonal communication about the news remains strongly related to understanding the news in both U.S. samples after all other measured factors are taken into account. Moreover, the interpersonal discussion variables survive a larger MCA much better than does newspaper reading, or other mass media usage. In that larger analysis of the national data, the respondents' estimates of how closely they followed the news was entered as an additional predictor to those examined in Table 4.9. These results suggest that the reason heavier newspaper readers score much higher in Table 4.9 is in large part due to readers following the news more closely.

There is another finding to be considered in the American data, namely the extent to which television's lack of relationship to comprehension holds across the board, that is, for less-educated respondents as well as for the better educated. The possibility that television might act as informational leveler for less literate segments of the population who are more directly reached by television was suggested in our concluding analyses in Chapter 3. That aspect of the data is examined in Table 4.10, which shows differences by media exposure between educational groups *after* MCA control in the American results.

Once again the larger differentials by newspaper and by magazine exposure tend to hold across all three education levels. The most dramatic differences, however, occur for television: In both studies, the TV differentials are positive for the least-educated groups (less than a high school degree) and *negative* for the college-educated group. Although the group differences are generally not statistically significant, this intriguing pattern is consistent across both studies *and* with the result presented in Chapter 3 for political information. Thus, television may very well be playing its hoped-for educational role among the less well-educated segments of society. On the other hand, it appears as though TV has the opposite effect on comprehension scores among the better-educated viewers who depend on it. In short, then, TV news indeed may be more of a *main source* for the less well educated.

SUMMARY AND DISCUSSION

In summary, then, what can be said about the public's awareness and comprehension of the news over a week's time? Perhaps the most obvious observation to be made is to point out the striking similarities between the findings in the three surveys presented here and those in Chapter 3. Key predictors of comprehension, such as prior knowledge and print media usage, are the same in both data sets; gender and age differences are rather consistent as well. Most differences by TV news viewing, particularly in the American results, are either insignificant or in the wrong direction—that is, comprehension scores are lower among those who view, or who say they depend most on, TV news.

Yet there are important differences in the British results. Print media differences tend to be lower, and broadcast media differences somewhat larger, than in the American results. These conclusions are reinforced by results from a more recent British news comprehension survey conducted with 535 London residents by the Independent Broadcast Authority in 1984 (Gunter, 1984). That telephone study was

TABLE 4.10   High-Low Media Use Differences in Comprehensive Levels
Among Educational Groups (U.S. Data)

		High School Incomplete	*High School Graduate*	*College Education*
(a)	National Data	(90)	(260)	(161)
	newspapers	+1.7	+1.9	+1.6
	magazines	+.4	+1.2	+1.9
	radio	−.5	+1.4	+.2
	TV	+1.5	−.2	−.1
(g)	Regional Data	(77)	(120)	(210)
	newspapers	+1.4	+.7	+1.8
	magazines	+.6	+1.1	+.4
	radio	+.3	+.8	+.5
	TV	+.6	+.6	−.4

more similar in research design and execution to the two phases of the American study than the BBC study examined in this chapter. It examined identification of eight political figures and three news stories that had been given extensive media exposure in the previous week; respondents obtained correct scores for slightly under half of these items. The study found gender and age patterns similar to those in the BBC study, but somewhat larger educational differences than in Table 4.8.

The Gunter study also found sharper differences across the news media use variables. After multivariate control, the extent of national news viewing was the main predictor (partial $r = .14$), being slightly higher than listening to radio news programs ($r = .10$), radio discussion programs ($r = .10$), and *type* of newspapers read ($r = .11$); simple frequency of newspaper reading was unrelated to comprehension ($r = .03$).

The fact that national television programs are more predictive in the British context, even if only slightly more, puts our American research in important cross-national perspective, and suggests that the American results may be unique to the media system in our country. This suggestion is further reinforced by Schulz's (1982) results from West Germany, in which TV news exposure (and radio news exposure) were again more important predictors than newspaper exposure, particularly for the reading of local and tabloid German newspapers.

Schultz's results are limited by the fact that he examined only younger news users. But there are some striking parallels with Gunter's British results, especially regarding the importance of type of newspaper usage, and there is also the possibility that national TV news programs in West Germany are closer in structure to British newscasts than American newscasts.

Nonetheless, there was a more striking parallel with Gunter's British results and those found in the American data in Table 4.9. That concerns again the variable of personal discussion, which emerged from the British data as *the* most important media predictor after multivariate control (partial r = .21). Talking about the news with others, then, seems to have at least as powerful an effect on comprehension as exposure to the news media.[2] This is perhaps not surprising given what is known in general about the role of interpersonal communication in clarifying manifest message content and creating a consensus of shared meanings. But the fact remains that interpersonal communication is a factor that has been too often neglected in discussions of the main source.

Finally, there continues to be a disturbing "bottom line" to our findings: Much less than half of the week's "most important" news in all these studies is getting through to the audience. That conclusion has serious implications for journalism, public understanding, and the democratic process, but we will save our remarks and suggestions until Chapter 9, after we have considered how comprehension research more generally fits into journalistic norms and practices.

NOTES

1. However, that is not the case once the prior information is inserted as a predictor. When that happens, education disappears as a predictor—as it did in the British data in Table 4.8. This point is discussed in more detail in the next chapter, where the prior knowledge variable once again overpowers the education variable as a predictor of accurate information. There is an important problem in the prior knowledge variable in the U.S. data in that it was too closely tied to personalities who were in the news that week. Thus, one of our prior information items asked respondents to identify Paul Volcker (as head of the Federal Reserve Board); subsequently respondents were asked why Volcker was in the news. This unfortunate confounding of the prior information and news comprehension variables led us to discard this as a plausible "independent" variable in the Table 4.9 analysis.

2. Schultz (1982) did not include personal conversations as a separate variable, but did find a highly significant correlation (r = .49) between news awareness and political participation.

Chapter 5

COMPREHENSION OF A
SINGLE EVENING'S NEWS

JOHN P. ROBINSON
DENNIS K. DAVIS

The research in this chapter focuses not, as in Chapter 4, on the week's news but rather on a single newscast on a particular day. It asks, What is the impact of that newscast on those who view it? Of the information in that newscast, how much shows evidence of having been comprehended or "digested" one to three hours after broadcast? What kinds of viewing variables are most closely related to that comprehension? Unlike the research in Chapters 3 and 4, then, we are able to study the cognitive impact of a specific news media source.

This news source research focuses on the national TV newscast, in particular specific newscasts for specific days. At the conclusion of that evening's news, we had interviewers knock on the doors of homes around the country to identify viewers who had seen that specific network newscast that evening. Households were selected in these national probability samples using the "random route" method of sampling.[1] Respondents in these national probability samples who indicated that they had viewed that newscast were then interviewed for about 25 minutes concerning as much of the information they recalled and understood from the newscast. Respondents were also asked to provide information concerning their levels of attention to the news, their attitudes about the newscast, other news media that they had used during that day prior to the newscast, and their demographic background (e.g., age, race, education).

Heavy reliance was placed on a respondent's answers to open-ended questions; this allowed analysis of comprehension in a respondent's own interpretive framework. Both general and specific information questions were included in the study and were precisely tailored to the content of that newscast, their wording having been finalized and telephoned to interviewers only about two hours prior to the broadcast. The researchers had developed the questions from consultations during the day with the editors and writers who put together that evening's news. This ensured that the most important points on that evening's newscast were represented in the survey.[2]

These same field procedures were used for four evening newscasts in Great Britain in June 1978 and for three evening newscasts in the United States in June 1979. In the British study, a total of 489 viewers of the 5:40 p.m. newscast from BBC (or about 120 per evening) were interviewed. In the U.S. study, the sample size was 447, or about 150 for each of the three networks (ABC, NBC, CBS) examined on those evenings. In order to keep sampling and field costs at a manageable level, rural areas of the country were excluded from the U.S. sample; thus sample respondents were probably somewhat higher in educational background and, hence, in news comprehension ability than the United States as a whole.

These samples are too small and limited to characterize with much precision audience comprehension for a particular evening (the usual 95% confidence limits being plus or minus 10% for any single evening's newscast); but when pooled, the samples should be sufficient to identify systematic differences across stories or types of people. This is particularly true for differences that are replicated across both the British and American settings—and that are also in Chapters 3 and 4.

MEASUREMENT OF COMPREHENSION

Both studies used the same basic approach to measurement of comprehension as used in Chapter 4. Comprehension is not an easy variable to conceptualize, let alone measure. Indeed, many scholars argue that it is impossible to measure in any final sense. As Trenaman (1967: 25) suggested,

> In the sense defined by the Oxford English Dictionary—'the faculty of grasping with the mind'—comprehension cannot be tested, for we cannot witness such a process in action. What we can measure is the use to which comprehended material can be put.

The most common empirical approach to demonstrating comprehension is the ability to answer questions related to the main points or gist of the story material.

We felt that most earlier empirical attempts to tap viewers' store of news information were inadequate, incomplete, and also unfair. First, much of that research (or the reporting of that research) failed to discriminate between *recall* and *understanding*. Even a person who had paid close attention to and understood most of the information in a newscast might be able to come up with only one or two stories when asked point-blank to recall them. Conversely, remembering individual details from a story does not constitute evidence that the individual understood what the story was about. Further, understanding does not necessarily require recall of certain factual details about the story, such as the exact geographical location of the story or the specific identification of the news personalities involved.

We were interested less, then, in how many stories viewers could recall or the story details than in whether respondents had gotten the gist of the story—that is, the main point(s) of interest that the newsmen themselves claimed to have put into the story. Hence, we proceeded on the assumption that if individual viewers could be shown to be able to recall what the *newscasters themselves* had identified as the "central point" of a particular news story, then comprehension had taken place.

In order to employ such a definition in the survey setting, we felt it important that viewers be given extensive opportunity to demonstrate that comprehension. This meant going beyond "unaided recall"— that is, questions that simply asked viewers to recall freely what they could from the newscast without any aids to memory. We found in our preliminary focus-group studies in England (see Appendix B) that even in high attention situations, few viewers could spontaneously recall much of what they had seen. Unaided recall produced results that seriously underestimated the rich array of information that viewers were later able to demonstrate that they *had* gleaned from the newscasts—a conclusion demonstrated both in their individual responses to our direct questions and in their free-form conversations in subsequent group discussion. Similar results had been found in the earlier recall studies when more specific follow-up questions were asked (Neuman, 1976).

This experience was corroborated in our national in-home surveys when we began our interviews with an unaided recall question. Fewer than two items on the newscast were freely recalled—far lower than we were to find with our more in-depth methods.[3] After the unaided recall question, we proceeded to give national survey respondents one or two short word descriptors ("bullets") for each item in the newscast. As an example, we used the bullet "Flogging" for a British news story on two oil employees who had been flogged and imprisoned in Saudi Arabia for breaking strict Islamic laws against alcohol. To qualify as having comprehended the central point of that story, viewers had to mention in their open-ended response to "Flogging" that the two men had been punished because they had broken the strict Saudi laws on the use of alcohol—which was the "central point" of *this* story (in contrast to other central points that may have appeared in other media reports of this story) according to that evening's news editor. Responses to that effect would put the viewer at level 5 on the scale described in Figure 5.1. Viewers who in their open-ended answers mentioned only details of the punishment (e.g., the instruments used, the exact nature or duration of the punishment, or the usually longer prison term for the original incident) without the central point were scored at level 4 on the scale. Viewers who mentioned such details *in conjunction with* the central point were scored at levels 6, 7, or 8, depending on the number and correctness of the details mentioned. Our scoring scheme thus put a premium on the main point of the story that the news writer or news editor had put into *that* story, and not, as we discuss in more detail below, what viewers may have picked up from other media accounts.

Viewers who could give neither the details nor the central point of the story were scored at the four lowest levels: level 0 (for recalling a story not on the newscast), level 1 (could not recall story), level 2 (said they recalled the story but then could give no specific information), or level 3 (vague recollection). An example of a level 3 response for the flogging story would be mentioning the general location or the individuals involved with no reference to the actual incident (e.g., "something in the Middle East," "some oil workers").

One basic advantage of the coding scheme in Figure 5.1 is its flexibility. In our analysis, we have chosen to use level 5 as the minimum for comprehension. Several researchers have told us they would feel more comfortable with responses we coded at level 4 (or even level 3) as the comprehension threshold. Others would raise the threshold to levels 6 or 7 on the scale because viewers were able to place the story in some correct context. The coding scale shown in Figure 5.1 can easily accommodate such differences in criterion levels for comprehension without the need for recoding the original data.

Our bullets (or brief headlines) for each story were prepared in the afternoon preceding the newscast after extensive discussion with the

Score	Type of Response to Information Stimulus ("Bullet")
0	Recall wrong story, information not in the newscast
1	Cannot recall; no reply; don't know
2	Recall something but then can give no details
3	Vague, general responses related to the story
4	Some details of the story, but not the central point
	Comprehension Threshold
5	Central point of the story, no further important details
6	Central point of the story, plus one further important detail
7	Central point of the story, plus two further important details
8	Central point of the story, plus three or more further important details

Figure 5.1   Basic Coding Scheme

senior editors for that newscast at each network. The discussion focused not only on which items were likely to be included but also on the main points and content of each news story. The researchers and editors then developed a suitable bullet description from one to five words that all agreed would best characterize but not "tip off" the central point of the story. The bullet usually identified either the location, the general actors, or the central action involved in the news story.

To supplement this aided recall approach, the researchers and editors also devised a set of six specific questions about the information in six of the stories in the newscast. The purpose of the specific questions was to act as a further check on whether the information leads provided in the bullets were sufficient. Examples of these follow-up questions are, "What reason did the Saudis give for punishing the Britons in Arabia?" "What topic did the Prime Minister discuss in Parliament today?" "What reason did the army give for conducting the raid?"

These bullets and questions had to be completed two hours before the newscast so that they could be telephoned to the interviewers across the country. Each of the two researchers contacted field supervisors with these final details of question wording, and the supervisors relayed them to each interviewer in their region. The interviewer then transcribed the required question wording into those portions of the interview schedule that had been left blank for that purpose.

Because late-breaking events changed the newscast right up to the broadcast time, not all news items that were telephoned were eventually broadcast. As noted above, such unused news items provided a useful set of "control" stimuli in the study. On the basis of the respondents' answers to such "placebo" stories, we were able to gauge the extent to which answers contained information actually in the newscast, rather than plausible conjectures or information picked up from the other media.

CODING

Once the questionnaires were completed, edited, and returned from the field offices to the researchers, the verbatim comprehension responses were transcribed and coded, with extensive help from the news editors. The editors had already indicated to us what they thought were the central points of each story, and we used these central points as the main criterion in coding each verbatim response into one of the nine categories shown in Figure 5.1. The actual coding, however, was done by the researchers, because we were the most familiar with the construction and aims of the coding scheme. The verbatim responses were then retranscribed onto separate sheets, in the order of the category into which they fell. That is, all the "0" category responses were typed onto a page listing, then all the "1" responses, and so forth, up to the code "8" responses.

At this point we returned the grouped responses to the editors and asked them to agree or disagree with our codings. Editors agreed with over 80% of our codings, and most of the disagreements concerned changes across only one category level. News editors occasionally had second thoughts about the central point of a few of the stories. In those instances, we reexamined the actual newscast transcript and made any appropriate changes in definition and coding. This was necessary for only about a tenth of the stories in the study.

The final score on the 0-8 comprehension scale, then, was our measure of comprehension for each story. If there were 11 items on the newscast, a respondent could score anywhere from 0 (wrong information on each item) through 55 (central point only for each item) up to 88 (score of eight on each item). Although on some evenings more items were broadcast than others, this was controlled by entering evening of broadcast as a variable into the regression analyses that follow.[4]

INDEPENDENT (PREDICTOR) VARIABLES

These analyses first relate our viewers' comprehension scores to several separate types of predictor variables. News stories that had higher comprehension levels and their relevant characteristics are discussed in Chapter 8. The three sets of viewer predictor variables analyzed in this chapter are

(1) *Demographic and Background Factors:* These include the usual background factors of age, education, and social class as well as date of newscast and prior information. The prior information variable was measured by four name-recognition items.[5]
(2) *Prior Media Exposure:* These include newspapers read and radio or TV reports heard earlier on that day as well as general perceptions of how much respondents felt they knew about the newscast's stories prior to broadcast.
(3) *Psychological Viewing Factors:* These mainly include measures of the "uses and gratifications" viewers said they derived from newscasts, either for enlightenment or curiosity, or for reassurance and support. These items were adapted from Levy's (1978a) measures of gratifications associated with viewing television news. Those items were based on earlier British studies (McQuail, Blumler, and Brown, 1972) and have been shown to be generally applicable to the gratification experiences of both American and British audiences (Levy, 1978b). Also included in this list of variables are attention to the newscast (or "freedom" from distraction) and self-perceived ability to understand the news: Viewers were asked whether they had paid complete attention to the newscast from beginning to end or whether there had been interruptions in viewing and the nature and length of those interruptions.

In the analyses that follow, each set of these independent variables is treated separately.

RESULTS FROM THE BRITISH STUDY

Respondents obtained a score of 5 or better for slightly over a third of the BBC news stories broadcast; the central point of a typical story, then, reached about a third of the audience. The proportions of comprehension ranged widely: from 3% for a story on U.S. Secretary of State Cyrus Vance's comments on Africa to 81% for a story about a mountain climber killed in the Himalayas. (See Chapter 8 for a fuller breakdown of comprehension differences across the nearly 100 stories examined.) For all stories in a given evening the average ranged only from 29% for the lowest evening to 40% for the highest evening, indicating general regularity in comprehension across the four evenings studied.

The overall comprehension *score* on the 0-8 scale in Figure 5.1 averaged about 28 (27.7 to be exact) per evening from a possible average score of 88 (for 11 news stories) across all evenings.[6]

Background Factors

Table 5.1 shows variations around the mean of 27.7 by the major demographic predictors of comprehension. Of these, *prior* information—that is, information concerning news personalities who had been prominent in the news but who were not mentioned during these newscasts—was clearly the variable with the largest spread in scores and thus the most important correlate. Those who correctly answered all four of the prior knowledge questions obtained a score of 39.0, almost twice as high as those unable to recognize any of the four (20.8).[7]

Education differences were not as large as for the prior information variable, varying between only 35.2 for those who had left school at age 21 or older, versus 26.3 for those who had finished their formal education at ages 16-17, and 27.1 for those who had finished prior to age 16. Occupational class differences varied between 20.2 for unskilled workers and 34.2 for lower-level professional-technical workers; however, high-level professional workers (28.5) hardly differed from moderately skilled blue-collar workers (27.4) in levels of comprehension.

Systematic differences by age were also difficult to locate, the only noteworthy difference being found for viewers under age 25, who scored almost five points below average (22.9). Scores were somewhat lower (24.1) for the June 15 newscast than for subsequent newscasts, but that factor is controlled in later analysis.

Media Factors

Table 5.2 shows differences in comprehension by how much the viewer had used other mass media for news prior to the newscast. Generally, exposure to other news media showed much lower differences on comprehension scores than the background factors examined in Table 5.1. For media differences that did occur, it was the type of medium and not exposure per se that made more difference. Thus respondents had higher comprehension scores (33.0) if they had read any serious newspaper (*Times, Guardian,* etc.) than if they had only read other types of newspapers (27.4).

Similarly, if they had listened to the news on BBC's Radio 4, they scored higher (34.4) than if they had listened to other news broadcasts on that day (29.3); moreover, those who had heard no radio newscast (25.9) scored almost as high as those who had heard two or three (28.7). Those who had seen the lunchtime news on television scored only about one point higher than those who had not.

TABLE 5.1 News Comprehension as a Function of Background Factors
(Four Days Combined, British Data)

Total Sample (489)		Average Score = 27.7
Age		
under 25	(68)	22.9
25-34	(88)	30.6
35-44	(83)	28.4
45-54	(54)	29.4
55-64	(73)	26.2
65+	(122)	28.0
High-Low*		+5.1
Education		
Leaving age: 14-15 and under	(289)	27.1
16-17	(117)	26.3
18-20	(49)	28.3
21+	(34)	35.2
High-Low		+8.1
Social dlass		
unskilled, unclassified	(78)	21.8
semi-skilled	(44)	26.5
moderately skilled	(88)	27.4
skilled	(112)	27.7
highly skilled	(59)	28.7
lower professional	(78)	34.2
higher professional	(30)	28.5
High-Low		+6.7
Prior information (out of four items)		
none	(201)	20.8
one	(142)	28.4
two	(68)	36.0
three	(44)	35.9
four	(34)	39.0
High-Low		+18.2
Date of newscast		
June 15	(137)	24.1
June 19	(147)	29.0
June 20	(122)	28.3
June 22	(83)	30.8
High-Low		6.7

*High group score minus low group score; sign shows expected group difference.

Finally, although those who felt they knew most or all of the stories prior to the newscast scored higher (29.4 and 30.0) than those who knew hardly any of the items (24.7), they did not score higher than those who felt they had known "less than half" of the news items beforehand (30.9).

TABLE 5.2   News Comprehension as a Function of Other Media Usage
(Four Days Combined, British Data)

		Score
Total Sample (489)	Average Score =	27.7
Read newspaper		
no	(215)	24.2
yes	(274)	30.5
High-Low*		+6.3
Which type of newspaper		
none	(215)	24.2
popular	(210)	27.4
serious	(64)	33.0
High-Low		+8.8
Heard radio bulletins		
none	(277)	25.9
one	(105)	31.9
two	(39)	28.7
three +	(68)	28.6
High-Low		+2.7
Which radio stations for news		
none	(277)	25.9
local and commercial	(55)	26.9
radio 1	(30)	23.7
radio 2	(39)	31.6
radio 4	(88)	34.4
High-Low		+8.5
Watched lunchtime news		
no	(430)	27.6
yes	(59)	28.4
High-Low		+.8
Felt knew stories prior to this newscast		
almost all	(44)	29.4
more than half	(54)	30.0
about half	(171)	27.7
less than half	(103)	30.9
hardly any	(117)	24.7
High-Low		+4.7

*High group scores minus low group scores; sign shows expected group difference.

In contrast to Table 5.1, the only groups showing deviations of over 5 points from the average for these media variables in Table 5.2 were for the Radio 4 listeners (34.4) and for serious newspaper readers (33.0).

Psychological Viewing Factors

The psychological viewing factors shown in Table 5.3 generally had less predictive power than the media use factors in Table 5.2. The differences were in the expected direction, however, with viewers who said they watched the news for reassurance scoring lower on the comprehension scale than those who did not, but the difference was only about 4 points. Similarly, viewers who said they watched the news to feel informed scored higher than those who did not, but the difference was less than 3 points. On the other hand, viewers who said they watched news for other "cognitive" reasons (out of curiosity and for comparison of their ideas with the newscasters') scored *lower* than those who said they did not watch to obtain those gratifications.

Conversely, and as would be expected, respondents who at the outset of the interview said they gave the newscast their full attention from start to finish scored 6.6 points higher (32.2 vs. 25.6) than those who were distracted from the set by other activities during the newscast. But the largest difference in Table 5.3 is between those viewers who *felt able* to comprehend almost all the news (31.8) and that minority who felt they *could* understand half or less than half of the news stories (16.8). This 15-point difference is only exceeded by the 18-point difference by prior information in Table 5.1.

Figure 5.2 summarizes the results from Tables 5.1 through 5.3 in a single diagram. At the top of the diagram are the groups that scored most above average: those with high prior information (39.0), those completing school after age 21 (35.2), and Radio 4 listeners (34.4). At the bottom are those groups scoring most below average: unskilled workers (21.8), those with no prior information about any news personalities (20.8), and those who felt they understood half or less of the newscast items (16.8).

Multivariate Controls

Not all of the factors in Figure 5.2 act independently of one another. People who were better educated tended to be better informed. People who were better informed read more serious newspapers and listened more to in-depth coverage of the news on Radio 4. Heavier users of these media felt they were also able to understand TV newscasts. There is the need, therefore, to use MCA to keep the various multiple factors in those tables statistically separate from one another and to provide "purified" estimates of each factor, estimates that represent what each factor contributes to comprehension on its own. The MCA

TABLE 5.3   News Comprehension as a Function of Psychological Viewing
Factors (Four Days Combined, British Data)

	%	Score
Total Sample (489)	Average Score	= 27.7
Watch news for reassurance		
low	(186)	29.5
medium	(196)	27.0
high	(107)	25.6
High-Low*		+3.9
Watch news for curiosity/comparison factors		
low	(186)	27.8
medium	(191)	28.0
high	(112)	26.9
High-Low		−.9
Watch news to feel informed		
no	(103)	25.6
yes	(386)	28.1
High-Low		+2.5
Attention paid to newscast		
partial	(318)	25.6
complete	(171)	32.2
High-Low		+6.6
Feel able to understand news		
almost all	(328)	31.8
more than half	(68)	23.6
about half or less	(93)	16.8
High-Low		+15.0

*Scale reversed to show expected differences.

program generates average values for the groups in Tables 5.1 through
5.3 that are controlled for the effects of other variables (such as date
of the newscast, education, and distraction).

As shown in Table 5.4, the gaps shown in Figure 5.2 are reduced
considerably when MCA is applied to the data. Rather than being 18
points above the "no information" group, those with the most prior
information are only 12 points above the lowest group after MCA adjustment. At the same time, the 9-point gap for another important
factor (education) is reduced to less than 1 point when other factors
(particularly prior information level) are taken into account. The unskilled occupational group similarly moves from 8 points below
average (before adjustment for other factors) to only 3 points below
average after adjustment, and the under 25 age group moves from 5

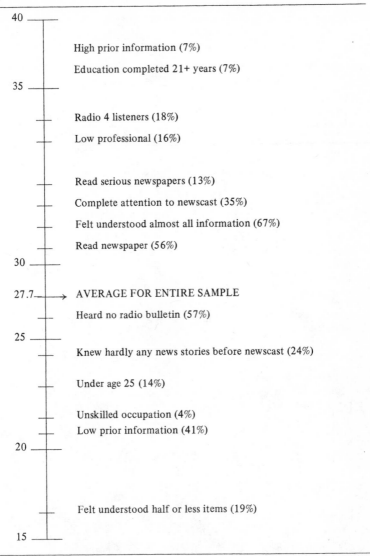

Figure 5.2   Summary of Variations in News Comprehension
              (percentage of total British sample group in parentheses)

points below average before adjustment to only 1 point below average after adjustment.

Similar shifts in results occur for the media exposure variables. Differences by type of newspaper do not hold up after adjustment, and the effect of having read any newspaper is reduced from a 9-point dif-

TABLE 5.4 News Comprehension Scores for Various Groups After Adjustment by MCA

Background Factors		Media Factors		Psychological Factors	
Total Sample Score (27.7)					
Age		**Newspaper read**		**Reassurance reason**	
under 25	26.7	no	25.3	low	29.1
25-34	29.3	yes	29.7	medium	27.0
35-44	27.4		+4.4	high	26.7
45-54	28.3				+2.4
55-64	24.6	**Newspaper type**		**Curiosity reason**	
65+	28.8	none	25.3	low	25.6
	+2.1	popular	27.8	medium	28.2
Education (years of schooling)		serious	26.7	high	27.2
14-15	28.0		+1.4		+1.6
16-17	27.5	**Radio bulletin**		**Informational reason**	
18-20	24.6	none	25.8	no	26.5
21+	28.9	one	28.0	yes	28.2
	+.9	two	28.5		+1.7
Social class			+3.7	**Attention**	
unclassified, unskilled	25.0	**Radio station**		partial	26.4
semiskilled	28.5	none	25.8	complete	30.2
moderately skilled	28.7	local/comm	31.3		+3.8
skilled	27.5	Radio 1	29.4	**Able to understand**	
highly skilled	26.3	Radio 2	37.0	all	30.2
low profession	30.2	Radio 4	36.4	>half	24.7
high profession	26.9		+10.6	<half	19.5
	+1.9	**Lunchtime news**			+10.7
Prior information		no	27.6		
none	22.7	yes	28.4		
one	28.8		+.8		
two	33.9	**Know stores before**			
three	32.2	all	27.7		
four	35.1	>half	27.6		
	+12.4	<half	27.8		
			.1		

ference to a 4-point difference. For radio listening, we find less difference by having heard a newscast than by the type of newscast heard, with scores well above average for Radio 4 (and Radio 2) listeners. The generally higher scores of those who felt they knew most of the stories before the newscast virtually disappeared after MCA control for these other factors. The difference between those who paid complete and less-than-complete attention to the newscast moved from 7 points to 4 points after MCA control.

Among other less important MCA predictors were reading of serious newspapers, viewing of the lunchtime news, and the psychological viewing factors of watching to feel informed and not watching to feel reassured—that is, watching out of curiosity or for comparison (which *was* higher than average after MCA control). The factor of age tended to be curvilinearly related to these comprehension measures, with those in the middle age groups (25-34, 35-44, 45-54) showing higher comprehension than those under age 25 or over 54 (especially those aged 55-64).

In summary, then, after control for prior information and perceptions of being able to understand the news, the only noteworthy predictor of comprehension of more items in the (early evening) BBC newscasts was listening to Radio 4 and Radio 2 newscasts. Very few predictors of what viewers comprehended from the news in Tables 5.1 through 5.3 retained much predictive power, including the viewer's formal education, usage of other media, or motivations for viewing. The accelerating process by which the already informed become more informed, then, seems to overshadow all other factors in the process of news comprehension according to these British results. And of the factors involved, it will be noted that the most powerful predictor is not respondents' level of formal education but their prior news information level.

Nor were these results solely dependent on our main measure of comprehension. They were almost exactly replicated when three other independent measures of comprehension were employed as the dependent variable in these analyses.[8]

Briefly, on *each* of these separate measures of comprehension, scores also increased mainly as a function of prior information and perceived ability to understand the newscast. Second-order predictors of these information measures included listening to news bulletins on radio, but also the degree of attention paid to the newscast, and the education variable (especially having completed formal schooling after age 20).

In general, then, these analyses confirmed that our Table 5.4 results were not simply an artifact of the main measure of comprehension we employed. It should be noted, however, that one indicator of comprehension did not produce the same pattern of results as the other four. That was the number of items freely recalled at the outset of the interview—that is, without any memory aid from the "bullets." Because that measure has been the one emphasized most often in prior studies of news comprehension, its poor performance here brings into serious question the validity of conclusions reached in the earlier studies. This is particularly true regarding their major implication—namely, the inability of viewers to follow much of what is being reported in newscasts. As noted at the outset of this section, news viewers seemed able to grasp about a third of the major points of stories in the newscast—perhaps a disappointing performance by some standards, but not as poor as prior research studies have led us to believe.

AMERICAN STUDY RESULTS

Respondents in the American study also obtained a score of 5 or better on about a third of the stories broadcast. The proportions of comprehension varied almost as much as for the British studies: from 5% or less comprehension for stories about prospective wage and price guidelines or about progress on the SALT II talks, to nearly 90% for stories on all three newscasts about resumption of flights with the DC-10 aircraft after one of them had been involved in a major air crash in Chicago. (Again, a more extended discussion of differences in comprehension by story is given in Chapter 8.)

The average comprehension score per evening was 43.3 from a possible score of 104 (13 stories per average newscast multiplied by the perfect score of 8 per item). In Tables 5.5 through 5.8, we have also included scores on the six-item direct question quiz asked for particular stories; the average score on this "quiz" measure was 18.2 out of 48 (6 items having 8 as the "perfect" score).

Because of missing data on certain variables, the effective sample size for these multiple classification analyses of the American data is only 387 respondents and not the total of 447 who were interviewed.

Background Factors

As shown in Table 5.5, prior information was again the main predictor of comprehension on both of our newscast comprehension measures. In the case of average story comprehension, the high-low differences on prior information were 14.4 units, compared to 11.4 units for high-low comparisons on the factor of education; in the case of the comprehension quiz, the scores varied by 8.8 points for prior information and 8.6 points for education. In other words, the differences again were generally lower than for prior information—although education level differences in the American study were sharper and more systematic than they were in the British study.

Differences by age were neither large nor significant. As in the British results, some curvilinear patterns were again observed with youngest and oldest respondents scoring lower on the quiz information measures than those aged 30-59. In the case of the story comprehension measure, viewers over age 60 scored lower than average, but those under age 30 scored higher than average. Differences by evening of newscast, while not significant, are statistically controlled in the analyses that follow.

Media Factors

As was the case with the British data, the differences in comprehension levels by media factors in the American study were much less significant than the background factors in Table 5.5. Thus, although viewers who had read a newspaper prior to the newscast did score higher than those who did not, the difference was only 1.6 points on the story comprehension score and 1.6 points on the quiz comprehension score (in contrast to the 11- and 9-point differences by education in Table 5.5). The differences by radio listening were even smaller, and in the case of story comprehension, viewers who had heard a radio news program prior to the TV newscast were slightly less informed after the newscast.[9]

In the case of viewers who were readers of news magazines, the differences were considerably higher but still well below differences by prior information and education. Viewers who read news magazines scored 3.3 points higher than nonreaders both on the story comprehension score and on the comprehension quiz. In the case of perceived awareness of the news stories (from these and other news sources), viewers who felt most aware also scored (2.2 points) higher on the quiz but less than 1 point higher on the story comprehension measure.

Thus the major media factor emerging in Table 5.6 is magazine usage, and although the other media usage factors were associated with higher scores, none of these differences is either large or consistent.

TABLE 5.5   Variation in Evening News Comprehension by Basic
            Background Factors (U.S. National Sample:
            Three Days Combined, Unadjusted Data)

		Story Comprehension	Quiz Comprehension
Total Sample (387)		43.3	18.2
Education			
grade school	(42)	35.8	13.2
high school graduate	(119)	42.5	16.3
some college	(119)	44.1	18.4
college graduate	(107)	47.5	21.8
High-Low		+11.4	+8.6
Prior information			
low	(145)	36.1	14.0
medium	(150)	46.4	19.5
high	(82)	50.5	22.8
High-Low		+14.4	+8.8
Age			
18-29 years	(97)	44.0	17.3
30-44 years	(110)	43.1	18.4
45-59 years	(98)	45.5	18.9
60+ years	(82)	40.4	17.8
High-Low		−4.0	+0.5
Days of newscast			
day 1	(132)	46.1	19.4
day 2	(129)	42.7	16.6
day 3	(126)	40.9	17.9
High-Low		5.2	1.5

Psychological Viewing Factors

Among the five factors examined in Table 5.7, three least useful predictors were the uses and gratification questions, which, in the case of the expressed reason to keep informed, were actually associated with lower comprehension scores. In the case of watching out of curiosity, virtually no differences were found. In the case of watching for reassurance, those agreeing that this was a reason did score lower than average as predicted, but the difference was only 2.5 points on the story scale and 1.6 points on the quiz score.

In contrast, differences by perceived ability to understand the newscast and by paying closer attention to it were associated with

TABLE 5.6   News Comprehension as a Function of Other Media Usage
(U.S. National Sample: Three Days Combined,
Unadjusted Data)

		Story *Comprehension*	*Quiz* *Comprehension*
Total Sample (387)			
Average Score		43.3	18.2
Read newspapers			
no	(185)	42.4	17.1
yes	(202)	44.0	19.3
High-Low		+1.6	+2.2
Heard radio bulletins			
no	(274)	43.5	18.0
yes	(113)	43.0	18.7
High-Low		−.5	+.7
Read news magazines (in general)			
no	(249)	42.2	17.1
yes	(128)	45.5	20.4
High-Low		+3.3	+3.3
Fully knew stories prior to newscast			
almost all	(81)	44.7	19.8
more than half	(80)	45.0	20.0
about half	(116)	42.9	17.4
less than half	(110)	43.6	17.6
High-Low		+1.1	+2.2

three to seven times as much variation in scores. Viewers who paid full attention to the newscast scored 9 points higher on the comprehension measure than those who watched only partially; and although not shown in Table 5.7, comprehension did decline steadily as viewers mentioned that they missed proportionately larger portions of the newscast. In the case of perceived ability to understand the newscast, the scores also declined monotonically and significantly with greater perceived inability to understand.[10]

Multivariate Controls

As with the British data, we subjected the data in Tables 5.5 through 5.7 to MCA and the results shown in Table 5.8 again tended to reduce considerably the high-low differences noted at the bottom of

TABLE 5.7   News Comprehension as a Function of Psychological Viewing
Factors (U.S. National Sample: Three Days Combined,
Unadjusted Data)

	Story Comprehension	Quiz Comprehension
Total Sample (345)*		
Average Score	43.3	18.2
Watch news for reassurance		
no (244)	44.0	18.7
yes (101)	41.5	17.1
High-Low	+2.5	+1.6
Watch news for curiosity factors		
no (93)	42.4	17.9
yes (252)	43.6	18.3
High-Low	+1.2	+0.4
Watch news to feel informed		
no (60)	43.6	19.1
yes (285)	43.3	18.0
High-Low	−.3	−1.1
Attention paid to newscast		
partial (223)	39.7	16.6
complete (122)	48.7	21.0
High-low	+9.0	+4.4
Feel able to understand news		
almost all (170)	46.4	19.8
more than half (70)	45.8	18.2
about half (52)	39.5	15.9
less than half (53)	30.9	14.2
High-Low	+15.5	+5.6

*Smaller than in Tables 5.5 and 5.6 because of more missing data on these questions.

these two-variable tables. One important exception to this trend was
the factor of age: After MCA controls, both measures indicate highest
comprehension of network news by the youngest age group and lowest
comprehension for the oldest age group.

Of the two major background predictors of prior information and
education, information held up more strongly after controls. In fact,
in the case of story comprehension, education level was practically
eliminated as a predictor after control for prior information. This was
similar to the pattern found in the British study, and we will elaborate
on this noteworthy finding in our concluding section.

TABLE 5.8 News Comprehension Scores for Various Factors After Correction by MCA (U.S. National Sample)

Background Factors

Average Score = 43.3 (Story)   18.2 (Quiz)

	Story	Quiz
Education		
grade	40.6	14.9
high	44.0	17.1
some college	44.3	18.5
college graduate	42.3	20.2
High-Low	+1.7	+5.3
Prior information		
low	33.6	15.0
medium	46.9	19.6
high	48.9	21.0
High-Low	+12.3	+6.0
Age		
18-29	46.4	18.5
30-44	43.3	18.2
45-59	43.8	18.1
60+	39.0	17.5
High-Low	-7.4	-1.0
Evening of newscast		
day 1	43.5	19.0
day 2	43.3	17.0
day 3	43.1	18.0
High-Low	+.4	+2.0

Media Factors

	Story	Quiz
Radio bulletin		
no	44.0	18.3
yes	41.5	17.4
High-Low	-2.5	+.4
Newsmagazines read		
no	43.5	17.9
yes	42.9	18.8
High-Low	-0.6	+0.9
Know stories before		
all	44.9	18.3
>half	42.8	18.6
<half	43.7	18.1
High-Low	+1.2	+.2
Newspaper read		
no	43.8	17.9
yes	42.8	18.4
High-Low	-1.0	+.5

Psychological Factors

	Story	Quiz
Informed reason		
no	42.4	17.8
yes	43.5	18.3
High-Low	+1.1	-.5
Attention		
complete	47.6	20.6
partial	40.8	16.8
High-Low	+6.8	+3.6
Reassurance reason		
no	43.7	18.4
yes	42.4	17.7
High-Low	+1.3	+.7
Curiosity reason		
no	43.5	18.7
yes	43.1	18.0
High-Low	-.4	-0.7
Able to understand		
all	44.6	18.4
>half	46.2	18.7
half	39.7	17.4
High-Low	+4.9	+1.0

Each of the media use factors discussed in Table 5.6 shows further reductions in effectiveness after the MCA control in Table 5.8. The already small differences in comprehension levels for prior newspaper, radio, and magazine news exposure in Table 5.6 are in most cases almost halved after control. The factor of perceived awareness of the news stories before the newscast, a significant predictor in Table 5.6, shows virtually no associated difference in comprehension after multivariate control.

Much the same is true for the uses and gratifications questions in Table 5.7. Even the question on perceived ability to understand the news, a major predictor in Table 5.8, is reduced to a fraction of its original explanatory power for the quiz measure after multivariate controls. The one factor that *did* maintain predictive power was the level of attention to the newscast. It will be remembered that this factor also survived relatively well as a predictor in the British data in Table 5.4. This is important because it indicates that attention to the newscast does play some role in increased comprehension.

SUMMARY AND CONCLUSIONS

Thus, in both the British and American studies, we find the following convergences in results:

(1) The major predictor of comprehension of newscast information is prior information.

(2) Prior information seems to exercise considerable influence over the primary predictor of comprehension in earlier research—namely, level of education. Nonetheless, both factors can act in concert to produce something of an "accelerating knowledge gap" between the informed and uninformed. Both refute Neuman's (1976) finding of no knowledge gap between better-educated viewers and less-educated viewers, one of the few general studies in the literature that has not found such a knowledge gap.

(3) Of the second-order factors in terms of predictive power, attention to the newscast stands apart from media use and psychological factors as an important predictor. Moreover, the greater the extent of described distraction from the news (that is, the lower the attention), the lower the comprehension. This is important because only about a third of news viewers in both countries said they watched the newscast without interruption from start to finish.

(4) In the case of British data, listening to a radio news channel and perceived ability to understand the newscast are also important predictors.

(5) Several factors related to news media use prior to the newscast were unrelated or only weakly related to comprehension levels. Along with

the evidence of very low comprehension levels of stories that were scheduled to be on the newscast but did not appear on the actual newscast, this indicates that the primary source of information provided by respondents was that newscast and not some other news source.

(6) In general, motivational or psychological viewing variables played a relatively minor role in predicting comprehension levels in both countries. Among the motivational variables, watching for reassurance reasons was associated with lower comprehension levels; that minority in the American study who said they felt stories should depend less on visual material and who were less critical of the newscast had higher information scores from the newscast.

From these six conclusions we single out two for more extended discussion. First, with regard to the performance of the prior information variable, it would appear that most previous information-flow studies have depended only on the factor of education to substantiate the "increasing knowledge gap" hypothesis and thus have overlooked the prior information variable (for which educational level may be considered a "proxy"). In other words, it may be less the factor of education that is responsible for the "gap," than the fact that those who are most informed are also those who are most educated. This suggests that being well educated is not sufficient to absorb news information; one must have used that educational background and skill to have absorbed the information that allows one to pick up additional information from the news media. Thus it appears that people's education must be combined with personal interest or abilities in a topic area to lead to more absorption of news information—and to produce the increasing gap between the information rich and the information poor noted in earlier studies. Put more succinctly, the knowledge gap is not a simple by-product of the educational process but is influenced by some personal investment of interest and ability as well.

The second point is that viewers *do* become informed from viewing TV news. This follows from our simple finding that viewers are able to understand and answer the comprehension questions we ask them. It is made even clearer by the consistent finding that viewers who watch with fewer interruptions or distractions score notably higher on all of our comprehension measures. And it is reinforced by the finding that news stories not eventually included in the newscast were comprehended at dramatically lower levels than those that were broadcast. Viewers therefore do pick up some information from newscasts.

However, this conclusion is not necessarily inconsistent with the findings in the previous chapter regarding TV news viewers' unimpressive scores as measured by weekly news comprehension levels. In that analysis, news viewers emerged with equal or lower scores than those who viewed few or no national TV newscasts. However, to score well on these *weekly* news questions, one must be able to remember content across several days. In the studies reviewed in this chapter we examined only one day. It would appear that either TV news presentations of short-run (daily) news stories do not effectively highlight their story's main points in relation to broader or to longer-run (i.e., weekly) types of informational frameworks or that they present them in such a short, fleeting, or nonredundant manner that the items make less impression on the audience's memory than having encountered the same information in the print media. These results would be consistent with Graber's (1984) and Robinson and Clancey's (1984) characteristic finding about the low staying power, or "teflon quality," of the information presented in TV newscasts.

Put in McLuhanesque terms, the presentation of news information on TV may be too nonlinear to register with our measuring instruments that examine linear information. Although this is an area that clearly requires further study and verification, the data in this chapter continue to reinforce our earlier doubts about TV being the main source of news information. That is not to deny that the public may not be made aware of news stories more quickly from television, but it also suggests that subsequent exposure, by reading in newspapers or magazines or by interpersonal discussion may be required for the point of these news stories to make a lasting impression on the viewer's memory.

NOTES

1. The random route method consists of selecting a particular street address at random from a master list and having the interviewers screen respondents at that address for people who had viewed that newscast. If no one had, interviewers continued with the next address to the right of that house and to the next house on the right, and so on, until a viewer was found. In general, it took about ten addresses to locate a viewer of a particular newscast. In some neighborhoods, however, no viewers of that particular evening's newscast were found after more than 50 households had been screened.

2. Not all the news stories that the editors were considering actually appeared on the newscast. Those that did not constituted an interesting "control group" of stories that were useful in indicating how much information respondents had learned about those subjects from stories that had only appeared in other sources.

3. The unaided recall question was, "Do you happen to remember any of the stories that were on the 5:30 News, or what they were about?"

4. In the case of comprehension for a particular story, a single comprehension score is the proportion of 5, 6, 7, and 8 scores over all respondents. In the case of the content-analyzed data on story characteristics (see Chapter 7), we also used the proportion of respondents who had scored 5 or above on that item. If no one had noted the central point, the score was 0 (for 0% comprehension); if half the viewers had noted it, the score was 50 (for 50% comprehension); and if all respondents had noted the central point, the score was 100.

5. The four names in the British study, for example, being (1) labor leader Moss Evans, (2) Doctor Coggan, Archbishop of Canterbury, (3) U.S. Ambassador to the United Nations Andrew Young, and (4) U.N. Secretary General Kurt Waldheim. None of the four had figured in any of the news stories covered on the four evenings, and this information thus remained independent of news information held by respondents prior to the newscast.

6. A score of about 28 per evening could possibly be obtained in several ways. For a 12-item newscast, a respondent could obtain that score by getting four 5s and eight 1s, for a 12-item newscast, or by getting nine 1s, one 3 and two 8s. As noted above, the scores did not vary widely by evening of broadcast, and such differences that did occur were controlled in the multivarate analyses that follow.

7. Because of the large number of group comparisons in Tables 5.1-5.8, as well as later in the report, we are unable to provide figures for tests of significance—particularly for the MCA programs described later in this chapter. As one rough rule of thumb for the data in Tables 5.1-5.8, a difference of over 5 points for two groups of 100 respondents would be statistically significant beyond the .05 chance level. In the high versus low comparison for prior information, the difference of 18.2 (that is, 39.0 − 20.8) was almost three times as large as that. In the case of educational attainment, only those leaving school past age 21 scored over 5 points higher than the other groups in Table 5.1, but those leaving school at ages 18-20 did not score higher than either those leaving at age 16-17 or under age 16.

In general, then, prior information looms far larger as an overall predictor of comprehension than the other factors. Highest scores were obtained for those high on prior information (39.8) and for those leaving school after age 20 (34.8). Viewers scoring lowest were those with no prior information items correct (20.8) and those in unskilled or unclassified occupations (21.3).

8. These measures were as follows: (1) The number of correct answers given to the *six direct questions* asked about information on the newscast (e.g., "Why did the Saudis punish the Britons in Arabia?" "Did the government figures show that unemployment had increased, decreased or stayed about the same?"). These were scored using the same scoring scheme outlined in Figure 5.1. Average score was 19.4 out of a possible 48. (2) The simple number of news items that respondents *said they remembered* from the newscast after the description of the "bullets." Average number of items remembered was 5.5 out of a possible 8-12. (3) The correct number of *specific pieces of information* present in the respondent's verbatim responses to each bullet. This scoring system differed from the Figure 5.1 scheme in that 1 point was scored for each correct piece of information that corresponded to the script for the newscast. This number varied according to the length of the story; in the flogging story, for example, separate points were given for mentioning that it took place in Saudi Arabia, that it involved infringing on strict Islamic laws, and that the laws concerned prohibitions on alcohol.

9. Because of the more localized nature of newspapers and radio stations in the U.S. sample, we were unable to collect data on the "quality" dimension of the specific newspaper or radio stations in the American sample.

10. Although not shown in Table 5.7, we also examined the effects of several other psychological or motivational factors. For example, we asked respondents whether they generally favored more or fewer visual elements in newscasts, more or less explanation of background information on news stories, and more or fewer stories on newscasts. Although none of these questions was a significant predictor, the one on visual material was most predictive—those in favor of fewer visuals being more informed, as might be expected among people who prefer to follow the news without the aid of pictures. Those who favored more explanation were also better informed. However, both those who favored more news stories (with less detail) in a newscast and those who favored fewer stories scored higher than those satisfied with the present number of stories. In the case of another set of questions that were asked, viewers who were least critical of the newscast (in terms of rating that evening's newscast performance as good or excellent, rather than fair or poor) scored higher on both comprehension measures, as did viewers who admitted that they did find some of the news stories confusing, and viewers who said that *some* of the news stories affected them personally. None of these worked particularly well as predictors after MCA control, however.

Chapter 6

INFORMATION-PROCESSING THEORY
AND TELEVISION NEWS

W. GILL WOODALL

Previous chapters have dealt with news information flow using survey research. Although the survey method has the advantage of dealing with "real" news stories and information and of being conducted in the natural setting of the respondent's home, the degree of scientific control in such surveys is limited to what occurs naturally. Without such control, we are left with considerable uncertainty about whether our obtained results would hold if all other factors were equal. Thus we may observe that group A is better informed than group B, or that story A is understood better than story B. But we are never sure what it is about story A or story B that gives it such an advantage.

Experimental and observational research provide that degree of leverage on what leads to better comprehension. It allows us to view the information flow with greater precision and control by varying only one or two elements in the process in situations in which one group sees one version of a program but a second group sees a second version. It allows researchers to focus more clearly on the central factors that affect comprehension by ensuring that only one factor varies between groups.

There is a further advantage in the experimental research that has been conducted in relation to TV news comprehension: It is research tied to a growing and promising body of knowledge referred to as information-processing theory.

It is particularly important to note that researchers and theorists in cognitive psychology and information processing now see the emergence of a broader-based field of research ("cognitive science" or "social cognition") that is less tied to traditional, controlled, basic research and is more concerned with everyday information-processing tasks as they occur in the "real world." As noted elsewhere (Woodall, Davis, and Sahin, 1983), comprehension of television news fits well within such parameters and promises to be one area in which knowledge gains can be made in both the nature of everyday information processing and television news comprehension. Graber's (1984) recent in-depth work provides an example of how information-processing concepts can be invoked to explain comprehension of televised news in a field setting, as do our less theoretically oriented focus-group studies (discussed in Appendix B of this book, which includes examples of a more observational approach to micro-level studies of news comprehension).

Several observations can be made at the outset of this chapter. First, there is a relatively small amount of experimental evidence on television news comprehension; thus, what researchers can say about television news comprehension in a direct causal sense is rather limited. Second, a great deal of the available micro-level experimental research has been done by European researchers (see Findahl and Höijer, 1981a), whose work remains unfamiliar to many American mass communication researchers. Third, cognitive psychology has an extensive and long-term experimental literature on comprehension from which TV news researchers can draw and influence the direction of experimental work in television news comprehension. Fourth, although there are many information-processing concepts available to apply to TV news comprehension, application should be done in a careful and considered way.

Much of current information-processing theory has been developed and tested only in narrow, strictly controlled experimental paradigms, and different concepts imply different views of how news information is cognitively processed. The appropriateness of applying any given information-processing concept to TV news comprehension will have to be carefully justified.

Finally, it should be noted that much has been taken for granted in television news broadcasting. One of the basic premises of television news is that certain journalistic practices will aid viewers in comprehending what is broadcast. We have attempted to place this and other related premises under empirical and theoretical scrutiny (as has been done in the rest of this book). This chapter will review work that aids such scrutiny, consider what information-processing theory suggests about the current state of television news, and speculate on which directions further research might take.

SOME EXAMPLES OF INFORMATION-PROCESSING
STUDIES RELATED TO JOURNALISTIC GUIDELINES

Broadcast journalism generally follows certain guidelines in the production of television news, and these guidelines can be examined in the context of information-processing theory. For example, there are guidelines concerned with the content of given news items, with the ordering of news items in the newscast, and with the use of visual materials in newscasts.

New item criteria. The most traditional rules of thumb for news items center on the who, what, why, where, and when criteria. Although these criteria were originally developed for print journalism, they have been adapted to broadcast journalism as well. Although the appropriateness of this adaptation of print to broadcast guidelines may be questioned (as suggested elsewhere in this book), it is instructive to examine the several assumptions underlying these criteria. One presumption is that covering all five elements in a news story is sufficient to allow viewers to comprehend the story. Current evidence from information-processing literature suggests several other factors that need to be considered: the viewer's level of prior knowledge, the level of attention paid to the news story, and a number of story attribute factors that affect news comprehension (see Chapter 8).

A second presumption is that each of these criteria is equally important for a viewer to comprehend the story. However, it appears that viewers weigh these criteria differently. Work by Findahl and Höijer (1981a), for example, has shown that the *why* or *causal elements* of a news story have the most influence on viewer comprehension because they allow other elements to be cognitively integrated into an overall story theme. It is unlikely that other story elements alone could result in much viewer integration and comprehension of news information.

A third presumption is that information on each of these criteria is presented in all news stories. Once again, content analysis of news stories by Findahl and Höijer show that this is not the case. Rather, most often the who, what, where, and when details of news stories are reported but the why elements are not. As Findahl and Höijer argue, possibly the most important story element in terms of viewer comprehension is the one most often left out. Finally, taken as a whole these criteria seem equally applicable and important to all stories. However, although there is no evidence on this point, it is unlikely that each of these criteria is equally important given varying news story structures and content. Some kinds of news stories (accident accounts, for example) may require special emphasis on who, where, and what details for viewer comprehension; other kinds of news stories (reports on foreign diplomatic negotiations, for example) may require special emphasis on why and what elements.

In sum, these guidelines about individual news items appear to be much less central to viewer comprehension of news story content than to standardization of its production. In addition to story-order criteria, a second guideline about the order of presentation of news items suggests that stories of a similar nature be clustered to provide a more coherent structure to the newscast by using natural bridges from one story to the next. However, as available evidence indicates, this practice may actually undermine instead of aid recall of certain news stories. Gunter, Berry, and Clifford (1982) review a series of investigations on order effects in television news comprehension. They have been specifically concerned with the buildup of "proactive interference" among TV news items, which impedes the recall of those items. Proactive interference occurs when a series of similar stimuli are encoded by a subject, and the earlier stimulus reduces the probability of recall of the later stimuli because of similar encoding properties lessening the ability to discriminate among the stimuli. Increasing numbers of similar stimuli result in further buildup of proactive interference (see Wickens, 1970, 1972).

As the clustering of similar news items is a common practice in TV news, Gunter, Clifford, and Berry (1980) used an experimental design based on proactive interference research to examine buildup of proactive interference over four news items similar in topic. Buildup and release from proactive interference were demonstrated in both immediate and delayed-recall situations. In a second study, the researchers demonstrated a buildup and release from proactive interference by changing the visual format of the news items from a studio-only format (newscaster reading the news) to a studio plus still picture format (newscaster with still pictures as illustrations).

Thus it appears that release from interference effects can be triggered either by change in topic or by change in visual format (although it should be noted that a release effect was obtained only from a shift from studio-only plus stills format, and not vice versa). Once again, these effects were obtained for both immediate and delayed recall. In a series of follow-up studies (Gunter et al., 1981), the researchers replicated the proactive interference buildup and release effects in both immediate and delayed-recall situations, and demonstrated the effects for cued recall as well.

This line of research clearly indicates that clustering of similar news items within a broadcast may impede recall, and that different kinds of similarities (topic-content, visual-format) may produce proactive interference. Gunter has recently suggested that

> This research indicates that, if one wishes the audience to take in information, it may be inadvisable to present news packages consisting of groups of news stories about very similar kinds of events or issues. The result may be extensive forgetfulness. The persistent tendency of television news editors to employ "packaging" in an attempt to enhance clarity and learning may not so much improve the viewers' memory for news as actually impair it [1983: 170].

Importantly, these conclusions are quite consistent with what we have found in our own field surveys of news comprehension, as will be discussed in Chapter 8.

Visual Materials

A third set of guidelines concerns the journalist's heavy dependence on visual materials (film, still pictures, graphics, etc.) in the television newscast. As Gunter (1983) has noted, TV news journalists believe in using the visual potential of the medium to its full extent, with film and videotape materials favored over still photos and graphs in portraying news stories. News producers appear to subscribe to the adage that "a picture is worth a thousand words" and that film and videotaped material are needed to provide the most complete and comprehensive story, given that television is such a visual medium.

At first glance, the evidence on the effects of visual materials is mixed. In his initial investigation, Gunter (1979) found that recall of brief television news items (short television news bulletins) was significantly better in video than in audio modes, and that within the video mode, news items that were illustrated with film clips were recalled significantly more often than items illustrated with still pictures; these were in turn recalled significantly more often than no-insert items (a newscaster reading the news). In addition, the analyses detected serial-order effects for recall of the news items in the audio mode, still picture and no-insert items, but not for film items. The results were interpreted to indicate that visual information can enhance recall of TV news items and possibly ameliorate serial-order effects in TV news recall.

A second follow-up study (Gunter, 1980a, 1980b) largely replicated the results of the earlier study, with recall of brief news items being significantly higher in film clip items than no-insert items, and recall for still picture items higher than for no-insert items (although there was no significant difference in recall between film clip and still picture items). Recall of items illustrated by film or still pictures was significantly higher in the video mode than the audio mode; however, no-insert items were recalled significantly better in the audio than the video mode.

A third investigation (Gunter, 1980a) extended the research of the previous investigations using a different methodology in which subjects were presented with much longer news items that more closely resembled typical TV news items. Instead of free recall of news items, subjects' memory for news information was measured by multiple-choice questions that assessed information gain. The results of this study indicated no significant differences between visual treatment (newscaster only vs. newscaster plus still vs. newscaster plus film) conditions for information gain items.

Gunter explained the discrepancy between these results and the previous studies' results as due to differences in learning task requirements between the last study and the first two. According to this explanation, the first two studies required subjects to process information only superficially because the news items were brief, but the last study required deeper and more semantically involved processing due to the greater length of the items. Thus, in the first, shorter study, the accompanying visual materials may have had a superficial, but important enhancing effect; however, these accompanying visual materials had an effect only in the case of longer stories if they were somehow semantically relevant to cooccurring news content. Since the visual information versus verbal content connection was not controlled for in the design, Gunter suggested that visual format effects washed out.

Although Gunter's evidence concerning the effects of visual format may appear to be inconsistent, one conclusion can be drawn: The research on visual format effects does not support the "use at all possible times" rule employed in producing the visual portions of TV news. Rather, the ways in which visual formats may enhance or detract from news comprehension appear to be complex and probably dependent on information-processing principles and properties. The current practices that determine the use of visual materials in TV news appear to proceed on a hit-or-miss basis, and visual format irrelevancy or distraction undoubtedly occurs much more often than TV news producers expect.

This analysis, as well as other research reviewed in Gunter, Berry, and Clifford (1982), suggests that there is a very large gap between what news producers think are the outcomes of their production practices and principles and the actual outcomes. Clearly, not *all* of the factors that increase TV news comprehension are under the direct control of news producers (as we note in Chapter 8), but some are.

More important, TV news comprehension itself is an amalgam of cognitive processes that are only beginning to be understood. Although it is probably premature to expect a great deal of research application to TV news, some applications (such as more careful ordering and clustering of news items to prevent proactive interference) are possible. Our main task, however, is to better explain TV news comprehension. To that end, we now review other research related to news comprehension.

A SUMMARY OF OTHER EXPERIMENTAL FINDINGS ON NEWS COMPREHENSION RESEARCH

Although the current experimental evidence on news comprehension is scant, a brief review of what has been found is still worthwhile to indicate the major gaps in the research and the directions for further research. The findings tend to cluster around five variables: (1) production and stylistic variables (primarily visual format variables, (2) repetition of news items, (3) news content, (4) individual difference variables relevant to viewer comprehension, and (5) knowledge level of viewers. More detailed reviews are given in Findahl and Höijer (1981a) and Berry, Gunter, and Clifford (1982).

In addition to the production variable studies just covered, several studies of visual format have been conducted. Although some research (Edwardson, Grooms, and Pringle, 1976) has found no facilitative recall effect for visual format, other research has done so (Findahl, 1971; Gunter, 1979; Edwardson, Grooms, and Proudlove, 1981). Two confounding factors that need closer control here are the different kinds of visual formats investigated (still pictures vs. graphs vs. film clips) and different news formats (short headline style items vs. longer conventional news items). Findahl and Höijer (1976, 1981b) have raised an important theoretical point concerning the comprehension effects of visual formats—namely, the link between visual information and news story content in visually enhancing news comprehension. Their research has shown that visual illustration of *person* and *place* elements of a news story enhances recall of those elements of the news but not other story elements. Visual formats and illustrations linked to cause-and-effect story elements, however, tend to enhance recall of all of the story elements overall.

Although these findings could be explained by a number of information-processing principles, the important point is that these findings show that it is not production variables alone that affect news comprehension but the way certain variables allow information to be cognitively processed more effectively. Lending support to this point is a study by Drew and Reeves (1980) that found that the main predictors of childrens' learning from TV news items were their *perceptions* of the program's believability, likability, and function. Thus a child's cognitive reactions, and not production variables, are more likely to determine what is gathered from television news. Although this finding needs replication with an adult sample, it does further suggest that cognitive variables are important mediators of production variables' effects on news comprehension. Presently, we will consider a number of information-processing concepts that may determine the impact of video production.

Future news producers will have an increasing array of visual format techniques from which to choose. As Berry et al. (1982) have indicated, the sophistication of video production is increasing as many new technical feats become available to news producers. Techniques such as "Chroma-key" and computer-generated graphics are increasingly being used on the news, and, like the techniques before them, the only rule that may govern their use is "use for use's sake." Future research efforts can evaluate when and whether these new visual production techniques will have utility for viewer comprehension and suggest uses based on criteria other than simple aesthetic or "gee-whiz" value.

Repetition of news content is an increasingly common technique that news producers use in order to bolster viewer comprehension. For example, news "recaps" at the end of news segments or shows are used to review the day's news headlines. However, the little research that has been reported suggests minimal efficacy of certain forms of repetition. Findahl and Höijer (1972, 1976) studied the effects of reemphasizing and reformulating the central points of news broadcasts via both verbal reformulations and reemphasizing the main points of the news through verbal and visual means. Their research indicated that although verbal reformulations did increase recall of news details, reemphasis of person and place details enhanced recall of those details only. Reemphasis of cause and consequence details, on the other hand, enhanced recall of more details of news story content. Combining both visual and verbal reemphasis of the news further enhanced recall if cause-consequence information was used.[1] Similarly, Perloff, Wartella, and Becker (1982) found that repetition of newscast story elements increased recall of those newscast elements both immediately after exposure as well as one week later.

An obvious concern for those who study news comprehension is the news *content* in the stories. Although some critics charge that there is little content *worth* comprehending on television news, that is surely not true for all news. At least journalists seem to operate on the assumption that, on balance, there is a good deal to comprehend in the news, which makes this communication interesting to study in and of itself given that journalists comprehend the news so much better than their audiences (Robinson and Sahin, 1984).

Some facets of news content should make it easy to comprehend. News content is produced in a rather routinized way, and many stories have common story structures or elements, such as who, what, why, when, and where. Time constraints force stories to be written in concise format using simple language. Different kinds of news stories generally cluster into a fairly well-defined set of content categories, such as Graber's (1984) categories of government or politics, economic issues, social issues, and human interest. Further, unlike many other incidental learning situations, news content is often repeated across a period of days as a given story remains current or "hot."

It would appear reasonable, then, to expect viewers to comprehend the news at a fairly high level. What mitigating factors about content might inhibit news comprehension? As indicated earlier, one possible factor is Findahl and Höijer's (1979) finding that news stories emphasize person and place elements but not causal story elements, with the outcome being scattered recall of story details, but little overall integrated recall. Similarly, the Swedish researchers indicate that the news often provides little or no background or contextual information for news stories, making it more difficult to find "hooks" for comprehension. Emphasizing such causal elements of a news story may, in fact, go against the norms of professional news training that dictate that journalists should report only "the facts," or the specific details of what, who, when, and where, and not lead the audience into areas that cannot be proven definitively. Thus, questions of the causal elements in a news event might lead to news reporting that damages journalistic objectivity and credibility. There may be inherent contradictions between what viewers need to comprehend in the news and what journalists see as their role in providing the news.

One other mitigating factor is use of terms that are technical, specialized, or otherwise beyond the vocabulary of many viewers (Robinson and Sahin, 1984). Terms such as "bilateral agreement," "economic embargo," or "leading indicators" are examples of newscast language that stand in the way of comprehension. One of the most important reminders about news content from an information-processing perspective is to call attention to the cognitive processes and abilities that it takes to comprehend any given content. Only by switching the emphasis to an analysis of the interaction between the media message (the news, in this case) and the viewer's cognitive abilities is any progress likely to be made.

Individual Difference Variables

These variables are also likely to affect viewer comprehension of news. In one study, Gunter, Jarrett, and Furnham (1983) investigated how individual arousal is affected by time of day. Earlier research in cognitive and experimental psychology had determined that immediate memory performance (recall soon after exposure) is superior in the morning compared to the afternoon and that this effect may be based on physiological processes, such as arousal, that change across the day. The results of their study indicated that immediate memory for TV news items, as measured by immediate free recall, cued recall, and recognition tests, declined at a significant rate across the day: from 9:30 a.m. to 1:30 p.m. to 5:30 p.m.

Gunter and his colleagues also found that immediate recall of information about the causes of events declined more rapidly than did recall of concrete details about the news items. In a follow-up study, Gunter, Furnham, and Jarrett (1984) investigated time of day and personality difference (introvert-extrovert) effects on delayed recall of TV news items. Although earlier research found immediate memory to be superior earlier in the day, other research determined that delayed memory (recall after some period of time) was superior later in the day. This, again, could be tied to arousal changes through the day, given that arousal increases during the day and may negatively affect memory. At the same time, arousal appears to be beneficial to delayed memory (Craik and Blankenstein, 1975); thus delayed memory for TV news may increase through the day.[2]

One of the most consistent findings in TV news comprehension research is that TV news viewers with *high levels of knowledge* comprehend and recall the news significantly better than those viewers who have lesser levels of knowledge. This research evidence indicates that those who bring more information to news viewing comprehend the news significantly better.

Most survey evidence in Chapters 3 through 5 supports this conclusion, and this conclusion has been supported by several other researchers as well. In Sweden, Findahl and Höijer (1976) found that individuals with high levels of current issue knowledge were able to recall more news program content than those with low knowledge levels. Stauffer, Frost, and Rybolt (1978) also found that "literate" TV viewers scored higher on unaided recall than did "illiterate" viewers. Graber (1984) also found that the panelists in her study who knew more initially learned more than those panelists who were knowledge poor. Prior knowledge appears to play so pivotal a role in news comprehension that Findahl and Höijer (1976) have characterized television news as "news for the initiated."

Several variables may, in fact, stand for and be correlated with different levels of prior knowledge. Education and socioeconomic status could account for differences in news processing because these variables may represent differentiated knowledge levels to some degree across variable levels. Current issue knowledge tests as reported in Chapters 4 and 5 and by Findahl and Höijer were used to assess prior knowledge, but these methods probably only scratch the surface of the several knowledge domains that could be relevant to news comprehension. There is little doubt that prior knowledge is an important determinant of television news comprehension, and as the results in Chapters 4 and 5 indicate, it functions independently from the factor of education. This is an issue to which we shall return shortly.

One final point can be made to illustrate the urgency of researching the news comprehension process. Jacoby and Hoyer (1982) studied the converse of comprehension of televised messages—that is, the *miscomprehension* of televised messages. Their experimental study found that TV communication content in general is miscomprehended at a rate of 23% to 36% per content unit. Further, they found that TV content from entertainment and network news programs was miscomprehended at a lower rate than advertising content. Although further work needs to be done on television and miscomprehension in general, as a starting point this study provides a useful exploration of TV content outside of news.

Even this cursory review of current research indicates that much research is needed even within the confines of the five variables discussed. Yet there are equally important unresearched variables and issues suggested by information-processing literature, and we now turn to a consideration of them.

INFORMATION-PROCESSING THEORY AND TELEVISION NEWS: EMERGING ISSUES

As research in television news comprehension develops, an increasing number of information-processing concepts, models, and theories are being brought to bear on news comprehension issues. Like many research areas in early development, it is somewhat unclear what the main defining issues are. Unlike many research areas in early development, there is already a large body of relevant theoretical work to draw on. As a result of these conditions, there are several emerging issues that TV news researchers who take an information-processing view will have to address in the near future. In order to best frame those issues, current theoretical concepts are first reviewed, followed by a discussion of emerging issues.

It is useful at the outset to reassert those information-processing concepts we have argued to be relevant to TV news comprehension (Woodall, Davis, and Sahin, 1983). We have made four basic points about information processing and TV news. The first point is that attention, as an initial stage of processing information, can be characterized by at least two modes: *bottom-up processing,* in which information flows from perceptual features of input information that serve as the focus of attention, leading to larger information units being built, and *top-down processing,* in which a knowledge structure guides attention and determines the interpretation of low-level perceptual features (see Anderson, 1980). Paying attention to TV news is likely to be characterized by both of these modes.

This view of attention is different from earlier views of it in cognitive psychology in which attention was seen as selective, narrow, and limited in information capacity, and part of the one-way information flow that led from attention to comprehension. Attention here is cast as a more flexible stage of information processing, one that can be driven either by input information or by previously held knowledge. Like other researchers (see Salomon, 1979), we suggest this view of attention as most appropriate for socially based information-processing tasks, such as watching TV news.

A flexible view of attention is particularly important when considering experimental evidence on TV news processing. As noted earlier, survey evidence indicates that viewers' attention to a newscast is at best intermittent. However, under experimental conditions, it is likely that viewers pay almost constant attention to news stimuli due to demand characteristics. The Jacoby and Hoyer (1982) study, for example, found only about 30% miscomprehension levels for the network news stories they examined, suggesting about twice as much story comprehension in the experimental setting as in the field studies in Chapter 5. As a result, the base rate of attention, and therefore other features of news processing, are raised above normal. When designing experiments in this area, it may be worthwhile to consider design features that allow some approximation of typical attention levels (i.e., more casual viewing conditions, incidental viewing situations in which viewers are exposed to news information with no forewarning, field experiment studies).

It should also be noted that under experimental news viewing conditions, viewers may adopt only one mode of attention, that being a top-down mode. Viewers might watch and pay constant attention to the news stimuli because "they were supposed to" given the experimental situation. As a result, the normal variation among top-down and bottom-up modes of attention and no attention would not be obtained, again affecting subsequent stages of processing. Clearly, as attention is the initial stage of information processing, it needs to be considered carefully, in terms of how it is both studied and conceived.

Remembering Versus Understanding

The distinction between remembering and understanding information underlies the second and third information-processing concepts that we offered as relevant. Ortony (1978) has claimed that *remembering* information and *understanding* information are separate and different cognitive processes. Memory processes involve the storage, retrieval, and access to prior information; understanding involves the linkage between new information and prior information stored in memory, so that stored prior knowledge is used to make a set of inferences that go beyond the new information. We have presumed that this distinction is valid and crucial for cognitive theory and have speculated on plausible memory and understanding models. When reviewing such models, some interesting implications of this distinction become evident and make the term "comprehension" more difficult to define. In the literature to date and in this chapter, comprehension has referred to both memory and understanding. For example, much of Gunter's research on retrieval of news information (especially the work on proactive interference) is clearly *memory* related. On the other hand, much of Findahl and Höijer's research program is focused on how viewers *understand* the news, as their emphasis on the effects of prior knowledge and story elements indicates. The research in Chapters 3 through 5 has examined mainly the understanding side of processing, although the graphs developed in Chapter 8 show both aspects on a single diagram.

We have proposed two models of processing and storage, one more relevant to remembering the news and the other more relevant to understanding it. The model more relevant to memory, termed "episodic memory," is based on work by Tulving and his colleagues (Tulving and Thompson, 1973; Watkins and Tulving, 1975). Episodic memory models are concerned with memory for events and may include behavioral and situational details, the temporal orderings of activity within an event, and "raw representations of what an observer thinks transpired in a particular episode" (Carlston, 1980). Two reasons this memory model is particularly applicable to TV news are, first, that the newscasts' event-like structure allows viewers to experience and store TV news information as events, and, second, its contextual cues. Research on episodic memory has shown that recall of events is highest and most efficient when contextual cues (cues that are relevant context for news content, in this case) are used to prompt recall. The episodic memory model can explain, then, why cued recall levels are somewhat higher in TV news research. We have further speculated that the relevant context for TV news may often be visual-format cues, and that some of the visual-format research could be explained using this principle. The model has general features that make it quite relevant to recall of TV news as was detailed in Woodall, Davis, and Sahin (1983).

The model we have proposed as providing an explanation for *understanding* the news is a semantic network model (Quillian, 1968; Collins and Loftus, 1975). This model views semantic networks as a complex network of interrelated "nodes" (words, concepts, properties, and their interrelationships) that are linked together by types of relations. Some relationships may be of the class or category type; others relate time and place; and still others are more associationistic in nature. These networks represent the "mental thesaurus" of the human cognitive system, containing the sum of preexisting knowledge that an individual brings to a situation. This model sees the process of understanding as an interaction between new incoming information and preexisting semantic network information. Some subset of nodes of information becomes activated by incoming information, and a set of inferences can be generated based on the interaction between activated prior information and new input information.

The semantic network model is particularly relevant to news comprehension because of its emphasis on preexisting knowledge and the role it plays in understanding. It is consistent with the findings on the importance of prior knowledge in TV news comprehension research. Moreover, the semantic network model emphasizes that understanding is *not* an all-or-nothing process, but that it occurs to a greater or lesser extent. A subarea of research in semantic network models has examined "depth of processing" (see Craik and Lockhart, 1972), and suggests that information processed at greater depth ("deep processing") entails more elaborate and involved semantic processing than does information that is not (i.e., "shallow processing"). Clearly then, whether incoming information from TV news is processed in a shallow or deep way is of central concern to those interested in TV news research.

Although all the factors that prompt deep processing have not yet been identified, Ortony (1978) has suggested that the context in which information is encountered is an important one. In the case of TV news, visual context could be seen to play a role by prompting deeper processing of news content, assuming that other factors that prompt or inhibit activation of semantic network information can be identified (we will return to this point shortly).

Visual Factors and Their Attributes

As we noted earlier, the role that visual information may play in the news is of great interest to both researchers and news producers. We have contended that the information-processing properties associated with visual production in the news play a far more important role in news comprehension than the sheer force of video technique. There are at least three information-processing factors to consider here, the first two concerning the attributes of visual information itself. The *vividness* and *concreteness* of visual information have been shown to predict retention of information experimentally (Paivio, 1971; Nisbett and Ross, 1980) and are also likely to predict news retention (Berry et al., 1982; Woodall et al., 1983). Vividness of information has to do with the properties of information that compel attention and encourage the creation of powerful mental images that can be used to interpret information. Concreteness can be defined as the degree of detail and specificity about actors, actions, and situational context.

The impact of vivid and concrete visual information can be considerable, as the analysis in Chapter 8 shows. Vivid or concrete visual information is likely to be retained and remembered by news viewers. As a result of that high memorability, vivid or concrete visual information is also likely to influence inferences viewers draw about the news, and thus their understanding of it.

The third and equally important factor is the *link* between visual information and news content. As the results of Chapter 8 suggest, the impact that vivid or concrete visual information has on retention and understanding is mitigated by the link between visual information and news content. Vivid or concrete visual information that is loosely linked to story content is likely to be remembered, but the story content will not be. In effect, a visual distraction outcome is obtained under these conditions in the sense that what is remembered is not story content but visual context. On the other hand, if vivid or concrete visual information is well linked to cooccurring story content, then enhancement in retention and understanding of news content should take place. Although the nature of the visual information-story content link needs further analysis, Findahl and Höijer's work indicates that one particularly strong link is visual information linked to the causal elements in the story.

All three of these factors need to be considered in order to determine the impact of visual information on news retention and understanding. Previous research has not done so and instead has mostly assumed that visual effects on news comprehension are a function of some aspect of video technique (i.e., visual format, amount of visual information, simple presence of video channel, etc.). This may partly explain the inconsistency in the literature's findings. Future research needs to consider carefully which particular aspects of video production result in visual information that is vivid, concrete, and linked or not linked to the news story content.

Schema Theory

Another major theoretical position that has been used to explain the processing of television news is schema theory, particularly Schank and Abelson's work on *scripts* (1977) and script processing. *Schemas* have been described by Anderson (1980) as "large, complex units of knowledge that organize much of what we know about general categories of objects, classes of events, and types of people." Scripts are a particular type of schema concerned with the structure and nature of events, primarily representing stereotypic sequences of action. As Schank and Abelson have shown, scripts can play an important role in the understanding of stories and texts.

As Graber (1984) has pointed out, these concepts have a great deal of relevance for the processing of television news. Schemas and scripts are a powerful way of describing prior knowledge that a viewer may bring to the TV newscast and can strongly affect the way news information is processed. Graber argues that schemas (or scripts) carry out at least four functions in (1) determining what information will be noticed, processed, and stored and consequently be available for retrieval from memory; (2) aiding in the organization and evaluation of new information so it fits already established perceptions; (3) making it possible for people to go beyond the immediate information presented to them and fill in missing information; and (4) aiding in problem solving by providing likely scenarios and suggesting ways to cope with them.

Graber uses schemas primarily to show how news viewers with varying backgrounds can use their beliefs and general knowledge (political beliefs mostly, as represented in schema form) to distill essential and basic meaning and to draw inferences from news stories.

One unconsidered possibility in applying schemas to TV news is that journalists themselves use schemas to formulate and present stories to the news audience. Although it is difficult to anticipate what the range of schemas used by journalists might be, one broad schema used is the who, what, why, where, and when structure. As pointed out earlier, this structure currently routinizes news information more than any other approach. Another example of a schema used by journalists is that of the "human interest" story. Here, a schema that emphasizes the personal, humanistic, and often prosocial attributes of news information is used to package the story from that point of view. When journalists present a story from a particular point of view, or "angle," or attempt to give the story a certain kind of "spin," it can be assumed that some schema is being employed by the journalist. Research in TV news would benefit from an analysis of the kinds of schemas that journalists might use.

It is unlikely that the use of a particular schema by a journalist prompts the news audience to use exactly the same schema to understand the story. However, it is likely that a journalist's use of a schema predisposes or "primes" the audience to use similar schemas to interpret the news story (somewhat similar to what Iyengar, Peters, and Kinder, 1982, have suggested as priming in agenda setting). Interestingly, it may be that such schema use has little impact on how deeply a given news story is understood by the news viewer. Despite the schema being a very powerful tool for text comprehension, schemas currently used by journalists may not aid viewer comprehension much at all. Not only do we need to understand better what schemas journalists use but we also need a thorough analysis of schemas and schema properties that promote viewer understanding of the news.

Discourse Analysis

Another approach to the processing of news information has been advanced by van Dijk (1983) and has come to be known as *discourse analysis*. Now a broad interdisciplinary field, discourse analysis is concerned with the comprehension of text by analyzing it on several different levels. Principles from linguistics, sociolinguistics, philosophy of language, and cognitive psychology (including many of the same principles as discussed above) are employed to explain how texts of various types can be comprehended.

Although van Dijk has so far examined only print news, he discusses how broadcast media can be analyzed from a discourse analysis point of view. One main difference between discourse analysis and an information-processing perspective lies in methodology. Discourse analysis relies on qualitative methods rooted in linguistics (for example, content analyses of texts designed to elucidate propositional structure) rather than quantitative experimental methods. Thus discourse analysis provides an avenue to investigate news processing other than the information-processing analyses on which we focus.

It should be noted that several other areas of research in information processing may be relevant to an explanation of news comprehension, but their exact relevance is as yet undetermined. One example is the work on sentence comprehension (see Thorndyke and Hayes-Roth, 1979). That work, as valuable as it is, is devoted to a narrow focus, that being the explanation of how the structure of individual sentences affects the recall of information. As such, this work is tangentially related to a broad comprehension process, such as understanding and remembering news text and stimuli. Other examples of potentially relevant factors include the syntactic and semantic cues in language that aid in parsing sentences and therefore affect comprehension, the amount of lexical and structural ambiguity a comprehender must deal with, the amount of information that is presumed known in order to comprehend, and text structures—about which little is yet known (for a review of these factors, see Anderson, 1980). What has been covered here are those theoretical concepts that have direct relevance to explaining TV news comprehension.

Unresolved Issues

These various theories and models raise several issues. First, regarding metatheoretical issues, there seems to be some danger in relying too heavily on the concepts of schema and script in TV news comprehension research. It should be pointed out that despite the current widespread popularity of the schema concept, there is no standard or consensual definition of the term. The schema concept has a long history in the psychological literature and means different things to different researchers and theorists. Unsettled details about schemas and scripts include whether they are or must be hierarchical in structure, under what conditions schemas are activated and utilized, how much individual variation exists in schema knowledge, what links exist between schema structures, and in what ways schemas are acquired and modified. As useful as schemas and scripts are theoretically, they are still somewhat fuzzily defined and can only be applied with some caution—although attempts are being made to further explicate these concepts.

Based on this confusion, overreliance on schema or script concepts seems unwise, as indicated in the following passage in Graber:

> When people fail to learn or create appropriate schemas for certain types of news, that news cannot be absorbed. Socialization of average Americans apparently leaves a number of gaps in schema structure. These gaps then make it difficult to focus public attention on some important problems. News about most foreign countries and news about science are examples. Even when such news is presented in simple ways, much of the audience fails to make the effort to absorb it because appropriate schemas did not form part of past socialization [1984: 206].

Given what has been said above regarding schemas, this position seems untenable. Clearly, failure to absorb the news rests in part on the lack of appropriate schemas to process it with, but also may depend on a host of other factors as well (e.g., lack of relevant information held in semantic memory, distracting visuals, proactive interference effects).

Another schema-related concern has been raised by Anderson (1980), who points out that not all story and text comprehension can involve the use of schemas. Schemas and scripts are most appropriate when input, or incoming information, has standard and stereotypic features. However, as Anderson suggests, not all stories and texts have standard or stereotypic features. Rather, some texts and stories are novel and unique, involving new and interesting combinations of events and facts. Cognitive processes that do not utilize schemas may be required to understand these stories. How often these novel stories occur in TV news is an important point to ponder because news information often has a rather stereotypic structure, as discussed earlier. Nonetheless, it is important to be able to specify theoretically when schemas and scripts are useful to information processing and when they are not.

Another concern directly linked to schemas and their use is the ability to demonstrate empirically *when* they are invoked in the processing of information. Traditionally, cognitive and social psychologists have been relatively sure about when schemas and scripts were being utilized by subjects because subjects could be prompted to invoke schemas in processing via controlled experimental procedures. However, as researchers have moved away from controlled experimental situations to survey and content analysis techniques, the certainty with which a researcher can assert that schemas were used in any processing instance has become much smaller. Close attention needs to be paid to the rationale and methodology used in such cases to claim that scripts and schemas were used by news viewers. Simply saying that schemas are used (as in Graber's work, for example) does not make it so because humans have a broad range of strategies to process or not process news information.

A final metatheoretical caution is that we should not see the theories and models discussed so far as necessarily opposed or competitive explanations of TV news comprehension. If anything, the various principles discussed here are still not explicated clearly and extensively enough to be pitted against each other—even if it is ever philosophically possible.

Rather, it appears that some concerns are exclusive and some overlap among the different theories and models. For example, at first glance it may appear that semantic network and schema theories represent competing explanations or understandings. However, semantic network theories rely mostly on depth of processing and factors that influence processing depth in order to explain understanding, whereas schema theories wish to explain understanding via use of different kinds of knowledge structures. Not only are these two theories not inconsistent in explaining news understanding but, in fact, some information-processing models employ *both* schema and semantic network concepts (Kintsch, 1979; Ortony, 1978).

Schemas are probably one of a set of factors (input context being another) that determine the spread of activation through a semantic network and that provide a partial answer to the activation question posed earlier by Ortony. Even though both are concerned with long-term memory, semantic network theories are chiefly concerned with the *representation of information* in long-term memory, whereas schema theories are more concerned with the *organization* of information. Recent models of text comprehension have shown that both concepts are necessary to explain text comprehension. Models of TV news understanding are also likely to employ both concepts. In summary, it seems premature to see these theories or models as competitive or to rule out some concepts in favor of others in news comprehension research.

FUTURE RESEARCH POSSIBILITIES

Although work to develop and test information-processing models of TV news comprehension has only begun, several issues go beyond what researchers and theorists have considered so far and are likely to be pertinent to any information-processing model that could be developed. Three in particular are identified here. The first issue concerns the different kinds of information domains relevant to understanding TV news. The term "information domain" refers to large content areas of information that are cognitively stored and that can be represented as subnetworks within a semantic network. So far, current theoretical work has suggested two relevant information domains, these being *general world knowledge* (or current events knowledge) and *schema, script,* or *procedural knowledge.* Other information domains must be relevant, however (as detailed below). The advantage and importance of being able to specify those domains are as follows: (1) further clarification of the role of prior knowledge in news comprehension; (2) ease of assessment of knowledge levels of news viewers through knowledge of which domains are relevant to a given news story; and (3) more effective expansion of news viewers' knowledge through knowledge of which information domains are relevant.

One broad information domain likely to be relevant to TV news is social knowledge. Viewers' knowledge of who other individuals and groups are, why others behave the way they do, and other relevant social information can be very important to understanding news stories, especially those concerned with human behavior as events. Recent work in social cognition (see Hastie, Ostrom, Ebbesen, Wyer, Hamilton, and Carlston, 1980; Higgins, Herman, and Zanna, 1981) suggests this information domain to be quite broad and complex for most humans. Some subsets of this information domain that may be particularly relevant to understanding the news may be found in people who have a high level of information about political behavior and are thus able to process and understand more deeply stories about political and government-related events. Graber's work also suggests that person schemas, stereotypes, and other social information (especially concerning politicians) are highly relevant to processing political news.

Other specialized information domains are also relevant to news understanding. Viewers with high levels of information about economics or statistics should be better able to interpret news stories in these areas than those with little prior knowledge about these topics. Similarly, news viewers who have a well-developed set of information about the processes of TV news production, such as journalists or specialists in public relations or advertising, may be better able to understand the news. They should be better able to infer why certain news stories were chosen for broadcast, why they were placed in certain slots within the broadcast, and so forth. Clearly, further work needs to be done to identify relevant information domains, as understanding any particular news story in any depth may require information from a number of domains.

Another issue likely to emerge in information-processing models of news comprehension concerns the kinds of inference making utilized in understanding the news. Graber (1984) has indicated some relevant modes of inference making based on previous work in cognitive psychology. She has focused mostly on the ways in which news viewers relate news stories to already stored information. She primarily discusses two types of matching strategies: *straight matching* and *matching of story spinoffs*. Straight matching involves a comparison of incoming information with preexisting information (in schema form, in this case) in order to determine whether incoming information is in any way similar or related to prior information. How closely related incoming information must be to prior information for a match to occur is unclear, although Graber suggests that similarity on a limited number of categories will suffice. Matching of story spinoffs, on the other hand, involved viewers deducing the consequences (spinoffs) of a news story and then matching these consequences with prior knowledge. Graber points out that although this kind of matching process lends stability to judgments, it also may lead to improper generalizations because viewers may ascribe inappropriate consequences to news events.

Other theoretical principles recently formulated by Nisbett and Ross (1980) may also be brought to bear on the area of inference making and TV news. These authors have combined attribution principles with the classic work of Kahneman and Tversky (1971) and Tversky and Kahneman (1973) on decision-making heuristics in order to assess inference strategies used in everyday social situations. The judgmental heuristics of primary concern here are the availability heuristic and the representative heuristic.

The *availability heuristic* affects people's judgments where they are required to make inferences concerning the relative frequency of particular objects or the likelihood of events. Those inferences will be affected by the relative availability of information about such objects or events in the processes of perception, memory, or construction from imagination (Nisbett and Ross, 1980).[3]

Television news can be a source of information for the availability heuristic. Thus, a news item about government figures on the rate of unemployment may directly contradict one's personal sampling bias in encountering employed and unemployed workers. Nonetheless, such a news item needs to be presented in a salient way in order to make it highly available to employed workers. Often, however, these kinds of stories are not presented in ways that increase the availability of the information to viewers. However, when TV news does present information in a way that results in high availability of the information, and when that information is strongly correlated with the objective frequency of events, we can expect viewers to draw valid inferences from these stories.

At the same time, TV news can also present stories that result in high availability for viewers but that are uncorrelated with the objective frequency of events. For example, the presentation of major crime stories on the news may incorrectly lead viewers to infer that certain types of crime are on the rise in their local communities, as in Gerbner's "scary world hypothesis" (Gerbner, Gross, Signorielli, Morgan, and Jackson-Beeck, 1979) about television. Although further work will be needed to determine how often viewers utilize the availability heuristic to process news, it seems likely to be one strategy for making inferences from news content.

The *representativeness heuristic* is described by Nisbett and Ross in the following way:

> The representativeness heuristic allows the individual to reduce many inferential tasks to what are essential similarity judgments. An object is assigned to one conceptual category rather than to another according to the extent to which its principle features represent or resemble one category more than another. . . . The problem with the heuristic is that it is sometimes used as the only judgmental strategy when it cannot alone provide an accurate judgment. When the known features of an object cannot categorize it definitely, statistical considerations become more important to correct categorization. In particular, the relative frequency of the categories in the population under consideration becomes the normatively appropriate guide to categorization to the extent that the known features of the object are ambiguous guides to categorization [Nisbett and Ross, 1980: 7].

People use this heuristic, then, when incoming information is ambiguous and its assignment to a given category rests only on appearances of similarity or features that resemble characteristics of a given category.

As Nisbett and Ross point out, this heuristic can lead to misjudgment in at least two ways. First, when persons attempt to explain some outcome or event, they may consider antecedents that are most *representative* in the sense that the antecedents *resemble* the consequences in some way or another. Resemblance or similarity criteria can thus lead to a choice of possible antecedents for a consequent event that, in fact, have nothing to do with the event. For example, when news viewers process a story about a large drop in stock prices, they may search for causal factors that are similar in degree of magnitude and type, such as large corporate stock selloffs, large trade deficits in certain business sectors, or high frequency of failure in certain business sectors. In fact, other antecedents, such as small changes in interest rates or subtle changes in announced government regulations, may be responsible.

Second, the representativeness heuristic can come into play when people employ implicit theories and general knowledge as a way to explain events. In these cases, consequent events are related to tacit or explicit models of causal relations in some information domain. To the extent that such causal models that people hold have validity, judgments are likely to be accurate. However, in many cases the tacit models that people use to explain events have little validity and thus can lead to misjudgment. For example, news viewers may process a breaking story about corruption in local government by inferring that most, if not all, politicians in the local government structure are involved. Such an inference is based on a general "post-Watergate" schema of dishonest politicians being the source of corruption in government. In fact, the source of corruption may later be found to be a minor low-level bureaucrat who had been operating without the knowledge of any elected official. Several of the inferences found in Graber's results suggest this kind of reasoning.

Although the extent to which this heuristic is employed in processing the news remains an empirical question, it is likely to be used with some frequency given Findahl and Höijer's observation that the causal elements of stories are the ones most often left out. When viewers are often left to their own devices to explain stories, opportunities to use these heuristics seem optimal. Overall, news research should make more effort to integrate information about human inference making in everyday situations.

The final emerging issue, touched on only briefly here, is the role that attitudes play in news processing. Graber has examined how general attitudes toward the media influence news processing in terms of how interested viewers were in gaining access to the media. More specifically focused attitudes about particular media content should be considered as well. Some recent interest in the way attitudes affect social information processing has begun to surface (see Petty and Cacioppo, 1981; Woodall, 1984). One question this work raises is whether and how attitudes prompt deeper processing of information.

To conclude, the area of news comprehension research is likely to grow in the coming years. We have raised issues here from the information-processing perspective of the news viewer. The integration of these issues with more macro-levels of analysis continues to be a concern because any account of news comprehension must reflect not only information-processing factors but social and cultural context factors as well. Continued work in this area will result in more satisfying accounts of the way people get what they do from the news, as well as, it is hoped, an increased ability of people to learn more than they currently do from the news.

NOTES

1. Some order effects were detected in these analyses as well. When visual reemphasis of cause-consequence details was followed by verbal reemphasis of person-place details, only recall of person-place details was enhanced. Thus sequence and ordering may play some role in repetition of news stories.

2. Gunter et al. (1984) also contrasted introverts' and extroverts' delayed memory performance. Because introverts may be more functionally aroused than extroverts (Blake, 1967), it was expected that introverts would show stronger delayed memory effects than extroverts. Delayed memory was measured by means of free recall, a recognition test (identification of countries in which news events took place from a list of countries), general cued recall, and a more detailed depth cued recall. Expected time of day effects occurred only for recognition, indicating increased delayed memory later in the day. Significant differences between introverts and extroverts were obtained only on free and cued recall, with introverts recalling more than extroverts. Finally, significant introversion or extroversion × time of day interaction effects were obtained for free and depth cued recall, indicating that introverts recalled significantly more than extroverts only in later afternoon sessions. Although mixed, the results were taken as partial support of the expectation that delayed memory is better later in the day, and that introverts, due to higher arousal, recalled more delayed information than extroverts later in the day.

3. Nisbett and Ross give the following example as an instance of an inference in which the availability heuristic has been applied:

> A pollster who asks a sample of American adults to estimate the "percentage of the work force who are currently unemployed" finds an "egocentric bias." That is, currently unemployed workers tend to overestimate the rate of unemployment, but currently employed workers tend to underestimate it [1980: 19].

The explanation of this example is that the availability bias lies in initial sampling by employed and unemployed workers. Those who are employed tend to know and associate with other employed people (and thus the information is not available to them); similarly, those who are unemployed tend to know and associate with other unemployed people. The sampling bias at the personal experience level and the resultant availability of information about unemployment tends to bias the workers' estimates of unemployment. Nisbett and Ross point out that the availability heuristic can lead to accurate inferences when availability is correlated with objective frequency. But as in the example above, availability is often not correlated with objective frequency, and thus inferences are biased as a result.

Chapter 7

INFORMATION AND MEANING
Audience Explanations of Social Issues

MICHAEL GUREVITCH
MARK R. LEVY

The history of American mass communication research is to a large extent the history of the conceptualization and study of media "effects." The now familiar account of that history suggests that attention has shifted from an earlier preoccupation with the power of the mass media to influence and change attitudes and behavior to a more recent concern with the "cognitive" effects of the media—that is, to the possibility that the main impact of the media lies in their contribution to shaping audience members' perceptions of society, its problems, processes, and prospects. Not surprisingly, this interest in "cognitive effects" has led to much research on information seeking and processing and on issues of audience comprehension of the informational contents of the media.

One significant and growing influence on the thinking of American researchers in this area has been concepts and paradigms developed by European critical theorists and imported (or transplanted) to the United States within the past decade or so. Broadly put, the European critical tradition questions—indeed, dismisses—the notion of an autonomous, nonpolitical, and objective mass media. It specifically rejects the neutrality implicit in the concept of "information" and replaces it with notions of meaning and ideology.

This interaction of American and European perspectives has set the stage for yet another "new look" at the questions of the role and power of the media in society, a round of research that promises not to supplant the *old* "new look" at cognitive effects (Blumler and McLeod, 1974), but to place it in an alternative theoretical perspective. In that perspective, a central position is occupied by both macro questions of ideology and micro issues dealing with the construction of meaning by audiences exposed to media materials.

ASSUMPTIONS OF THE
"INFORMATIONAL" APPROACH

Most of the work reported in this book belongs to the tradition of the earlier "new look." As Davis and Robinson describe it in Chapter 2, much of that research centers on an empirical assessment of the effectiveness of television news as a source of information for average persons. Although their discussion aims to identify the "merits and limitations" of the theories that underlie the central focus of this volume, the notions of information rather than meaning and of the effectiveness—specifically of television news—in transmitting this information remain at the heart of the studies reported.

The conceptual limitations of that approach are by now well known. To begin with, the notion of "effectiveness" implies, as in the vintage Shannon and Weaver (1949) model or in what Carey has called the "transportation theory" of communication (1976), a process in which the message at the point of reception corresponds as accurately and precisely as possible to the message transmitted. It is a process in which message decoding is considered neither especially problematic nor capable of transforming the message's meaning.

In conventional usage, the notion of information also suffers the limitations concerning the problematics of "objectivity," the "news frame," and other factors that influence and constrain the production of informational materials in the media (e.g., Tuchman, 1978). At the audience end of the process, the idea of comprehension, when defined in terms of accurate reproduction of messages, ignores the complexities of diverse decodings and the potential variety of meanings constructed by receivers on the basis of information received (Hall, 1980; Morly, 1980).

However familiar the critique, there is no need to throw out the baby of comprehension with the bathwater of effectiveness. Assuming that the manifest function of television news is to convey unambiguous information still provides a useful point from which to launch empirical studies of the audience experience with television news and its role in forming audience understanding of the world. Dahlgren (1983: 6) observes that

> while the output of television news does convey "information," some of which is certainly retained by viewers, it is not the discrete units of information per se—the daily variation in content—which are at the core of the broadcasts' role in orienting the audience to the social world. Rather, it is the recurring, stable features of the programming (that is to

say the generic conventions, the structure and thematic content of TV news) as a cultural form which, over time, are the most significant.

Dahlgren identifies two intellectual sources for this view. The first are numerous empirical studies of news audience attention and recall that "suggest that the broadcasts are not exclusively, nor even primarily, an information absorbing experience for the audience," but rather part of the political socialization process. The second source is the results of semiotic and other holistic analyses of cultural texts. These studies, Dahlgren (1983: 7) concludes,

> have a strong critical dimension which highlights the ideological aspect of the broadcasts, [and] suggest that the signs and codes of the discourse embody a systematic bias in favor of the prevailing power arrangements. . . . [Thus] this line of research has been an invaluable development in the social analysis of TV news. Not only has it helped to take us beyond simplistic "informational" perspectives, but it has also illuminated the hegemonic tendencies of television programming.

One of the better-known attempts to identify the "preferred reading" (Hall, 1980) of social issues as presented in television news is the series of *Bad News* studies conducted by the Glasgow University Media Group (1976, 1980, 1982). Through careful content analysis of the coverage of industrial relations in British television news, these studies appear to have documented a promanagement, antiunion bias in that coverage. Not surprisingly, these conclusions were not sympathetically received by the British television establishment, and the resulting controversy pitted broadcasters and researchers against each other in a no-win war of words.

Policy controversies aside, there is an important theoretical gap in the *Bad News* research, namely the assumption that one can move from content-analytic findings to conclusions about audience understandings. There is, after all, considerable difference between documenting a "preferred reading" in television news (as the Glasgow group contends they have done) and demonstrating the hegemonic *consequences* of any text or body of texts. To document the latter requires evidence about *audience* readings of the texts, not simply an analysis of texts as cultural artifacts.

Indeed, even some critical researchers also accept the logic of this conclusion.

> To say that the mass media are saturated with bourgeois ideology is simply to pose a series of questions for investigation. To begin to answer

them, however, it is necessary to go on to show how this hegemony is actually reproduced through the concrete activities of media personnel and *the interpretative procedures of consumers.* This requires detailed and directed analysis of the social contexts of production and *reception* [Golding and Murdock, 1978: 350; emphasis added].

Thus, one does not have to endorse the theoretical assumptions and underpinnings of mainstream effects research to realize that members of the television audience may comprehend, process, or decode television news stories in different ways—and thus derive and construct different understandings from those materials. Hall's (1980) classification of different modes of audience decoding represents one attempt from within the critical approach to address this issue. Morly's (1980) work on the ways in which different groups relate to the BBC news magazine *Nationwide* attacks the question from an empirically based cultural studies perspective. Thus, even those researchers who work in the critical paradigm and who have justifiably been accused of paying insufficient empirical attention to media audiences (see, for example, Fejes, 1984) do occasionally recognize that the "pictures of the world" in audience members' minds cannot be assumed to be identical with media portrayals of social reality. In short, we would contend that the relationship between media representations and audience perceptions and understandings should not be taken for granted and must be the subject of empirical examination.

MEDIA REPRESENTATIONS
AND METAMESSAGES

We will now present the results of one such study. The project itself is highly exploratory and must be considered as a pilot for a long-term effort. Our discussion here is part theoretical and part methodological; and, as it should be, the theoretical and methodological arguments simultaneously inform and constrain each other.

In what follows, we will consider what our research group has come to refer to as "metamessages." By metamessages, we mean those latent meanings that are embedded in *audience decodings* of mass media messages and that link the aggregated structure of individually created meanings to macrosocial phenomena. Metamessages inhere in the meanings attributed to mass media messages by individuals who are trying to make sense of those messages. In short, the notion of metamessages is an audience-centered concept. We assume that like journalists who select, emphasize, and present the news based on "little tacit theories about what exists, what happens, and what matters" (Gitlin, 1980: 6), audiences too "frame" their understandings in accordance with "little tacit theories." By studying metamessages, we hope to describe and understand those taken-for-granted, common-sense theories, those explanatory frameworks—ideologies, if you will—that determine what people learn and know about their world from the mass media.[1]

Evidence about metamessages in general and evidence about audience members' understanding of social issues, which is the particular focus of our study here must, of course, be gathered from individual audience members. They alone can tell us what those messages mean to them. Yet the theoretical import of the metamessage concept can be judged only at the macro level in conjunction with notions regarding the media's role as initial constructors and disseminators of societal meanings. Thus, the concept of metamessage should be considered as a variable with "emergent" properties (Nagel, 1952), capable of being measured with reliability and validity at the individual level, but "larger than the sum of its parts" and theoretically more fruitful when so viewed.

As stated above, a full understanding of metamessages also requires evidence about media portrayals of reality and social issues. And such evidence could be derived from analysis of media texts, either through conventional methods of content analysis or via semiological or thematic approaches. But having performed such analyses, how would one link such evidence to data on audience perceptions?

The basic strategy we would suggest (and we are attempting to follow it in a separate project now under way) is to adopt essentially an agenda-setting logic. We recognize the enormous potential difficulties in attempting to locate causal, one-to-one relationships between media representations and metamessages. With that difficulty in mind, probably the best that one can hope for is to be able to identify similarities and perhaps overlaps between two bodies of evidence. Just as agenda-setting studies have often shown substantial similarities between categories of news on the media and public agendas, one could argue that similarities and discrepancies between metamessages and aggregates of media representations would represent, with varying degrees of accuracy and selectivity, the impact of media-explanatory frameworks on meanings created by individuals.

WAR/PEACE AND UNEMPLOYMENT:
A PILOT STUDY

Our first opportunity to study metamessages came in the two surveys described in Chapter 4. It will be recalled that those surveys were conducted during May and June of 1983, one in the Washington, D.C., area, the other a national sample. Two issues were selected for examination: first, the likelihood that the United States would become involved in a "hot" war, perhaps in Central America or the Middle East, and second, the high levels of domestic unemployment that were occurring in 1983.

To set the context for our choice of issues, it should be noted that the winter and spring months of 1983 had been characterized by increasing tension in Central America. President Reagan was actively campaigning for increased U.S. involvement in the region, and the struggles in El Salvador and Nicaragua were often portrayed as a conflict between the United States and surrogates of the Soviet Union. Elsewhere, the situation in Lebanon was deteriorating dramatically, with possible dire implications for world peace. With regard to domestic unemployment, during the first six months of 1983, the number of out-of-work Americans reached a record post-Depression high of 10 million, and stories about the state of the economy and unemployment in particular appeared with considerable frequency in the news media. Thus, in both cases we assumed that the public had been exposed to media portrayals, framings, and explanations of the issues, although most certainly in varying degrees.

Aside from their obvious topicality and substantive importance, these issues were selected for two other reasons. First, they represented two different kinds of stories—the question of possible war being one of international relations and foreign policy, with overtones of potential personal and national danger; the unemployment issue being a largely domestic, "bread and butter" concern.

Second, and of greater theoretical importance, we assumed that the two issues would be different with regard to how much firsthand knowledge about each might be available to our respondents. Specifically, we felt that whatever understandings people had about the "war and peace" issue by and large must have come either directly or fairly directly from news coverage. By contrast, it appeared far more likely that our respondents might have actually experienced real-world cues about unemployment. If this were so, then we might expect audience understandings of war and peace to be closer to media representations of that issue, although individual understandings of unemployment might result from the interaction of both direct experience and media messages.

In order to tap respondent understandings of these two issues, we decided on an open-ended form of questioning. Rather than providing respondents with researcher-generated alternatives, we felt it would be more fruitful to have respondents give their own explanations and understandings in their own words. Such an approach, it seemed to us, would be more likely to capture the possible range and qualities of audience understandings. Obviously, however, the telephone interviewing situation itself would place limits on the fullness with which respondents answered, and therefore our analysis would be constrained by the text at hand. Further, although extensive follow-up questions would have been highly desirable, it was impossible to construct such a conversation in advance, largely because each response would have required a unique set of probes and each would have proceeded along different lines of discussion.

Specifically on war and peace, respondents in the regional sample were first asked, "Have the chances that the U.S. will become involved in a war anywhere in the world increased, decreased, or stayed the same in the past few months?" Regardless of their answer, respondents were then asked, "Why do you say that?" For the unemployment issue, we first told respondents in the national sample, "There are many different explanations given for why we still have high unemployment," and then we asked, "What do you think are the main reasons for high unemployment?" That was followed by a brief probe, "Any other reasons?" Then, "And what do you think could be done about it [high unemployment]?" In addition, respondents were also asked standard demographic and media use questions.

Before proceeding to the findings, two limitations of the research design must be made clear. First, the absence from our data of any evidence of *direct* links between respondent answers and media portrayals of those issues renders it impossible to perform a micro-level analysis of media influences on public issue understandings. However, it should be recalled that our main concern is with the macro-level "ideological" role of the media, rather than with variations at the level of individuals. One aspect of the macro-level role of the media inheres in the assumption or claims that the media may achieve an "ideological effect" through the repetitiveness and the uniformity of their portrayals of social reality. Thus, the Glasgow University Media Group (1982: 59) contends,

> The content of the news is organized in such a way that coherence is
> given to only one set of explanations and policies. What we are in-

dicating here is not isolated pieces of "bias." The problem is much more profound than this. The logic of one group of explanations is built into the text.

The implication of this argument is that the "coherence of one set of explanations" is not only transmitted to the audience but is also largely accepted by that audience. At the same time, we have already noted the argument that allows for different modes of audience reading of media materials, in essence suggesting a semiautonomous decoding process. Following that line of reasoning, we would expect to find that the more autonomous the decoding process, the greater the diversity we would encounter in our respondents' explanations of the issues presented to them. Our data therefore ought to shed some light on the power of "one set of explanations" to impress itself upon audiences and lead them into accepting a relatively similar set of understandings.

A second limitation of the research design is that any assessment of the diversity of audience explanations needs to take into account the possible *absence* of competing or alternative explanations. By asking open-ended questions, we sought to capture respondents' understandings about war and peace and unemployment. It is possible, of course, that audiences hold other perceptions and explanations but simply did not offer them during the course of the interview. However, as the findings below clearly demonstrate, the open-ended questions produced a variety of responses, and we would assume that few, if any, important alternatives were overlooked.

One final point is in order. A universe of audience explanations that seems at one level of analysis to be quite diverse might simultaneously, and at another level of abstraction, actually be lacking in diversity. This "invisible" uniformity would be so if the apparently varying explanations stem from the same *general* explanatory framework. Genuine diversity of explanations, we suggest, is not necessarily reflected in the number of different kinds of responses to the same question. Rather, diversity of metamessages is demonstrated by the range of *alternative paradigms* from which the aggregated understandings stem.

FINDINGS

We will first present the results from the "war and peace" and unemployment questions separately, and then draw both sets of findings together.[2]

War and Peace

Three out of seven respondents (42%) in the Washington, D.C. metropolitan area survey thought the chances that the United States would soon be involved in a war anywhere in the world had increased. Some 18% thought the chances of the United States being involved in a war had decreased, but 31% said chances of war remained "about the same." One respondent in eleven was "not sure."

When respondents who had a definite opinion about the likelihood of war were asked to explain that opinion, a substantial majority (56%) gave answers that we classified as "process-oriented." By process-oriented, we mean responses framed in terms of social, political, historic, or economic factors or forces. Some 16% of justifications centered either on political leaders or on organizations that personified such leadership, and we labeled those "actor-oriented" reasons. Slightly fewer (14%) of all justifications were classified as "event-oriented." Event-oriented responses focused on a specific conflict or incident. One in seven (14%) respondents offered no rationale for their opinion.

Sixteen different categories of process-oriented answers were coded. The four most frequently offered account for almost one-third of *all* explanations. Of these four, one had a single-nation focus (growing U.S. involvements overseas), one centered on U.S.-Soviet relations (nuclear stalemate), and two (continuing world unrest and war-as-historical-constant) were not tied to the actions of specific nation-states. Although no mention of the Soviet Union was made in the survey question, respondents mentioned the Soviet Union (either acting alone or as part of bilateral relations with the United States) in six categories of process-oriented answers.

With regard to the five categories of actor-oriented rationales, coded, President Reagan and his administration received the largest number of mentions, many with a clearly negative valence. It should be noted, however, that in absolute terms, the total number of such explanations was comparatively small. About 2% singled out "inadequate" world leaders in general, but less than 1% of all the explanations offered mentioned Yuri Andropov, then Soviet Premier, directly by name.

Seven different categories of event-oriented rationales were also coded. For all practical purposes, only two geopolitical regions—Central America and the Middle East—were mentioned as real or potential "trouble spots." Virtually no respondents justified their opinion about the likelihood of war by referring to events in Europe,

TABLE 7.1 Reasons War Is "More" or "Less" Likely (N = 370)

	Percentage
"Process" reasons	
increasing U.S. involvements overseas	9
continuing general unrest, tensions	8
nuclear stalemate	8
war a historic constant	7
increased general unrest, tensions	6
continuing U.S. involvements overseas	5
empty political rhetoric	3
arms control talks	2
increased Russian involvement overseas	2
unchanged U.S.-Soviet relations	2
nuclear arms race	1
decreased U.S. involvement overseas	1
U.S.-Soviet confrontations	1
U.S.-Soviet détente	1
decreasing general unrest, tensions	*
"Actor-oriented" reasons	
President Reagan	11
current U.S. administration	2
inadequate world leaders	2
Yuri Andropov	1
Reagan and Andropov	*
"Event-oriented" reasons	
several countries/regions named	5
Central America in general	4
El Salvador/Nicaragua	2
Middle East in general	1
Lebanon	1
Iran	*
Afghanistan	*
"Don't know"	16
	100

*Indicates < 1%.

Southeast Asia, or the Third World more generally. This relatively constrained geopolitical focus may be interpreted as a form of media agenda setting, given that during the general time period of this study the American media were paying scant attention to areas outside Central America and the Middle East.

Respondents who said earlier that the likelihood of war had increased were significantly more likely to frame their answers in terms of either social actors or events. By contrast, respondents who offered process-oriented answers were no more likely than the sample as a whole to see war as increasingly likely.

Total news media use (i.e., the sum of exposure to newspaper, television, radio, and newsmagazines) was not significantly associated with whether a respondent would provide a "process," "event," or "actor" rationale. However, differential dependence on the news media was often significantly associated with the type of response, even when controls for respondent sex, age, education, and total news media exposure were introduced. Thus, for example, although two-thirds (67%) of television-reliant respondents framed their answers in terms of process, virtually the same proportion of newspaper-dependent respondents gave answers that were event-oriented. Regardless of news media dependence, respondents under 30 years of age were disproportionately likely to offer actor-oriented explanations.

Unemployment

On the first of the two unemployment questions, we found that almost one-fifth (19%) of our national sample had no explanation ("don't know") for the continuing high levels of unemployment. About half offered one explanation, one-quarter gave two reasons, and one in ten respondents replied with three or more reasons. Overall, 32 different types of causes were mentioned, with no single cause being mentioned by more than one-sixth of all respondents.

Explanations centering on economic forces (e.g., high interest rates, inflation, "vulnerable" industries) accounted for one-third of all answers excluding "don't know." About one-fifth of all causes focused on unions or workers with a slightly smaller proportion "blaming" politicians, government, or public policies. One-seventh of all responses dealt with foreign competition or imports, but only 6% of all answers (excluding "don't know") specifically faulted the business community or management.

In general, the number or types of explanations offered were not significantly related to the kind or amount of news media exposure or to news media dependency. However, male, younger, and better-educated respondents were somewhat more likely to give explanations centering on government or politicians and economic forces. Some 43% of women offered no explanation at all.

Asked for solutions to unemployment, 43% of all respondents said they either didn't know or offered the obviously tautological solution,

TABLE 7.2 "Causes" of Unemployment (N = 544)

	% Responses	% Cases
Economic forces		
high interest rates	8	11
inflation	4	7
certain industries vulnerable	4	6
recession	3	5
technology, automation	3	5
low consumer demand	3	5
public lack of confidence	1	1
worldwide economic conditions	1	1
industry relocating	1	1
high cost oil, materials	*	*
"unemployment inevitable," structural	*	*
Unions/workers		
unions/union demands	7	10
lack of desire to work	5	8
poorly trained workers	3	5
too many workers	2	3
Government/politicians/policies		
Reagan/Republican policies	6	9
federal debt, budget deficits	2	3
cuts in federal programs	2	3
monetary policy	2	2
taxes	1	2
excessive military/space spending	1	2
Carter, Democratic policies	1	1
anti-inflationary policies	*	*
government regulations	*	*
not enough military spending	*	*
Foreign competition/imports	11	17
Business sector		
unproductive U.S. industries	3	4
poor management/business practices	1	2
failure to plan	1	1
Miscellaneous		
"not enough jobs"	9	14
racial prejudice	*	*
God, fate	*	*
Don't know	12	19
	100	151

*Indicates < 1%.

"put people back to work." Still, 34 different categories of solutions were coded. The largest number, representing almost two-thirds of all solutions (excluding "don't know") centered on actions by government and politicians. Approximately one-quarter focused on either individuals or the public, with only a handful of solutions placing the responsibility for alleviating unemployment in the business sector.

News media use and dependence was not significantly associated with solutions offered. However, male, younger, and better-educated respondents were more likely to call for governmental or political action to solve the unemployment problem.

IS THERE A COHERENT SET OF EXPLANATIONS?

The principal question to be addressed is whether these findings suggest or confirm the existence of a "coherent set of explanations" held by mass media audiences. On the face of it, the range of responses certainly is wide enough to be construed as a diversity of understandings. Respondents invoked a variety of different "causes" and "solutions" in both the war-and-peace and unemployment issues.

This range of responses is reflected in both the specific explanations introduced as well as the different *dimensions* implicit in those responses. For example, many audience members responded in terms of "economic forces," some controllable, some not. By contrast, other respondents focused on specific social actors (e.g., unions or workers, government or politicians, business or management). A similar degree of diversity, in terms of both range of responses and dimensions of response, is apparent on the question of war and peace.

As further evidence of diversity, it is possible to order the subcategories on a rough scale of abstraction. Thus, we suggest that the category of process-oriented responses in the war-and-peace question and the economic forces category of explanations about unemployment contain responses framed in somewhat more abstract terms. On the other hand, actor or event responses to the war-and-peace issue and responses such as "unions," "government," and "business" with regard to unemployment are clearly couched in more specific and less abstract terms.

Further, the process-oriented war-and-peace responses generally contained the most complex and synthesized information. Thus, they represent the most abstract sense-making or decoding by audience members. By contrast, actor- or event-oriented responses to both

TABLE 7.3 "Solutions" for Unemployment

	% Responses	% Cases
Government/politicians/policies		
Protectionist policies	7	9
job-creating public programs	7	8
job training, reeducation	6	7
cut interest rates	5	6
cut public spending, welfare	3	4
more equality in wealth, taxes	2	2
get rid of Reagan	2	2
cut military spending	2	2
balance budget, reduce deficit	2	2
control inflation	2	2
decrease foreign aid	2	2
have a war; put unemployed in camps, etc.	1	1
rely on "free market" economy	*	*
keep plants from relocating	*	*
print more money	*	*
"refuel" the economy	*	*
fewer regulations on business	*	*
match workers with jobs	*	*
shift emphasis away from industry	*	*
tax large corporations	*	*
Unions/workers/public		
curb unions, worker demands	4	5
more discipline, readiness to work	3	4
"Buy American"	3	4
share existing jobs	1	1
help each other; be humane	*	*
Business sector		
produce more, better products	2	3
deny non-Americans jobs	1	2
higher pay for workers	1	1
encourage business to create jobs	1	1
improve technology	*	*
impose production quotas	*	*
Miscellaneous		
"Put people back to work"/tautology	6	8
"Ride it out," "no easy answers"	5	6
prayer	*	*
Don't know	30	35
	100	188

*Indicates < 1%.

issues contain less abstract and synthesized information. Respondents in such instances apparently have reduced the complexities of international relations and economics, either by a process of personification or simply by fixing their sights on "one damn crisis after another."

It could be argued that the more concrete responses are closer in quality to the notion of "messages" in the information-transmission model. They reflect the perceptions of audience members who, in processing the news, focus on concrete, informational bits of data and then construct their understandings of the issues in those terms. Responses couched in process or economic forces terms, however, seem much closer to frames of understanding and thus are likely to have been shaped *less* by the "discrete units of information per se—the daily variation in content" (Dahlgren, 1983) and *more* by the latent frameworks implicit in the news.

Recall now that the more abstract types of responses far outnumbered the more concrete categories of responses in our data. We do not interpret this to mean that in any absolute sense the average audience member is especially well informed about either international affairs or economics. There is simply too much evidence presented in Chapters 3 through 5 to suggest otherwise. Nor are we suggesting that the average member of the news audience is necessarily very capable of or especially interested in understanding the news in abstract terms. However, to the extent that a fair proportion of news users perceive social and political issues in abstract terms, and to the extent that these frameworks or contexts are constructed, at least in part, by a cumulative exposure to the "dominant meanings" offered by the news media, then our findings tend to lend some weight to conclusions about the frame construction function of the media.

PARADIGM DIVERSITY?

Finally, there is the question of the extent to which our data suggest diversity in the paradigmatic underpinnings for audience understandings. As we noted earlier, genuine diversity of understandings implies not only variations between responses but, more important, diversity in underlying paradigmatic assumptions. At the "supply" end of the mass communication process, "conflicting viewpoints of social issues are . . . the elements that structure most television programs," thus casting TV in the role of "cultural forum" (Newcomb and Hirsch, 1983). At the same time, Newcomb and Hirsch also acknowledge that such "variety works for the most part within the limits of American monopoly capitalism and within the range of American pluralism." Diversity, it seems, is clearly permissible within and contained by paradigmatic boundaries.

Thus, it is necessary to examine metamessages in paradigmatic terms. It is, however, far easier to state this precept than to assess it operationally. The major difficulty we encountered was how to make sense of respondents' explanations in paradigmatic terms. One difficulty lay with the data. The open-ended question format did not produce responses that were complete enough to allow very complicated analyses, most certainly not of the sort required here. This difficulty could, of course, be overcome with other methods, such as clinical or in-depth interviews.

But our experience with these limited data have convinced us that even if "richer" data were available, we would still face another, even knottier problem. Before respondent understandings can be classified according to paradigms, it is necessary to establish clear paradigmatic types. Although the classification of natural science theories and even certain social science theories may be relatively easy, the paradigmatic classification of commonsense or "working" theories (McQuail, 1983) is far more problematic. Criteria for classification are largely nonexistent, and when they do exist, their applicability is uncertain.

On the issue of unemployment, for example, economists we consulted generally refused to accept the idea that the notion of paradigm differences would be very fruitful. True, they said, there are different schools of economic thought, but these schools do not lend themselves to simple paradigmatic classification. For example, the term "market economics" can be applied to describe the economic process in both capitalist and socialist economies. Thus, even a seemingly basic distinction between capitalist and Marxist schools of economic thought is not directly applicable to our task. In short, concepts and methods for the identification and classification of real-world paradigms remain a major and largely unmet challenge.

In this chapter, we have presented first results of our investigation into audience understandings of reality. Unlike media materials as texts, audience members' accounts must be "created" before they can be analyzed. We have tried one approach and suggested others. What we have found is that those audience accounts that are most accessible to the researcher are also likely to be less rich in meaning and more difficult to analyze than related media texts. And we have encountered a host of conceptual and methodological impediments to that analysis.

Nevertheless, studies of how and what people understand of social life and its problems must be undertaken if we are to increase our knowledge of the role played by the mass media in shaping public consciousness. The promise of such work, if it is to continue, depends on successfully confronting the theoretical and methodological difficulties we have raised.

NOTES

1. Examples of possible metamessages created when audience members attempt to decode entertainment messages might include the "scary world" notion of Gerbner and his associates, or the idea that particular individuals (e.g., the president, parents, or other authority figures) are better at solving problems than other people. It should be noted that from our perspective, these explanatory frameworks should be considered metamessages only insofar as they can be linked to macrosocial issues such as power and social control.

2. Responses to the "war and peace" and unemployment questions were independently coded by three specially trained graduate assistants and the second author of this chapter. Based on Scott's pi, intercoder reliability for the "war and peace question" was 0.91, and for the two unemployment questions 0.89 and 0.92.

III   *Producer Factors*

Chapter 8

NEWS STORY ATTRIBUTES
AND COMPREHENSION

DENNIS K. DAVIS
JOHN P. ROBINSON

The typical television news broadcast contains a mixture of contrasting or even conflicting news stories. Newscasts frequently juxtapose reports on the actions of world leaders alongside human interest features that highlight dramatic incidents in the lives of average persons. Some stories provide matter-of-fact descriptions of routine happenings; others contain emotional outbursts from event participants. Given the varied content of news, it is likely that some news items will be better understood and remembered than others. But which items will stand out and be better comprehended by most viewers?

It has often been said that the attributes of news stories play a large role in determining a story's effects on viewers. Television news stories are quite varied in their structure and content, so it is to be expected that comprehension of stories will also vary. Powerful combinations of stimuli should be able to attract viewer attention to otherwise routine stories and induce the viewer to learn information. Similarly, significant stories may be so poorly structured that their theme is lost amid a flow of irrelevant detail. The news comprehension data collected in Britain and the United States for our study of viewer comprehension of single broadcasts permits us to make an exploratory assessment of the attributes of stories that were more or less well understood. This analysis can serve at least three purposes. It can provide some insight for news broadcasters who are interested in increasing the comprehension of different types of stories. It also allows an initial understanding of the impact that certain story factors do have. Finally, it provides some indirect insight into the decoding process that viewers use to make sense of news stories.

Previous survey research has generally failed to study links between the attributes of specific stories and learning. Gross measurements of story content are typically used by agenda-setting researchers (McCombs and Shaw, 1972; McCombs, 1981). The amount of coverage given specific issues over a period of days is matched up with audience rankings of issue importance. Diffusion researchers have studied whether stories that audiences (or researchers) perceive as important are likely to diffuse more rapidly. Uses and gratifications researchers have asked people whether they use media differently to seek news that serves different purposes for them (Katz et al., 1973).

News comprehension studies have found that although learning tends to fluctuate greatly over the course of a broadcast, it is only modestly linked to story position (Neuman, 1976; Stauffer et al., 1983; Robinson and Sahin, 1984). Although initial stories are generally better remembered, it is common for stories placed late in broadcasts to be well remembered also. Some survey research suggests that those stories that interest people or that are perceived as being personally useful are more likely to be learned (Gaziano, 1983). All such inferences must be considered tenuous in the absence of research that examines what is routinely learned from a large number of different types of news stories.

Experimental research provides one basis for predicting learning from individual news items. This literature has been summarized in Chapter 6. Learning has been linked to a variety of story factors: amount of visual content, position in broadcast, inclusion of causal explanations, story complexity, congruence between visual and verbal content, and positioning next to similar stories. Some rather strong effects have been found in laboratory experiments. But can such effects be found in home viewing?

The news comprehension data that we collected in Britain and the United States included measures that allow us to make an exploratory assessment of the comprehension of various types of stories. The relatively small number of news stories included in our research (40 in Britain and 49 in the United States) and our limited audience samples do not permit us to draw definitive conclusions. Nevertheless, our findings suggest that it may be possible to replicate many of the findings of experimental researchers using survey techniques. This should encourage others to undertake survey work in this area. It is important to begin to move story attribute research out of the laboratory and into the field. It is likely that many of the findings that are now well established by experimental work will not receive serious consideration from journalists until it can be demonstrated that they apply to actual newscasts watched by typical viewers in their homes.

Below we have suggested how findings like those reported in this chapter could be used by journalists as a basis for improving newscasts. Ongoing news research could continuously verify the success of such changes. Although significant refinement in research methods should occur before they are used to guide extensive changes in newscast practice, we believe that we have demonstrated the feasibility and potential of such research. The cost of such comprehension research should be significantly less than what is now being spent to study news viewer preferences and audience demographics. Its public service value is infinitely greater.

THE BRITISH AND AMERICAN SURVEYS

In Chapter 5 we described the objectives and overall research design of our comprehension research in Great Britain; that research was undertaken at the request of the BBC and involved the ongoing cooperation of BBC journalists and social researchers. A central objective of this research was to be able to identify specific news stories that had been comprehended well or poorly. A survey of 489 persons was conducted over a period of four days. During this time, 40 news stories were broadcast. On an average day, 120 persons were questioned about each of these stories. Comprehension scores were calculated for each respondent for each story using the technique described in detail in Chapter 5. Comprehension scores ranging from 0 to 8 were obtained for each story. These scores were averaged across the 120 or so viewers of each story to obtain an average comprehension score for each story. This average comprehension score was then used as the dependent variable in the analyses reported below.

In June 1979, the British research was replicated in the United States with some modifications. Interviews were conducted with 425 respondents over a period of three days immediately after viewers had watched a specific national network news broadcast. A different network broadcast was targeted each night. About 140 persons were interviewed each day in nine different U.S. cities. The probability sampling scheme used maximized the heterogeneity of the sample and assured inclusion of approximately the same proportion of persons of varying education, income, and place of residence as would be found in the news audience. Although the sample was too small and nonrural to be representative of the entire population of American viewers, it is quite adequate for an exploratory analysis.

The same method was used to measure comprehension of news stories as had been used in Britain (see Chapter 5). Cued recall data were content analyzed using a coding scheme identical to that used in England. Three members of our news research team coded each story. Senior news producers at each of the three network news operations assisted us in checking the accuracy of our coding. The producers were then furnished with all of the open-ended audience response data together with our coding of each into one of the nine points on our comprehension scale. (See Figure 5.1 in Chapter 5.) They responded by either agreeing with our codes or suggesting changes. Few changes were suggested and most of these changes were easily incorporated into our analysis. News producers often suggested that ratings of audience comprehension be lowered rather than increased.

The Independent Variables

Our independent variables were measured by conducting a content analysis of each story. The coding scheme used was based upon the multidimensional coding scheme proposed by Schulz (1976). He developed this scheme relying upon content analyses done in Europe and the United States. We developed a coding scheme that included the 25 story attribute items shown in Table 8.1. Many of these same items were used to analyze the U.S. stories as shown in Table 8.2. Some story attributes were dropped from the U.S. analysis and several new attributes were added. In general, the attributes that were dropped were found to be insignificant in the analysis of the British data, to overlap significantly with other items, and to be of less theoretical interest. The several items added to the U.S. analysis were based on a consideration of information-processing research as explained below.

A content analysis coding sheet was prepared that listed each of these story attributes in the form of five-point rating scales. In Britain, a team of three judges was chosen to analyze each story based on these rating scales. Two judges were BBC researchers and one was a senior BBC news editor. The judges used a consensual process to arrive at their final ratings. They first made independent judgments after viewing a videotape of each story. They then discussed differences of opinion and arrived at a single score to reflect consensual agreement on each scale. For example, if two judges rated a story "3" on human interest but the third rated it "4," a consensual score of "3" would have been recorded if no agreement could be reached. Serious disagreements arose on less than 5% of the codings; the judges' scores were usually identical or were within one point of each other.

In the United States, a team of three judges analyzed each story using the rating scales. The judges were all researchers involved with our news research team. Unlike the British analysis, a consensual process was not used to determine the final ratings. After each judge watched each story on videotape, the tape was stopped and the story was briefly discussed. Then each judge made an independent rating on each scale. The ratings were added together and a mean rating was calculated for each. Few differences were found in the ratings made by judges. Most ratings were within one point of each other.

STORY PLACEMENT AND LENGTH

Much previous research has examined the relationships between comprehension and both story length and story placement in a TV news broadcast. Length and placement have both been found to be positively related to comprehension. Although our research also finds modest relationships, length and placement were not found to be especially strong factors in comparison to other predictors. Figures 8.1 and 8.7 show how two different levels of viewer comprehension were found to fluctuate over the course of each of the seven broadcasts studied in Britain and the United States. The top line in each figure represents the percentage of audience members who recognized each story. The second line shows the percentage who were judged to have comprehended the main point of each story. Stories are arranged on the bottom axis according to their position in the broadcast. By looking across each figure, it is possible to note the fluctuation in story recognition and comprehension that occurred as each broadcast proceeded.

An examination of our figures reveals several common findings. First, both recognition and comprehension fluctuate markedly over the course of every broadcast. This occurs even when a single network, such as the BBC, is studied over the course of several evenings (Figures 8.1-8.4). Therefore, we do not interpret our findings for the U.S. networks (Figures 8.5-8.7) to mean that one network was better (or worse) at communicating information.

During several broadcasts, first and last stories were well comprehended, but this was not true for all. In several cases very large gaps can be found between the line that indicates recognition of stories

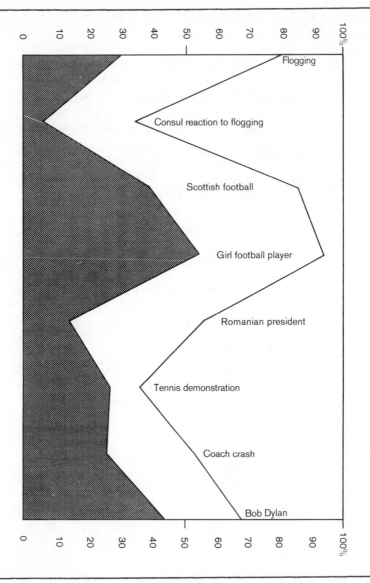

Figure 8.1   U.K. Awareness and Comprehension Levels for Evening 1

and the line that shows comprehension. The gap is smallest for the broadcasts shown in Figures 8.2, 8.3, and 8.6. In some figures, the gap is consistently large (Figures 8.1 and 8.7); in others, it widens and narrows over the course of a broadcast (Figures 8.4 and 8.6). On the basis

(text continued on page 188)

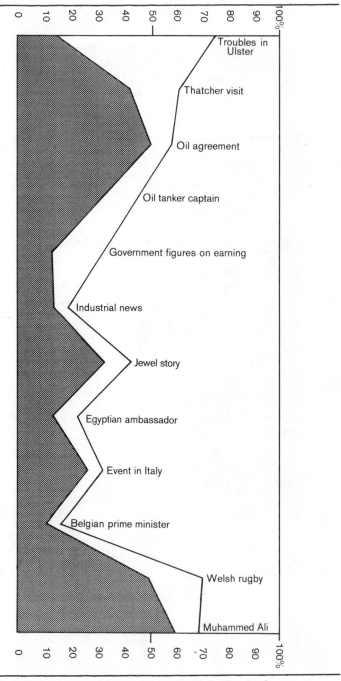

Figure 8.2 U.K. Awareness and Comprehension Levels for Evening 2

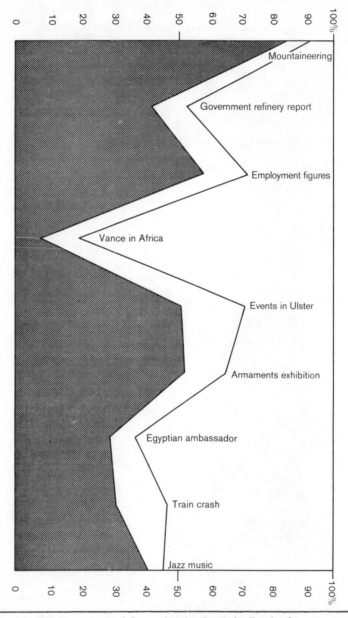

Figure 8.3 U.K. Awareness and Comprehension Levels for Evening 3

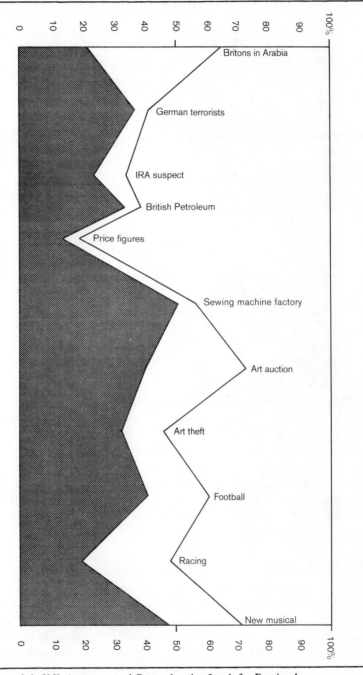

Figure 8.4   U.K. Awareness and Comprehension Levels for Evening 4

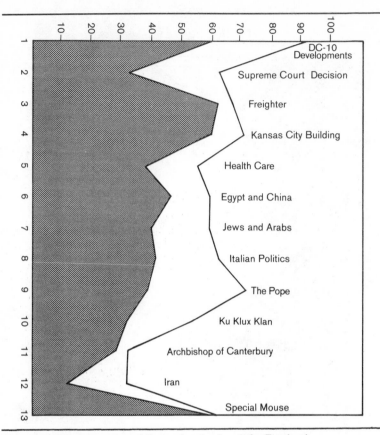

Figure 8.5   U.S. Awareness and Comprehension Levels for Evening 1

of our limited research, we cannot determine the degree to which such fluctuation is a function of the substance of the news stories on a given day, how much a function of the structure provided by a particular news producer, and how much a function of the journalistic skills of a specific group of reporters.

The Lead Stories

Our research does permit us to gain some insight into the most striking gaps revealed in these figures and to assess underlying causes. Lead items were quite poorly comprehended in several instances (Figures 8.1, 8.2, 8.4, and 8.7). Nevertheless, story position and comprehension were significantly associated in the United States ($r = .31$). We made a content analysis of each of these items to try to ascertain

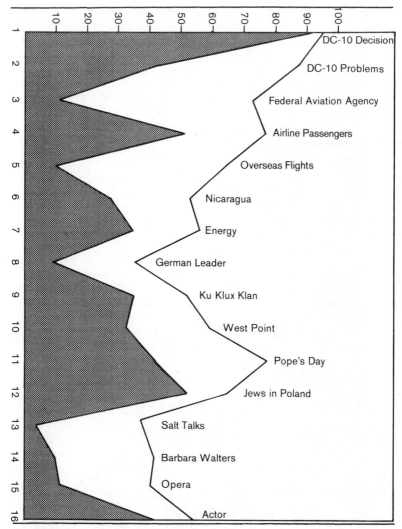

Figure 8.6   U.S. Awareness and Comprehension Levels for Evening 2

what led each to be poorly understood when positioning as a lead item should have assured relatively high comprehension. In each case there was evidence that problems were created by the inclusion of too much extraneous visual and verbal information. Each of the stories was long and included graphic visual as well as unrelated verbal content.

Another problem was created by the way in which BBC editors defined the main point of each story. Typically, their view of the main point differed markedly from the reports given us by audience

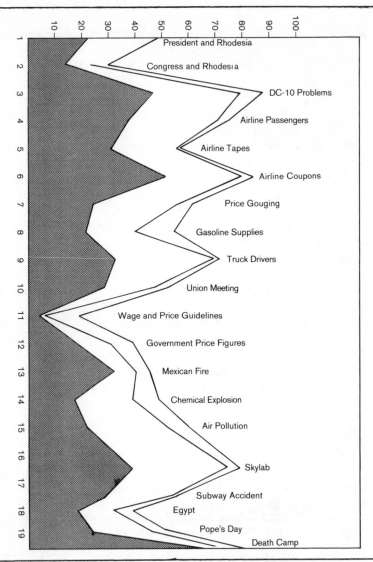

Figure 8.7   U.S. Awareness and Comprehension Levels for Evening 3

members. For example, the news editors stated that the two news
stories about Britons in Arabia (Figures 8.1 and 8.4) made the point
that there were dire consequences for British citizens who broke the
laws in the Middle East. Most audience members provided factual
reports of the details of the punishment given and the sentence com-
muted. They did not generalize from these details to the larger point

that the editors sought to communicate. Similarly, a story about troubles in Ulster introduced digressive elements and subplots about a hostage who had been freed. It described how he *survived* the incident and did not focus on the main point defined by the editors, who sought to communicate that several British soldiers had been killed that day. Fewer than 20% of audience members mentioned this point, but the remaining 60% recognized the story reported details relating to the hostage who had survived.

Figure 8.7 shows a lead story broadcast in the United States that was poorly comprehended. The story dealt with President Carter's announcement that he would not lift an economic embargo of Zimbabwe-Rhodesia because elections held there had not been "free and fair." The story was complex and used abstract or technical terms, which most viewers were not likely to understand. Our analysis of viewer responses revealed that few persons used the terms "economic embargo," "sanctions," or "Zimbabwe-Rhodesia" to refer to this story. Instead, they provided vague reports to the effect that Carter was unhappy with some African nation because it was not free. Several commented on an accusation that Carter was not acting like a Christian. The story was told with few visuals, but those that were included did little to communicate the main point. Visuals showed Carter speaking at a press conference. A map was used, along with pictures of leaders in Zimbabwe-Rhodesia. A long verbal description of the elections failed to reinforce the story's main point.

The Closing Stories

The figures show a far more uniform finding for the closing stories in each broadcast. These "signature" stories were consistently among the best-comprehended stories. They were almost always comprehended better than the stories immediately preceding them. In several cases there are quite dramatic rebounds from preceding stories. In every case, closing stories were highly visual stories with high human interest value. Several dealt with popular culture content or performers (Bob Dylan, Muhammad Ali, jazz music, a new musical, and the death of an actor from the *Wizard of Oz*). In almost every case, the stories were upbeat and visually interesting but dealt with essentially trivial topics. The sole exception was a story that dealt with the Pope's visit to concentration camps in Poland. On the basis of these data, we cannot state that closing stories necessarily will be better understood than lead stories. We are left with a chicken-and-egg argument: How much is it story placement per se that accounts for these signature stories being highly comprehended and how much the attention-getting appeal of stories that news professionals specifically choose so that their programs will end happily?

The Stories in the Middle

With regard to the vast majority of stories between the first and last stories, marked peaks and valleys can be noted in both recognition and comprehension. This finding is consistent with research by Gunter and his associates (see Gunter, Berry, & Clifford, 1981) that proactive interference may be built up by lumping similar stories together, thus depressing comprehension for subsequent stories. The valleys tend to occur for routine, brief stories on abstract reports or remote, rather minor events (e.g., Vance in Africa, Belgian prime minister, release of price figures, Egyptian election results, appointment of an archbishop of Canterbury). Similarly, reports of routine political unrest tend to pass unnoticed (e.g., demonstrations at a tennis match, demonstrations in Iran, arrest of another IRA suspect). Stories having some personal relevance were sometimes surprisingly well comprehended given their brief length and poor placement (e.g., an OPEC agreement on higher oil prices, unemployment figures, availability of discount airline coupons, price gouging by gasoline dealers, truck drivers on strike blocking major highways, a new plan for national health insurance).

Stories dealing with unique or notable individuals were well comprehended in both nations (e.g., the Pope in Poland, girl football player, Muhammad Ali, Bob Dylan), as were stories about unique situations (fall of Skylab, Jews in Poland, Jews and Arabs, closing of a sewing machine factory, art auction that produced record prices). One apparent difference between the United States and Britain was that in the United States, stories about disasters or accidents tended to be better comprehended than other types of stories. Stories about the DC-10 crash, an oilfield fire in Mexico, a subway accident, the collapse of an arena in Kansas City, and a burning freighter on the Great Lakes were among the best-comprehended items on the days they were broadcast. In Britain, accidents and disasters were not consistently among the best-remembered stories. It may not be safe to assume that British viewers are less interested in disaster, or that British TV news provides less dramatic portrayals of accidents; rather, it may be that the accidents and disasters that occurred in the United States during the period of our research were unusually interesting whereas those in Britain were especially routine.

STORY ATTRIBUTES AND COMPREHENSION

A significant difference was found between Britain and the United States when story length and story placement were correlated. In Britain, a strong correlation (r = .50) was found between placement of the 40 stories and their length. Longer stories were consistently placed near the beginning of broadcasts. In the United States a weak positive correlation of r = .19 was found between story position and length. Long feature stories were often placed near the end of the U.S. broadcasts, whereas groups of short items were placed just prior to commercial breaks.

In both nations, story length was significantly associated with comprehension. In Britain, the correlation was r = .55 and in the United States it was r = .27. The consistency in this correlation is noteworthy given the quite significant variation in story positioning noted above. Longer stories are better comprehended no matter where they are placed. Table 8.1 shows how comprehension and story length were related for the 40 BBC items. Of the 14 stories that had high comprehension, only one was shorter than 30 seconds; on the other hand, of the 12 stories that had low comprehension, seven were shorter than 30 seconds.

Tables 8.2 and 8.3 report the relationships between the various story attributes and comprehension for the British and U.S. data, respectively. In Table 8.2, only nine of the twenty-five attributes were significantly correlated with comprehension. Of these nine factors, five predominate with correlations above .45: length, proportion of time with newsreader on camera, human interest, personalization, and overall excitement. These five variables fall into two general categories: time length and human interest.

The U.S. data reported in Table 8.3 show a similar pattern. Stories with surprising information were more likely to be comprehended by audiences (r = .26 in Britain and r = .45 in the United States). One relationship was not found in the United States that was found in Britain. The British were less likely to comprehend items similar to preceding items. For Americans, this relationship was insignificant. In general, the story attributes linked to human interest (personalization, excitement) were somewhat less strongly linked to comprehension in the United States than in Britain. This may simply be due to the substance of the stories broadcast during the time of our research. For example, there were several rather dramatic hard news stories broadcast in the United States that were well understood. This was less true in Britain.

TABLE 8.1   Relation of Story Length to Comprehension
(Entries in the Cell Are the Bullets for Each Story)

| | | Comprehension (in Percentage Comprehending) | | |
		High (Over 40%)	Medium (20-40%)	Low (Under 20%)
Length (in seconds)	Long (95+)	Girl football player Mountaineering Government refining report Armaments exhibition New musical	Flogging Scottish football Football	Troubles in Ulster Britons in Arabia Racing
	Medium (31-95)	Bob Dylan Egyptian ambassador Thatcher visit Oil agreement Welsh Rugby Muhammad Ali Events in Ulster Jazz music	Industrial news Train crash German terrorists British petroleum Art auction	Vance in Africa
	Short (under 30)	Employment figures	Tennis demonstration Coach crash Oil tanker captain Jewel story Events in Italy IRA suspect Art theft	Consul reaction to flogging Romanian president Government earnings figures Egyptian ambassador Belgian prime minister Armaments exhibition Price figures

The results in these tables suggest that many story characteristics considered important by scholars and journalists may not be linked to comprehension. These attributes include conflict, physical proximity to the viewer, relevance of a story to society, ethnocentrism, prominence of persons in a story, and amount of interpretation. Two other factors were linked to comprehension: story structure and surprise. Story structure was an index of the degree to which a story was structured by a standardized story formula or whether it unfolded in an unusual manner. Surprise was an index of the number of unusual elements contained in a story. In general, Americans appear to be more sensitive to these two attributes than the British.

A test of the robustness and clarity of our British findings was made possible by the introduction of two alternate indices of comprehension into our analysis. The results are shown in columns two and three of Table 8.2. Comprehension was indexed by a measure of the number of story points mentioned and by the proportion of people who scored 5 or more on the comprehension scale.

TABLE 8.2 Correlation of News Factors and Percentage Comprehension

	Correlation (Pearson's r) with % Comprehension of Story	Correlation with Other Comprehension Measures	
		Information Points	% Items Over 5 Scale Points
(I.) Objective factors			
(1) Length of item (in seconds)	.50	.55	.22
(2) Percentage of item newscaster only	-.55	-.42	(-.18)
(3) Position of item in newscast (first-last)	(-.05)	(-.02)	(.10)
(II.) Ratings—"objective" factors			
(1) Depth of theme (1-5 long established)	(-.15)	.22	(.15)
(2) Duration (1 immediate-5 long-term)	(.08)	(.03)	(.00)
(3) Internal proximity (1 outside-5 near)	(.07)	(.06)	(.12)
(4) External proximity (1 far-5 U.K.)	(-.11)	(.10)	(-.04)
(5) Political-cultural proximity (1-5 near)	(-.05)	(.00)	(-.01)
(6) Centrality (1 minor-5 major powers)	-.24	-.26	-.21
(7) Prominence (1 ordinary-5 influential people)	(.04)	-.21	(.03)
(8) Losses (1 none-5 heavy)	(-.10)	.11	(-.04)
(III.) Ratings—"subjective" factors			
(1) Relevance (1 none-5 great significance)	(-.10)	(-.26)	(-.16)
(2) Story length (1 one day-5 over a year)	(-.04)	(-.08)	(-.11)
(3) Surprise (1 routine-5 unexpected)	.26	.32	.22
(4) Structure (1 stereotyped-5 no known pattern)	.23	.22	.23
(5) Portrayal (1 simple-5 complex ideas)	(-.06)	(-.10)	(-.12)
(6) Conflict (1 none-5 overt major conflict)	(.01)	(.07)	(-.13)
(7) Criminality (1 none-5 life-threatening)	(.02)	.25	(-.03)
(8) Success (1 none-5 great break-through)	(.10)	(.08)	(.15)
(9) Personalization (1 none-5 people sole focus)	.45	.57	.39
(10) Ethnocentrism (1 foreign-5 British)	(.07)	.21	(-.10)
(11) Human interest (1 none-5 heavy)	.58	.72	.48
(12) Overall excitement (1 none-5 extreme)	.52	.64	.53
(13) Connection to preceding item (1 none-5 extreme)	-.24	-.30	-.22
(14) Amount of interpretation (1 none-5 extreme)	(.16)	(.15)	.21

NOTE: Correlations in parentheses not statistically significant at the .05 level.

TABLE 8.3   Correlation of News Story Attributes
with Story Comprehension

Story Attributes	Correlation with % Comprehension of Story
Objective Factors	
(1) Length of story (in seconds)	.27
(2) Position of item in newscast (first-last)	.31
Ratings–"Subjective" Factors	
(1) Relevance (1 none–5 great)	(.16)
(2) Duration in news (1 one day–5 over a year)	(−.18)
(3) Surprise (1 routine–5 unforeseen)	.45
(4) Structure (1 stereotyped–5 no known pattern)	.36
(5) Portrayal (1 simple–5 complex)	(.01)
(6) Conflict (1 none–5 major)	(−.03)
(7) Criminality (1 none–5 life-threatening)	(−.10)
(8) Success (1 none–5 great)	(−.11)
(9) Personalization (1 none–5 focus on people)	.36
(10) Ethnocentrism (1 foreign news–5 domestic news)	(.18)
(11) Human interest (1 none–5 heavy)	.36
(12) Overall excitement (1 none–5 extreme)	.50
(13) Connection to preceding item (1 none–5 extreme)	(.08)
(14) Amount of interpretation (1 none–5 extreme)	(−.17)
(15) Amount of visual content (1 none–5 large)	.47
(16) Abstractness of visuals (1 content–5 abstract)	−.24
(17) Vividness of visuals (1 weak–5 strong)	.44
(18) Strength of emotional content (1 weak–5 strong)	.55
(19) Direction of emotional content (1 negative–5 strong)	(.12)
(20) Uniqueness of visuals (1 usual–5 unusual)	.47
(21) Congruency of visual/verbal content (1 congruent–5 incongruent)	(.00)

NOTE: Correlations in parentheses not significant at the .05 level.

Visual Attributes and Comprehension

The attributes that were added to the U.S. analysis proved to be rather strongly associated with comprehension. Of the seven variables added, five were found to be significantly correlated with comprehension (see Table 8.3). The most interesting of these variables involves measures of visual content. These items were added to the analysis based on previous experimental research that found that visual factors were linked to news story recall. Some information-processing theorists have developed a dual coding theory to explain processing of audiovisual information. They argue that visual information is coded separately from verbal information using qualitatively different coding schemes. Given that the coding of these two forms of information occurs simultaneously, visual cues that trigger recall of visual information might assist recall of congruent (similar) verbal information. Similarly, verbal cues might trigger recall of congruent visual information. However, in either case, incongruent or dissimilar information would not be recalled. For this reason, highly powerful but irrelevant pictures in a news story would serve to distract viewer attention from verbal content, would impede learning of verbal information, and would not later provide a basis for assisting recall of the verbal content. We hoped to assess whether news stories that contained large amounts of powerful but irrelevant visual content would be as poorly remembered as dual coding theory predicts. It should be noted that it is not just the vividness of the visual information per se that may be at work here; rather, it may be the *link* between the vivid visual information and cooccurring story content that is important in producing such a distraction effect. Although further research will be needed to sort out these possibilities, the link between visual information and story content should be carefully considered by both news researchers and producers. More comment will be made shortly about this visual-verbal congruency link.

We included several new measures of the emotional content of news stories in an effort to extend our findings in the British data concerning the higher comprehension of human interest stories. We speculated that the most salient feature of human interest stories is their emotional content—the visual and verbal cues that tend to arouse strong emotions, such as sympathy, fear, sorrow, and delight. Such emotions can be both positive and negative. We wanted to know if the "good" news stories that aroused positive emotions would be better comprehended than those that aroused negative emotions. Would the direction of the emotions aroused make any difference in level of comprehension?

Interrelationships Among
Story Attributes

In our analysis of the U.S. data, we also sought to investigate the interrelationship of the various story attributes. This was done by calculating the intercorrelations for the attribute items as reported in Table 8.4. The strength of these correlations should reflect the degree to which stories tend to contain similar attributes. The clustering of items can be found by isolating sets of items that are strongly related to each other but not to other items. The strongest cluster of items includes the visual attributes as well as the human interest attributes:

personalization, human interest, overall excitement, amount of visual information, vividness of visual information, strength of emotional content, and uniqueness of visual information. Each of these attributes was individually linked to comprehension, and their high intercorrelation makes it difficult to assess the relative power of each in enhancing comprehension.

We identified ten stories that possessed all of these attributes at rather high levels. Five dealt with the Pope's trip to Poland, and others dealt with the DC-10 crash in Chicago, the death of actor Jack Haley, a freighter fire, the collapse of a Kansas City arena, and a race between computerized mice. It is not surprising to find that so many stories combine strong visual attributes with strong human interest attributes. Epstein (1973) reports that news program producers select stories based on the presence of such attributes. With human interest news, there will frequently be a number of equally relevant (or trivial) stories available for broadcast, so it is logical to choose those that include attractive visuals.

Our findings suggest that this combination of human interest and attractive pictures is quite successful in communicating information. However, it is important to keep in mind that the learning induced by such stories may be lost quickly. We measured learning within three hours of each broadcast, but further research is necessary to assess how long this learning is likely to persist. The main points of such stories are usually very simple and concrete—someone famous died, a building collapsed, a ship burned, or the Pope went somewhere. Such points can be easily shown in pictures that graphically portray the main point of the story. When direct visual coverage is lacking, drawings or the graphic descriptions of eyewitnesses can be used. Such stories are ideally suited to communication via television, but is the learning they induce likely to persist and prove useful to viewers?

Other clusters of attributes were less strongly related to comprehension and include fewer items. The following items are intercorrelated at the .45 level or more: surprise, unusual structure, and level of excitement. In general, this combination of attributes is found in breaking news stories about accidents or disasters. For such events, facts about causes or principal actors are unknown or highly speculative. Mysteries raised by the events cannot be resolved. Unusual facts may be presented even though explanations cannot be offered. Conventional story formulas simply may not permit adequate organization of facts. Visual information may be lacking, so that dramatic eyewitness descriptions may be substituted. In our study, examples of such stories included news about the impending fall of Skylab, a subway accident

TABLE 8.4 Intercorrelations Between Story Attributes: 12 Selected Attributes—U.S. Data

Attributes	1	2	3	4	5	6	7	8	9	10	11	12
(1) Surprise	1.0											
(2) Structure	.59	1.0										
(3) Conflict	.25	.37	1.0									
(4) Criminality	.25	.22	.72	1.0								
(5) Personalization	.18	.43	−.03	.09	1.0							
(6) Human interest	.19	.41	.01	.15	.91	1.0						
(7) Excitement	.46	.54	.12	.08	.69	.75	1.0					
(8) Amount of visuals	.14	.53	−.14	−.24	.64	.63	.61	1.0				
(9) Vividness of visuals	.11	.49	−.12	−.19	.68	.72	.71	.92	1.0			
(10) Strength of emotional content	.34	.62	.08	.08	.72	.73	.77	.74	.81	1.0		
(11) Direction of emotional content	−.30	−.18	−.54	−.46	.27	.27	.08	.36	.32	.16	1.0	
(12) Uniqueness of visuals	.17	.49	−.12	−.22	.61	.66	.66	.90	.96	.76	.29	1.0

NOTE: The direction of attributes is given in Table 8.3. Correlations are Pearson Correlation Coefficients.

in which a young girl was pushed under a subway train, the FAA grounding of all DC-10s after an unexpected flaw was found in wing pylons, and the Pope's visit to concentration camps.

Another cluster of attributes combined conflict, criminality, and negative emotional content. Such stories are common. News frequently reports major crimes, especially if conflict of some kind is involved. But none of these attributes was significantly linked to comprehension. This contradicts the commonsense notion of many journalists that audiences are fascinated by crime and are avid consumers of "blood and guts." Crime reports have become commonplace. They are not likely to attract much interest if they have no pictures, originate from remote places, or involve routine mayhem. In our study, such coverage included news about the murder of a witness in a Ku Klux Klan trial and the subsequent arrest of a suspect. This coverage spanned two broadcasts and each time was among the least well-comprehended of news items.

Multiple Classification Analysis

In Chapters 3 through 5, multiple classification analysis (MCA) has been introduced and used to assess a series of multivariate relationships. MCA permits variables measured on nominal or ordinal scales to be used as independent variables or covariates. Only the dependent variables are assumed to be measured on an interval scale. MCA provides the nonlinear equivalent of regression or path analysis. We applied this same technique to the analysis of our story attribute data, using our measure of comprehension as the dependent variable for both the British and U.S. data.

Our selection of predictor variables was based upon the results of our bivariate analyses. We selected those variables that had been most strongly linked to comprehension and then used MCA to investigate the relative strength of each in relation to the others. Thus, MCA allows us to address questions such as whether length of story time makes much of a difference once other factors such as personalization, human interest, or excitement have been taken into account. Although such statistical control is not a perfect substitute for experimental manipulation, it does attempt to apply this same logic to the data and it does permit an exploratory assessment of predictive power across story characteristics.

Once predictor variables were selected, they were trichotomized to facilitate the MCA analysis. The cutting points were selected to create three groups that were nearly equal in size for each variable: a high group, a medium group, and a low group. Occasionally, the frequency distributions of the predictor variables were such that it was not possible to create groups exactly equal in size. Although we have only reported MCA analyses below, we did conduct comparable analyses using regression techniques and path analysis. The results of these analyses were quite consistent with the MCA results.

Table 8.5 reports the results of the MCA for the British data. Column one of this table shows the average comprehension scores for each of the trichotomized independent variables. These scores imply that there is a rather linear and monotonic relationship between these variables and comprehension. In general, the differences between the low and medium groups is smaller than that between the medium and high groups. There is sufficient nonlinearity to warrant the use of MCA.

Column two shows the comprehension scores after they have been corrected by MCA to take into account the influence of the other independent variables. Beside this column we have calculated the difference between the low and high groups. By looking down this list of differences it is possible to ascertain quickly which variables are most strongly linked to increased comprehension. Two of the variables are revealed to be quite weak in relation to the others: percentage of camera time on the newsreader and degree of personalization in the story. In both cases, the high group minus low group figure is negative. Both of these variables were highly correlated with story length and human interest, respectively. Apparently, they explain little additional variation in comprehension, but they do explain the inverse of their bivariate relationship. Both factors may actually reduce comprehension in stories that are brief or that lack human interest.

Degree of human interest emerges as the major MCA predictor of comprehension. A difference of 2.2 points separates the 14 stories scored low in human interest from the 10 that were scored high. Even though human interest and excitement were intercorrelated, excitement does independently explain considerable variance. The 14 stories scored low in excitement averaged 2.0 points, but those scored high in excitement averaged 3.5 points. Finally, story length is important, but it ranks third after human interest and excitement. A difference of 1.1 points separates the low and high groups on this variable. Thus, the British data support the view that human interest is the strongest factor affecting comprehension of news, followed closely by excitement and story length.

TABLE 8.5   Differences in Story Comprehension as a Function of
Ten Story Attributes—British Data
Average Comprehension for All Stories = 2.9

Attribute/Level	Number of Stories	Unadjusted Average Comprehension	Adjusted for Independents
Length of story			
low	16	2.4	2.4
medium	15	2.8	2.9
high	9	3.8	3.5
Low-high difference =		+1.4	+1.1
Percentage of newsreader on camera			
low	13	2.1	3.0
medium	11	3.7	3.6
high	16	3.5	2.3
Low-high difference =		+1.1	−.7
Human interest			
low	13	1.9	2.4
medium	10	2.7	2.6
high	17	3.8	4.6
Low-high difference =		+1.9	+2.2
Excitement			
low	14	1.7	2.0
medium	16	3.4	3.3
high	10	3.6	3.5
Low-high difference =		+1.9	+1.5
Personalization			
low	15	2.3	3.3
medium	13	2.5	2.0
high	12	4.1	3.2
Low-high difference =		+1.8	−.1

NOTE: The table reports a multiple classification analysis in which column one shows the average comprehension for each level of each attribute considered independently. The final column shows the average comprehension for each level of each attribute when MCA is used to statistically control for the other four independent variables.

A somewhat more complicated analysis of the American data was conducted. A large set of predictor variables was chosen based upon the bivariate analysis and our review of information-processing research. We wanted to see whether some theoretically interesting variables that were not good bivariate predictors might emerge as stronger predictors in the MCA. Tables 8.6 and 8.7 report the results of two separate but complementary analyses. In the analysis shown in

Table 8.6, one cluster of variables was entered as the main independent variables and a second cluster was entered as covariates. In Table 8.7, the same two clusters are shown, but they have been entered in reverse order so that the independent variables are now the covariates and the covariates in the first analysis are treated as the main independent variables. Table 8.6 reports the results found when the five strongest predictor variables were used as the dependent variables and five theoretically interesting variables were added as covariates.

Human Interest and Comprehension

These results complement and extend the British analysis. As was noted in our discussion of the bivariate results, visual factors were found to rival human interest variables in predicting comprehension. MCA permitted us to assess the relative power of these factors. The human interest related variables "excitement" and "personalization," which were found to be important in the British analysis, proved to be so weak that they were discarded from the final set of strong predictors. Their place was taken by three visual factors and an index of the strength of emotional content. The analysis reported in Table 8.6 can be interpreted as implying that these visual and emotional story attributes constitute more direct measures of the attributes of human interest content that link such content so strongly with comprehension. Thus, it is not surprising to find that the predictive power of "human interest" disappears when the other indices are controlled. All are highly correlated with human interest (see Table 8.4), and when they are controlled, there is little additional variance for human interest to explain.

These results suggest that the use of attractive pictures and the presence of cues that arouse emotions contribute greatly to the success of human interest stories. When MCA statistically controls for these variables, the relationship between human interest and comprehension disappears. It should be noted that the initial relationship between human interest and comprehension was considerably weaker than that found in the British data; still, additional research would be necessary to determine if control of visual and emotional story attributes serves to attenuate this relationship in Britain.

Visuals and Comprehension

An intriguing finding reported in Table 8.6 is that when the other story attributes are controlled, the relationship between "vividness of visual content" and comprehension is negative. This implies that

TABLE 8.6   Differences in Story Comprehension as a Function of
Ten Story Attributes — U.S. Data
Average Comprehension for All Stories = 2.7

Attribute/Level	Number of Stories	Unadjusted Average Comprehension	Adjusted for Independents	Adjusted for Independents and Covariates
Human interest				
low	13	2.4	2.8	2.8
medium	18	2.3	2.5	2.7
high	18	3.3	2.8	2.7
Low to high difference =		+.9	0	−.1
Amount of visual content				
low	17	2.2	2.0	2.1
medium	15	2.6	2.8	2.9
high	17	3.3	3.3	3.2
Low to high difference =		+1.1	+1.3	+1.1
Vividness of visual content				
low	17	2.3	3.7	3.6
medium	15	2.6	2.7	2.8
high	17	3.2	1.7	1.7
Low to high difference =		+.9	−2.0	−1.9
Strength of emotional content				
low	16	2.1	2.1	2.2
medium	15	2.5	2.4	2.4
high	18	3.3	3.4	3.4
Low to high difference =		+1.2	+1.3	+1.2
Uniqueness of visual content				
low	16	2.2	2.4	2.3
medium	16	2.6	2.6	2.5
high	17	3.3	3.0	3.3
Low to high difference =		+1.1	+.6	+1.0

NOTE: The table reports a multiple classification analysis in which column one shows the average comprehension for each level of each attribute considered independently. Column three shows the average comprehension for each level of each attribute when MCA is used to control statistically for the other four independent variables. Column four shows the average comprehension for each level of each independent variable when all of the other independent variables and a set of five covariates (story relevance, surprise, amount of interpretation, direction of emotional content, and congruency of visual and verbal content) are controlled.

when other visual factors are controlled, highly vivid visuals may reduce comprehension. This relationship is the strongest one reported in the table—a difference of almost two points between the high and low groups—and the relationship is monotonic and linear. This finding confirms a hypothesis that can be derived from dual coding theory. This theory argues that visual content must be coded separately from verbal content using a quite different coding scheme. When pictures are congruent and not visually compelling, they will be routinely coded and can actually facilitate recall of verbal content coded simultaneously. But when visuals are incongruent and vivid, an extraordinary effort must be made to code them. Because this effort must be made at the same time that verbal content is being coded, it may reduce the efficiency of the verbal coding and result in failure to code important verbal information properly. Although our results appear to support this theory, they must be considered quite tentative and in need of replication.

The two visual factors linked to increased comprehension are the amount of visual content and the uniqueness of visual content. Stories that contain either large amounts of visual content or highly unusual visual content appear to be better comprehended. When discussing these factors above, we noted that it is common for human interest stories to be chosen for broadcast precisely because these factors are present.[1] There is the possibility that the powerful pictures in human interest content divert viewer attention away from the effective processing of more important "hard news" stories; however, this deserves further research.

Emotional Content and Comprehension

The findings in Table 8.6 also indicate that news content that arouses strong emotions may increase comprehension. This effect appears to operate independently of the amount and type of visual content. The difficulty of interpreting this finding is increased by its strong association with vividness of visual content. As we have already noted, vividness of visual content appears to reduce comprehension when factors such as strength of emotional content are controlled. The two variables, though highly correlated, appear to have opposite effects upon comprehension.

We are also concerned about the interpretation of this finding due to the nature of the specific stories that we studied. At least one story each day dealt with the Pope's trip to Poland, and these were consistently rated by our judges as arousing high levels of emotion as well as including vivid visuals. At the same time, the main point of each of these stories was often quite simple and shown visually: The Pope went to the death camps, or was tired today, or spoke out against the Communist regime.

If our finding about the linkage between strength of emotional content and comprehension is accurate, it may lend support to another proposition from information-processing theory. One concern of information-processing theorists is to understand which attributes of content lead to deeper processing of new information (see Chapter 6 for an extended discussion). It is possible that content cues that arouse emotion will trigger deeper processing. Perhaps this process works best in the absence of vivid visual content. If vivid visuals are present, necessary verbal information will not be stored in short-term memory. If emotional arousal later leads to deeper processing, there will not be adequate information stored in short-term memory.

Table 8.7 reports an MCA analysis in which the choice of the five independent variables was motivated by information-processing theory. As column one indicates, none of these variables was an especially powerful bivariate predictor of comprehension. Two of these variables were considered in the British analysis: surprise and amount of interpretation. Surprise is an index of the degree to which an event is unexpected or nonroutine. It was found to be a respectable bivariate predictor in both the British and U.S. analyses. The MCA results suggest that it has some independent predictive power, but this power is rather weak when human interest-related and/or visual attributes are controlled.

In the bivariate analysis of the U.S. data reported above, amount of interpretation in the news story was linked to decreased comprehension. This finding contradicted information-processing experiments by Findahl and Höijer (1976) as well as the modest zero-order correlation found in the British data. It is clear from the MCA analysis that amount of interpretation as we measured it has little independent predictive power. It is possible that stories that include interpretations are, on the whole, more complex than those that do not. Stories that do not include interpretations may tend to be simple, concrete presentations of factual information or they may be touching human interest stories. The points of such stories may be easier to grasp than the points of more complex, abstract stories in which alternative viewpoints of events are presented.

TABLE 8.7   Differences in Story Comprehension as a Function of
Ten Story Attributes – U.S. Data
Averge Comprehension for All Stories = 2.7

Attribute/Level	Number of Stories	Unadjusted Average Comprehension	Adjusted for Independents	Adjusted for Independents and Covariates
Story relevance				
low	14	2.8	2.6	2.8
medium	17	2.4	2.4	2.4
high	18	2.8	3.0	2.8
Low to high difference =		0	+.4	0
Surprise				
low	20	2.3	2.2	2.4
medium	14	2.7	2.7	2.6
high	15	3.1	3.3	2.9
Low to high difference =		+1.1	+1.1	+.5
Amount of interpretation				
low	18	2.9	2.9	2.9
medium	17	2.5	2.3	2.5
high	14	2.7	2.6	2.7
Low to high difference =		−.2	−.3	−.2
Direction of emotional content				
negative	16	2.6	2.3	2.4
neutral	16	2.7	2.7	2.6
positive	17	2.7	3.1	2.9
Low to high difference =		+.1	+.8	+.5
Congruency of visual and verbal				
low	13	2.5	2.7	2.6
medium	20	2.7	2.5	2.4
high	16	2.7	2.9	3.2
Low to high difference =		+.2	+.6	+.6

NOTE: The table reports a multiple classification analysis in which column one shows the average comprehension for each level of each attribute considered independently. Column three shows the average comprehension for each level of each attribute when MCA is used to control statistically for the other four independent variables. Column four shows the average comprehension for each level of each independent variable when all of the other independent variables and a set of five covariates (human interest, amount of visual content, vividness of visual content, strength of emotional content, and uniqueness of visual content) are controlled.

The ability of interpretive content to enhance information processing clearly deserves further study. Much may depend upon the context in which interpretations are routinely offered. In our study, one poorly comprehended story dealt with competing interpretations of the progress being made to reduce air pollution. The story was long and made extensive use of visual content but still was not understood. The inclusion of competing explanations may have confused rather than assisted viewers. Although the direction of emotional content had a very small bivariate relationship with comprehension, this relationship was increased when other variables were controlled. This finding tends to confirm the view that audiences respond better to good news than to bad news. Perhaps the arousal of positive emotions is more likely to trigger deep processing of information than is the arousal of negative emotions.

Story Relevance and Comprehension

The measure of story relevance was found to be a poor predictor of comprehension, even when other variables were controlled. It is important to remember that this is not an index of the relevance assigned by viewers. Thus, this finding does nothing to contradict experimental research that has found strong links between story relevance and learning. The finding does suggest that stories that academic researchers consider to be important to society are not being communicated any more effectively than are routine human interest stories.

Congruency and Comprehension

We were encouraged that our index of "congruency between visual and verbal content" improved as a predictor when other variables were controlled. A small but linear relationship can be noted in column three. This is sufficient to make it the best predictor among our second set. This association was predicted by information-processing theory, and several experimental studies have found evidence to support it. Nevertheless, more survey research will be necessary to determine if this association can be found in field settings.

THE CHALLENGE TO JOURNALISTS
AND RESEARCHERS

Our findings confirm some long-held notions of journalists but disconfirm others. Television emerges as a powerful visual medium that can use pictures effectively to induce learning of information. Attractive, unique pictures that arouse positive emotions and are congruent with verbal content may add considerably to the power of a story to induce learning. On the other hand, routine pictures that arouse negative emotions *and* that are incongruent with verbal content may impede learning.

Pictures may be more likely to enhance human interest stories regularly given that such stories will be produced and broadcast largely because "good" pictures are available. A great deal of luck and/or journalistic skill may be necessary to put such pictures into a breaking, "hard news" story. Nevertheless, our findings imply that such an effort may have considerable audience payoff. There may be a very real danger that "good" pictures will drive out or overwhelm good verbal information in the competition for viewer attention and information processing.

Our preliminary results illustrate the difficulties of the task that journalists face each day as they strive to serve audience needs and interests. It may be relatively easy for them to create the ideal human interest story, which in turn is very well received and appreciated by average viewers (Turow, 1983). But it is not easy to develop and present complex and relatively abstract hard news stories about breaking events. It is all too easy simply to string together a jumble of quickly assembled pictures and words and use the excuse that time does not permit an effective story to be constructed. It can also be easy to take a complex set of facts and simplify them so greatly that average viewers gain misimpressions concerning events. Pictures and words taken out of context can easily mislead rather than inform.

Our findings suggest that it is worthwhile to seek to develop journalistic strategies that improve the quality of hard news coverge. Each day news viewers face a deluge of pictures and words from which they must sort out the useful elements. Our findings and those of other researchers suggest that average viewers are not coping as well with this flood as they might if program producers were more sympathetic to their plight.

The results reported are exploratory in nature. Research will be necessary that expands upon this beginning and seeks to provide definitive results that can be trusted to guide news production. Development of information-processing theory and of both experimental and survey methods will be necessary. We are only beginning to understand why television has proved to be a relatively ineffective medium for transmitting news or public information. Television no doubt possesses a largely untapped ability to communicate significant amounts of useful information systematically and effectively even to apathetic or poorly informed viewers. Television may already be reaching such viewers, but the quality and substance of the learning that it induces is likely to be inadequate and superficial. The information now routinely learned from TV news may be doomed to rapid decay in short-term memory.

NOTES

1. Typically, a large pool of human interest stories is available. This pool is growing as affiliated stations compete to supply their networks with stories. Although affiliates may have little control over the quality of the hard news that they generate because this is so dependent upon the events involved, they can strive to produce attractive human interest content. Turow (1983) provides an excellent discussion of the "soft news" production process by local affiliates.

Chapter 9

NEWS COMPREHENSION
AND THE WORKING JOURNALIST

MARK R. LEVY
JOHN P. ROBINSON
DENNIS K. DAVIS

Like workers in other industries, we communication researchers often view the world from the vantage point of our professional and disciplinary fortress. We would like to believe that others share our intense interest in our research topics and discoveries. We would like to believe that our work is of some long-run practical importance to an improved society. In the case of television news, we would like to see news organizations take our results to heart and change their news policies accordingly.

To some extent, our hopes were partially realized during the research we conducted at the BBC in 1978. For a few weeks, we talked daily with journalists about their news stories and discussed the messages they wanted to convey to their audience. We then collected relevant audience data and provided fairly immediate feedback to the journalists (sometimes the next day) about how well these messages were received and understood. Most editors were intrigued, if somewhat depressed, by the results—because for the first time they had hard evidence about the real-world impact of their work. With the passage of time, however, their interest faded under the pressures of getting out the day's news.

Like members of cargo-cult tribes, we now look back at those "good old days at the Beeb" and wonder if they were not just an accident of history, something unique whose time is long past. We do not think so, because although we did not participate in the study, there is also an American precedent for our hoped-for journalist-researcher cooperation. The American experiment was called "Nightly-

Nightly," invoking both its periodicity and its focus. As an all-out collaboration between NBC's audience researchers and the journalists responsible for producing the network's *Nightly News with John Chancellor*, the Nightly-Nightly project was arguably the first attempt by an American broadcast organization to study viewer comprehension of the news. Each weekday night, Nightly-Nightly researchers conducted telephone interviews to find out, among other things, what viewers had learned from watching the news *that* night, which news stories they liked or disliked, and why. By early afternoon the next day, the previous night's survey findings had been presented to the news executives for use in planning their coverage. The Nightly-Nightly project required an enormous commitment of research dollars, staff time, and goodwill. At least according to the researchers, it was a "great success." But Nightly-Nightly "ran" for only one month in 1975. Since then, to the best of our knowledge, nothing like it has been tried at NBC—or any other U.S. network.

The point of these two anecdotes—the BBC interlude and the Nightly-Nightly experiment—is this: From time to time, the broadcast journalism community has taken *some* cognizance of the news comprehension issue. But for a host of reasons, including organizational inertia and the professional values of newsworkers, the public's understanding of the news has not received the extended attention it deserves.

We have studied the public's news awareness and comprehension for more than twenty years. Although most of that work has focused on the public-as-audience, we have always been aware that our research had important implications for the practices and policies of the news profession, particularly broadcast journalism. Indeed, we have conscientiously tried both to involve working journalists in our research and to make our findings available to the men and women who make the news. Our work is grounded in a belief that television news has the greatest responsibility to serve those persons who are not effectively reached through any other medium. Barber (1979: 16) has noted that "we need to look at television news as the educational medium most promising for reaching and teaching the less informed what they need to know to do democracy well."

To say that the conclusions from our past research have been greeted with less than total enthusiasm by even the most responsible and self-aware members of the journalistic community is to understate our frustration. Some journalists have shown a passing interest in what we and others have learned, but many have reacted with hostility or, worse yet, indifference.

It is not merely a case of hurt feelings or academic hubris that fuels our frustration. After all, the competitive and economic pressures that journalists face are severe. Entrenched newswork practices and long-held professional ideologies seem to get the job done. The time and rewards required for "philosophical" discussions about the role of the news in a democratic society are in very short supply in most newsrooms.

Still, we believe more firmly than ever that journalists *ought* to be aware of, understand, and apply the findings of the news comprehension research. We rest our case on the following arguments:

(1) Some commonly accepted normative theories that guide press behavior permit and possibly require journalists to take an active stance toward informing the public.

(2) These normative demands can be met without detrimental effects to professional autonomy.

(3) Newswork might be less alienating and professionally more satisfying if journalists were more self-conscious about audience comprehension—and could point to examples in their work where their self-awareness was put into practice and made a difference for the public.

(4) News that informed as it "told" might in the long run actually attract larger and more enthusiastic audiences.

(5) Finally, when all is said and done, only journalists can shoulder this obligation to make the news comprehensible. No one else is in a position to improve the understanding of news, except newsworkers themselves.

We are not especially optimistic that journalists will quickly "buy into" either our analysis or our prescriptions. In the pages that follow we will attempt to make as compelling a case as we can. The problems are multiple, but at their core they revolve around occupational ideologies and institutional imperatives.

NEWS VALUES AND AUDIENCE RESEARCH

There are long-standing and respectable philosophical traditions that say it is not the news media's obligation to be overtly concerned with the audience—neither monitoring audience reactions nor tailoring the news product to audience needs or capacities. But the news media do affect audience needs and perceptions, whether or not journalists attempt to affect them, and journalists need to be aware of the consequences of their work.

In fact, there is a clear and important division of opinion between those news professionals who see it as their responsibility to "inform the public" and those newsworkers who see their obligations as going no further than to "make information public." This latter view would restrict journalists to producing a record open to the public but not to catering to the public's needs or capacities. It is, to lean on a metaphor, a view that would lead the public to news but not force it to think.

Although there is some merit, and certainly less guilt, in such an "audience-free" philosophy, it is a point of view that we find basically narrow and unrealistic. All news is ultimately addressed to some audience, even if it is only the newsworker's own conscience or "image" of what the audience ought to be. What of value can be lost in finding out how these performance standards compare to what actually happens to news in the real audience? As Barber (1979: 16) puts it: "If . . . journalism has a responsibility for telling the truth, journalists also have a responsibility for telling it in a way that people can learn it."

Clearly, our sympathies lie with those editors who would undertake the broader "democratic" role of informing the public. However, as we have consistently documented, they face an extremely challenging task. Many of their readers and viewers lack the basic informational skills and background to appreciate or understand the news. Many others are distracted by their own personal problems, pressures, and concerns—even (as we showed in Chapter 5) while they are watching TV news programs.

Nonetheless, we see these obstacles as more formidable than insurmountable. The research in this book, as is true of parallel news research in other countries, suggests several ways in which the news media can better reach and inform the public. Many news editors to whom we have talked have themselves suggested other plausible methods for achieving this goal. The major problem is that there is currently so little, if any, professional incentive even for trying. How likely is it after all that news editors would have their salaries raised or receive a Pulitzer prize "just" for improving public knowledge by 50% or 100%? Which news organizations would risk ratings points or advertising sales by attempting to develop news content that could be more broadly understood? And finally, would a public soured on journalism suddenly heap praise on the bearers of (comprehensible) bad news or—in a larger sense—see any direct connection between being better informed and the quality of their lives?

PREVIOUS RESEARCH ON THE
AUDIENCE PERSPECTIVE OF JOURNALISTS

It could be argued that American television journalists must know their audiences quite well because they have easy access to data concerning the demographic properties of the potential and real audiences. Indeed, the ratings system guarantees that basic audience data will be widely available to most television journalists or at least to their bosses. Moreover, reports of findings of public opinion polls have become staple news items, occasionally raising the eyebrows of news reporters who find out that the opinions and values of the public do not necessarily conform to their own.

Yet, researchers report that network journalists hardly pay attention to such information (Gans, 1979). Earlier research also suggested that few journalists had sharply defined conceptions of their audiences (Pool and Shulman, 1959; Gieber, 1964). Some researchers have reacted with surprise at the extent of journalistic ignorance about public opinion in general and the nature of the audiences in particular (Bagdikian, 1971; Crouse, 1973; Gans, 1979).

Many journalists, on the other hand, have a fatalistic attitude toward developing any worthwhile insight into the audience. Gans (1979: 234) reports,

> Story selectors are actually cowed by the magnitude of their audience and by the responsibility of producing news for it. "If we had to think about how our readers feel, all twenty million of them," one top editor said, "we'd freeze."

Finally, journalists may be defensive about confronting findings that contradict their own impressionistically formed images of the audience. Journalists frequently assume that they can successfully use their *own* reactions to stories as the basis for predicting audience reactions. Although some journalists produce their stories for a select, generally up-scale audience, this view flatters newsworkers into omitting background information that may not be known even by that preferred audience. Journalists who do consult colleagues, friends, and family members often generalize from these unrepresentative reactions to their audience as a whole.

JOURNALISTIC "IDEOLOGIES"

Neither occupational ideologies nor their specific components, such as the journalists' perception of their audiences, can be studied in isolation from their societal and institutional contexts. The myths, ideas, and images that make up such ideology take shape over long periods of time. They reflect the historical experience of the society in which they are embedded. An understanding of American journalists' view of their audience, for instance, must take into account the conflicting ideologies of libertarian, popular, and participatory democracy discussed in Chapter 2.

It is also necessary to be aware of the apparent contradictions between commercial imperatives and professional values. The flood of data gathered by commercial research firms is tailored to the needs of what is termed the "demand model." This model dictates that ratings and circulation figures are indicators of audience demand, and the manufacture of content is by and large adjusted to market requirements. Of necessity, such an approach caters to short-term consumer wants rather than long-term public needs, and provides a purely economic rationale for news decisions. The demand model does ascribe great importance to "knowing" the audience—not as enlightened citizens, but solely as consumers of the news product. Thus, the audience need be known only as quantifiable commodity for sale to advertisers on a cost per thousand basis.

The traditional occupational ideology of American journalism rightly rejects the demand model as an appropriate determiner of news content. Television journalists insist upon drawing a clear distinction between themselves and the producers of entertainment material, in this respect. As William Leonard (1978: 53), executive vice-president of CBS News, put it: "We have an obligation to report what's out there and what's important by the standards of trained journalists, whether or not it is what people want."

Yet, especially at the local level, news creation is very much attuned to the requisites of the demand model (Powers, 1977a, 1977b; Broadcasting, 1979; Newsweek, 1980). In the age of "news doctors" and "happy talk" formats, and with national news organizations too often open to bottom-line thinking, the cherished professional norms of the newsroom seem to be in increasing jeopardy.

This threat to professional autonomy has made news professionals of the "old school" extremely suspicious of research. We know of a onetime president of a major network news division, for example, who consistently refused to be in the same room as his company's own news audience researchers, and the executive producer of that network's principal evening newscast had a similar "no contact" rule for his *entire* staff. These journalists and others see research as a handmaiden of commercial interests, an instrument of mercantile encroachment. When newsmen refer to the "risk of being corrupted by research" (Rubens, 1980), it is not their souls for which they fear—it is for their power to insulate their editorial judgments from external influences. Ironically, most sophisticated news researchers, particularly at the network level, share this concern, having little interest in and fewer journalistic skills that would allow them to poach on the broadcast journalists' turf.

What is more, there are some journalists who do recognize the difference between the manipulative "doctoring" of news programs and the research that seeks to increase audience understanding of the news. One former president of a U.S. network news operation wrote to his colleagues that our news comprehension project "so clearly draws the line between the totally unacceptable kinds of research which fiddles around with cosmetics and, worse yet, dictates content and assignment of news personnel, on one hand and [this] kind of research relating to comprehension, on the other hand" (Salant, 1980). This position was defended by referring to the social function of the news profession. "*Since we are in the business of informing viewers*," wrote Salant, "I think it is important that we not spin our wheels and do as well as possible" (emphasis added).

THE BRITISH EXPERIENCE

British broadcasting has a long tradition of public service. It emerged from the class structure and cultural traditions of England and results in a less demand-oriented, more paternalistic view of the audience (Burns, 1969; Smith, 1973). In this context, the broadcasters are often reminded of their "obligation" to inform and educate their audiences. As Katz (1977: 61) noted in his report to the BBC:

If the job of news and public affairs is to create an informed citizenry, the most elementary obligation of public service broadcasting is to determine whether and what the citizens understand. At one level that means they understand the words and concepts used. At another, it means whether their understanding of their society, and the problems confronting it, has been enhanced by the particular program or by the particular mix of programs to which they have been exposed.

Yet this emphasis on understanding the news has not created a hospitable milieu for feedback into the news process from systematic research: what Katz calls "a missing link between news producers and news consumers." Schlesinger (1978) has reported in his study of the BBC news that British broadcasting journalists, like their American counterparts, prefer to rely on peer opinion, professional norms, and standards of performance. They believe that audience research is not needed because they can anticipate audience comprehension as well as audience standards and tastes. One television editor told Schlesinger that "we take it that if we can understand it, so can the public."

But our research at the BBC and our experience in broadcast journalism more generally points to an extremely significant gap in knowledge levels between television editors and their audiences. When ten BBC news staff members were questioned about the same eight leading stories from the previous week as the public had been asked (see Chapter 4), nine out of the ten staffers got all eight items "correct." The one journalist who did not get a perfect score missed one item, but he had been out of the country on assignment. By contrast, not one respondent in the British national sample of 507 persons described in Chapter 4 scored that well on the same test items. In fact, only 2% scored 6 or 7 on the test. Thus, for the week studied, the average BBC news editor was more knowledgeable about the news than most of his or her entire audience—an audience that is at the receiving end of "the blizzard of information that hits us daily and leaves the public undernourished and unaware" (Barber, quoted in Modern Media Institute, 1983: 53).

REACTIONS OF JOURNALISTS
TO OUR RESEARCH

In the past, when we showed our research findings to journalists at the BBC and at the American television networks, the journalists often reacted with disappointment that so few of their stories were "getting through." Some seemed threatened by this evidence of their "failure to communicate." Questioned about the usefulness of this type of research, their reactions also varied considerably. Although many journalists saw this research as a valuable professional learning experience, others simply dismissed the results out-of-hand. One common reason was the journalists' essentially negative conception of the audience. Some news reporters openly admitted that the audience was of no interest or consequence to them. Some took the position that their job was to report the news as best they could and that the audience was on its own to cope as best it could. Other news personnel blamed the "victims" by saying it was not the broadcasters' fault that the audience was so ignorant or uncomprehending. Most journalists despaired of finding any remedy short of massive citizen reeducation.

But this despair also has an up-side, for it represents one possible avenue for change—not by remaking the audience (that is far beyond what journalism is all about), but by giving a greater sense of purpose to newswork itself. The craft of journalism, particularly as practiced in large, elite organizations, is filled with many frustrations, both personal and professional. Many of our "successful" journalist colleagues see their work as kind of splendid agony: well paid and sometimes exciting, but too often alienating and devoid of larger purpose. In part, it seems the hostility of newsworkers to comprehension research may reflect that malaise. It is as if journalists are saying, "Things are already bad enough and now you are telling us we've failed as communicators."

SOME GENERAL ACTION STEPS

Reviving journalistic esprit will not be easy, but putting comprehension high on the reward structure may help. As the old adage goes, "Scratch a journalist and find a reformer." What better way to deal with that "itch" than to take seriously the duty of the profession to truly inform the public. Although there are necessarily limits to what journalists can or should be expected to do to help information-poor audience members remedy their deficiencies, it is certainly possible for the press to do more than it does now.

Here are a few *general* steps that could be taken. It would be relatively easy, for example, for journalists to attempt to anticipate some future events to prepare themselves better to communicate effectively about them. The Associated Press now routinely looks ahead to the most important "futures" that are likely to occur each month as well as to the issues that are likely to be featured in the news. National surveys could be conducted to assess how much information news audiences have about these events and issues, and news content could be created to seek to increase people's stock of relevant information systematically.

Of course, many journalists treat such background information as boring, not newsworthy—not something that gives "added value" to news accounts. From their point of view, these "facts" are simply history or civics lessons, better learned in high school. Moreover, most incorrectly assume that the public has been consistently exposed to as much current events coverage as journalists have. Journalists, of course, have a professional need to keep up with the news; the public does not. But as our research makes clear, it is this double whammy of failing to provide adequate background information and erroneously assuming that the audience knows the whole story that makes it so difficult for the public to comprehend the news.

Another somewhat more innovative idea would be to develop a special kind of ombudsman, who might be called the "comprehension editor." Assigned to monitor newsroom output, the comprehension editor would be a surrogate for the audience. All major news stories could be vetted for comprehensibility by such an editor. Armed with surveys like those we have reported in preceding chapters and acting with the clear blessings of news management, the comprehension editor would serve as a "reality checker" judging and correcting the performance of peers *as an insider*.

History, of course, suggests that the introduction of a comprehension editor will not be greeted with journalistic huzzahs. Journalists were quick to invoke "professional autonomy" and even quicker to ignore the research when attempts were made, starting in the 1940s, to apply "readability" studies to story creation. Similarly, the much-heralded ombudsman movement that got under way two decades later has been severely undermined by professional carping. Indeed, in those three dozen or so U.S. newsrooms that have ombudsmen today, most of these "people's advocates" are seen less as a mechanism for press responsibility and more as a means for keeping the public at bay (Mogavero, 1982). Still, a somewhat more optimistic reading of this history also suggests that there is some room for innovation, some limited openness to change.

If getting working journalists to accept a comprehension editor will be difficult, monumental difficulties will arise in winning the support of management. But here too, there is some leverage for change. First of all, the goals of news management are rarely monolithic (Tunstall, 1971). Prestige and public service count for something. As the current president of NBC News, Lawrence Grossman, recently told his network's affiliates:

> If we have any single priority for every one of our news shows in the months ahead, it will be to clarify, to explain, to write our scripts and file our reports in a style that makes what is happening as fully understandable as we can possibly make it to every one of our viewers [Broadcasting, 1985: 89].

More noble motives aside, we think there is at least one line of argument that might appeal to even those news executives whose eyes are more firmly fixed on the profit margin.

Although the conceptual details need to be worked out and the empirical support developed, it is certainly plausible to speculate that news—especially TV news—that successfully informs the public might also be a commercial success. Many of the recent successful commercial enterprises that have made "megabucks" have done so by packaging technical information in a way that "keeps it simple." Newscasts too would have much to gain by deliberately and conscientiously offering the public news that is comprehensible and useful. Viewers should find it both "easier" and more rewarding to watch. It should take less "effort" and give more rewards for them to tune in, to pay attention to what was broadcast, to stay tuned, and to watch on a regular basis. After all, how many programs that are neither memorable nor useful, that make little or no sense when viewed, would otherwise stay on the air? Only a glutton for video punishment would seek out that kind of program, and, to paraphrase the behavioral law of effect, people are not that stupid.

Without giving in to the vulgarities of "eyewitless" news, and without compromising legitimate professional values, it would still be possible even with limited funds to experiment with different forms and styles of news presentation. Despite the well-publicized success of public television's *Sesame Street,* and despite the commercial networks' long-standing use of formative research for entertainment programming, there are precious few instances in which this proven model for effective communication has been applied in a news context.

Indeed, the only American example of which we are aware took place at NBC News in the late winter and spring of 1985. In what was regarded by all concerned as a rare case of researcher-journalist interaction, the network's audience researchers were called in by the news division to help evaluate and resuscitate a deeply flawed news magazine for children. Among the network's concerns was whether children would understand the program's contents. Based on focus-group discussions and over-the-cable household tests of pilot episodes, substantial changes were made—not always willingly by the newsmen. At this writing, it remains to be seen whether "W5," as the show was known during its developmental stages, will be a ratings success or merely a *succès d'estime*. Still, we mention it to reiterate our fundamental point: A commitment to formative news research can go hand in hand with both the desire of journalists to inform the public and the need of all news organizations to attract large audiences. All it takes is a willingness to experiment and a conviction that the risks of innovation may yield substantial rewards—both on the ledger of public goodwill and on the profit-and-loss statement.

SPECIFIC IMPLICATIONS OF OUR
RESEARCH FOR JOURNALISTS

For journalists, the findings discussed in previous chapters contain good news as well as bad. The good news is that there is a news audience out there that is being informed—at least to a degree. Results from our present studies confirm our suspicion that unaided recall techniques have seriously underestimated what audiences comprehend from the news. We have found examples of news stories that achieved nearly universal recognition and comprehension, whereas we found no stories that were completely "missed" by the audience.

However, most news stories fail to reach a majority of the audience. Only about a third of news information seems to "sink in," and that should present a major challenge to the journalistic profession. It is not only our impression but that of most of the professional journalists with whom we have worked over the years of our research that more comprehensible news products can be developed—and with minimal commitment of time and resources from news organizations.

As we noted in the first chapter, much lack of comprehension results from factors outside the journalists' control. Some news stories have wide public appeal, some do not. Certainly it is easier to make exciting copy from exciting events and damnably difficult to create dramatic stories from statistical data, business deals, or routine diplomatic visits. But it is possible to improve the translation of the "objective" news that journalists see into the subjective interest of the news audience. We have encountered very few stories that with some simple reorganization of elements or changes in emphasis could not be improved in terms of audience comprehension.

Our findings suggest certain common problem areas and certain specific ways to deal with them.

(1) The need for more repetition or redundancy. It is clear from both our research and earlier work elsewhere that the news goes by too quickly for most people. Thus, the news needs to be slowed down. This is particularly true for television newscasts and it points up the importance of the verbal (audio) portion of the newscast. Recall the study (Katz et al., 1977) in which people who listened to the newscast with their backs to the set learned little less from the newscast than those who watched from the normal position. In our own TV news studies, what the news editors wanted to get across as the central point was almost always information conveyed by the script and not the pictures.

That means that journalists need to pay very close attention to how the news story is written if they want their audiences to grasp the significance of what they report. We think it would help audience comprehension to have news writers (the best of whom probably do it instinctively anyway) keep a central point at the forefront of each story and weave and relate the other elements of the story around that central theme. The question should be, "how pertinent is each story element for the comprehension of the central point?" We have found dramatic examples of stories in which comprehension apparently suffered as a result of discordant elements in a story—for example, a story on terrorist *deaths* in Ireland, which included a lengthy interview with a *survivor* of the incident. Redundancy is important to television news viewers simply because most viewers tune in to and out of the newscast.

Given the nature of television viewing, it may not be possible to write compelling stories that will overcome audience inattention. Quite possibly, although perhaps of little comfort, we should note that the audience pays even less attention to the entertainment programs it views. As Jacoby and Hoyer (1982) found, entertainment shows are often more poorly comprehended than news or commercial programs. However, the notion of TV news having a "captive audience" is unrealistic and self-defeating. Televised messages, perhaps more than other forms of communication, are at the mercy of the environment in which they are received.

By redundancy we do not mean simply repeating the same phrase or thought, or recapping the main points of a news story at the end. We mean building up to the main point with the copy preceding it, or explicitly stating the various implications of the story's main point.

The news package should be constructed as a cohesive whole, with all elements contributing to the central point rather than ambitiously and ambiguously moving in many directions.

(2) The need to emphasize why the story is important enough to be on tonight's news. Audience members need to understand why the journalist considers the story important. The more the news editor builds on that feature—why the story is newsworthy—the easier it will be for the audience member to grasp the story's significance. The more audience members know about the criteria by which a story has been deemed important, the better able they will be to understand news stories and to put them in clearer perspective. The same is true for highlighting the historical context in which stories are embedded. Perhaps the clearest difference of opinion we had with working journalists was with what we considered newspeople's myopic concern with today's news. There is very little "organized memory" or concern with the future that is built into the newscast. Barber (1979: 16) has called TV news "blanked-out history," noting how "clarifying information on analogous events in the past and on developments leading up to the reported event tend to be sacrificed."

(3) "Slowing down" the news. The need for such repetition and contextualization was further highlighted in the very high scores of the BBC newsmen on our weekly news quiz. Very few journalists, we suspect, appreciate how much more familiar with events in the news they are than the average audience member or than the most sophisticated portion of the news audience or even than other information elites (e.g., government officials, business leaders). Working over a news story for the third or tenth time may make journalists apprehensive about boring their audience or appearing to report "stale" news. This anxiety is probably unfounded. What most audience members really want, or can really use, is some explanation of why the story is important and not necessarily the "5th-Add." update. The competitive environment of news reporting may reward up-to-the-minute news, but long-term audience interests are better served by a more patient approach to news reporting.

Journalists are also afraid that if they slow down the pace they may lose the audience. However, this may be a misperception, as was clearly demonstrated when so many of the British viewers we interviewed mentioned the weekly summary that the BBC news prepared each Sunday for the hard-of-hearing. Many nonimpaired viewers of that program were reluctant to admit they watched, but the slower pace of its news presentations was appreciated because it gave them (and we presume the journalists who prepared it) more time and opportunity to reflect on the significance of the previous week's news.

Repetition does not mean that journalists have to lower their standards or to treat their audience in a condescending, patronizing manner. It means tighter, better-structured reporting and more demanding and reflective writing. It also means slowing down the rush to publish; stories that do not make *complete* sense to the journalist are unlikely to make much sense to the audience.

(4) The need for organizational rewards and incentives for increasing comprehension. Throughout this project, and in our interaction with British and American newsmen, it was clear that however much news personnel might care to increase audience comprehension, they were not likely to be rewarded for doing so. There were in fact several excellent and insightful suggestions made about that goal by the news personnel to whom we talked. Obviously, these ideas had not filtered very far up the organizational hierarchy.

Reporting news is a complicated process, and many basic criteria for sound journalism do take precedence. Making sure that a story is told in an accurate and unbiased fashion obviously must take top priority in putting together the news. So who will care, or who will know, if audience information needs are not being met? After all, the audience is unlikely to know or to complain if it is ill informed.

There are clear risks in this type of audience-centered news. No one has devised a news format with audience comprehension as its main goal. It is potentially in conflict with traditional journalistic priorities and is likely to encounter considerable resistance on these grounds alone. Additionally, there is no guarantee that such a format will necessarily sit well with the audience. Audiences do not like to be surprised or to see changes solely for the sake of change. More articulate audience members possibly may see more repetitive news products as boring or condescending.

Yet, there is a tacit agreement among most of the journalists we talked to that more comprehensible news products can be produced. The question, again, is whether it is worth the organizational effort in view of all the other day-to-day demands involved in producing the news. That is a question that only news management can answer.

Some TV-Specific Solutions

We make these recommendations with some reluctance because they may seem either vague or obvious, and because recommendations are often taken too literally and not in the sense of "other things being equal, try this.'' Our view is that research ought to free journalists from rules or guidelines that are outmoded or counterproductive and not institute new sets of rules that may impose new sources of ineffectiveness.

Nonetheless, we see potential benefits at low organizational cost from the following:

(1) Making news information as explicit as possible. In contrast to most media research findings, the evidence on whether implicit or explicit messages are more effective is quite unambiguous and straightforward (Weiss, 1969). Explicit messages are usually far more effective. Stories written "between the lines" stay "between the lines," because implicit messages require extra mental work on the part of the audience. For an implicit message to be comprehended, audience members must be thinking along with, if not anticipating, the direction the story is heading. Audience members must then relate that story to the same frame of reference as the reporter. In view of the many frames of reference that may apply to any given story, it is not difficult to see why implicit messages demand so much from their audience and are harder to understand.

(2) Separating similar stories from one another. The current practice, a deeply ingrained principle from print journalism, is to put similar stories together. The separation of similar stories can be accommodated easily on the printed page through formatting, lines, and boxes. The audience for TV news has no such "linear" aids, so that the newscast needs to provide these separations and distinctions verbally as well as visually. Otherwise, TV news runs the risk of story "meltdown," in which one item blurs into and is confused with a separate but closely following second story.

(3) Using graphics, especially for statistical or quantitative information. We have found considerable audience resistance to statistical data in the news. This aversion to "statistics" may be detrimental to citizen interests if they do not understand the factors upon which decision makers make or justify their public policies. Graphs that actually show upward and downward movement and not static representations can help the audience appreciate the numbers and possibly the policies based on them. Visual presentations of the actual numbers involved in the story (e.g., the number of unemployed, the number injured, the number of dollars spent) can help increase comprehension only when put into the context of the important elements of the story. Even very

crude visual representations—as long as they are not too abstract—can provide the viewer with some insight into the circumstances or setting of a story. Visuals are important even if they only convey to audience members the sense that they *can* understand what is happening.

(4) Using "human interest" angles on stories wherever possible or appropriate. Again, we are by no means suggesting a tabloid approach to television journalism. However, in putting together the newscast, news editors often become so preoccupied with getting the story right that they forget to tell their story in human terms. Human interest may involve no more than communicating to the audience a sense of why the news editor felt that story was important enough to be featured in the news, particularly (to the extent possible) how the news story might personally affect audience members.

(5) Explaining technical or specialized terms. Terms such as "economic embargo," "bilateral agreements," "leading indicators," "COLAS," and even "inflation" are quite technical and unfamiliar to most members of the audience. Barber (1979) cites over 30 examples of such "foreign language" that appeared in the single evening's newscast that he examined. Follow-up statements reinforcing the implications of technical language, however, are easy to craft (e.g., "The fact that both sides must come together on this *bilateral* agreement poses difficult problems, etc ...") and could significantly reduce the language barrier to comprehension.

CONCLUSION

Television journalists' and other communicators' images and knowledge of their audiences need to be the subject of continuing social scientific scrutiny. Our work with television journalists suggests important ways in which they are unable to communicate adequately or come to grips with their vast and diverse audiences. Many work with hazy and rather naive notions about the "mass" audiences they profess to serve. Others refuse to acknowledge any responsibility to audiences and prefer to justify their performance entirely in terms of the norms of their craft.

In brief, they are reluctant to pay attention to the evaluations of their work done by "outsiders." They perceive such efforts as a threat to their editorial judgment and an infringement upon their journalistic integrity. On those rare occasions when they do cooperate with researchers, they are often disappointed with what they learn about the effectiveness of their work. They are inclined to believe that they are doing the best job they can do under difficult circumstances; we are sympathetic to that argument.

Nonetheless, journalists' reluctance to develop more highly defined conceptions of their audiences also serves certain self-protective needs. When the audience remains an ill-defined mass—a phantom public—it can be made to fit different organizational and professional exigencies. The insulation and isolation of bureaucrats from the people they are supposed to serve is a phenomenon widely reported by journalists about other bureaucracies. But that same phenomenon is likely to hold true for news bureaucracies as well. Altheide and Johnson (1980) have argued that news bureaucracies also create "bureaucratic propaganda" that serves to legitimize their work and shield it from criticism. Reporters rarely investigate their own bureaucracy with the enthusiasm they reserve for the White House or City Hall. It could be that such "investigations" will need to be undertaken by outsiders. As Hoggart put it in his foreword to *Bad News* (Glasgow University Media Group, 1977: x):

> The sooner the newsmen and their superiors accept this starting-point, the better for them, us and 'the news.' In this way they can after all learn something from outsiders, even if outsiders don't know all the jargon of their trade, even if the outsiders are those always suspect academics or, worse, social scientist academics.

IV *Conclusions*

Chapter 10

TELEVISION NEWS
Beyond Comprehension

JOHN P. ROBINSON
MARK R. LEVY

> I never got involved. I am an artist. I am less likely to be that way from
> now on. I know now that we're all operating from the same material. ...
> My opinions are just as valid [quoted in Elkin, 1985].

So said Patricia Roth, an apolitical grade school art teacher after
her months as juror in the libel trial of *Westmoreland* v. *CBS, Inc.*
She had a rare opportunity to watch history play (and replay) itself
out. For Mrs. Roth, the trial was a high-tension blend of courtroom
drama, often boring First Amendment intricacies, and troubled in-
trospection about the Vietnam war. It changed, she later confessed,
the way she looked at the world—and at the news media.

Before the trial, Mrs. Roth says, she had "taken it for granted"
that the nation's leaders "knew what they were doing." And if they
did not, she assumed, America's hard-charging journalists would have
told her about it. After 18 weeks of testimony, Roth now says: "I lost
my awe of the top decision makers in government *and* the news
media" [emphasis added].

Although it would be wrong, of course, to make too much of the
reactions of just one person, we think Mrs. Roth's experience may be
symptomatic of a larger concern. Not only did Mrs. Roth have the rare
privilege of learning firsthand how the Vietnam war was fought and
lost, but she was candid and insightful enough to put what she learned
into the context of her own previous ignorance and apathy.

We do not know much more about Mrs. Roth than what we have
just outlined, and we certainly have no information about her use of
the mass media for news. Still, we do not think it would be unfair to
her—or to the rest of us—to suggest that much of the time we all are as

ignorant of the world's affairs as we were of the "Vietnam deception." Indeed, if we were as reflexive as Mrs. Roth, we might conclude that most of what passes for "important news" is in fact so remote and mysterious that it is, in the vernacular sense of the phrase, beyond comprehension.

Throughout this book we have asked why the world—or at least news accounts of it—is so poorly comprehended. Our review of the research in the past nine chapters has addressed many questions and taken us in many directions. Although we mostly have examined evidence from large-scale national surveys, we have also reviewed more local surveys, as well as experimental research and content analyses. We have considered studies done in the United States and in other Western European countries, particularly Great Britain; we have pondered this research from the perspective of the audience and in terms of its implications for broadcast and print journalists.

Our major conclusions can be summarized in five points. The first is as follows:

(1) Television news should not be considered the public's main source of news. Of the many studies examined in Chapters 3 and 4, not one indicated superior news information gain by television news viewers when compared to the gain by users of other media. In some research, TV news viewers emerged as less well informed than nonviewers, and that seems particularly true among those who claim that TV is their main source of news.

In earlier chapters, we described the barriers television faces in effectively transmitting news stories: too little airtime to tell most stories in sufficient depth; an easily distracted, often inattentive audience; the lack of viewer control over the pace of story presentation; the absence of clear separation between stories or story elements; inadequate historical perspectives or causal explanations to make the story meaningful; frequent inconsistencies between words and pictures; and the lack of redundancy to give content more than one perspective. Put another way, one should not be surprised to find that much television news is beyond comprehension when so few of its features were specifically designed to meet ordinary viewers' cognitive abilities and needs.

That is not to say, however, that television is a completely ineffective source for certain information, that people learn nothing from the television newscasts they view, or that TV news cannot be made more understandable. People who watch TV news do generally have slightly

above-average news information levels (see Chapter 3 and 4). They do
know more about TV entertainment figures (Chapter 3) and about
principles of weather forecasting (Robinson, 1972b). There is also
evidence that exposure to TV newscasts is a more potent predictor
among less-educated than among better-educated people, and less-
educated people are more likely to watch TV news (in contrast to their
lower use of print news media). In terms of both exposure and effect,
then, television does act somewhat as an "information leveler" between the better and the less educated. Moreover, in Chapter 5, we
showed that the comprehension levels for "unused candidate" stories
(that is, stories initially scheduled for broadcast but ultimately cut
from the newscast) were far lower than for almost all items that were
broadcast. Although these stories were more likely to be of lesser importance, the virtual noncomprehension of such material convincingly
demonstrates that if a story does not make it onto the TV news, it
has little chance of becoming news for much of the public.

The more the exposure to TV news, then, clearly the greater the
comprehension. But our evidence consistently shows that TV news exposure, either by itself or after controls for other factors, is not as important a correlate or predictor of news comprehension as exposure to
other media. In particular,

> (2) Heavier exposure to print media is generally associated with higher
> levels of news comprehension. In both Chapters 3 and 4, newspaper
> readers, and to a lesser extent magazine readers, were consistently found
> to be more informed than nonreaders. Print media use is not merely a
> surrogate variable for education, given that these differences held up
> after control for education and other predictors.

This is not to say, however, that print media exposure is a primary
determinant of news comprehension. In fact, the correlations are
rather modest in strength. In some studies that we reviewed,
newspaper exposure tended to be a better predictor among better-
educated respondents than among less-educated respondents, and the
"effects" of newspaper reading were greatly reduced after controlling
for interest or prior information levels.

It is also important to note that although the results in Chapters 3
and 4 are extremely consistent and tend to hold up after control for
levels of education and levels of news interest, these analyses do not
directly address those possible, subtle factors of self-selection that
may predispose some people to use newspapers or television as information sources. In other words, people who are more information

oriented may also be more likely to choose print over television as an information source.

The relatively modest differences overall by newspaper exposure are consistent with another major conclusion from our analyses—namely, that

(3) Interpersonal discussion of news may be at least as powerful a predictor of comprehension as exposure to news media. That interpersonal channels are more effective than mass media channels is not a new finding for communication research. But it is one that has been neglected in all the discussion and excitement over new media technologies and high-tech formats for news. It may also have been neglected because so few respondents think to bring it up in their response to survey questions, such as: "Where do you get most of your news?"

Once again, we cannot be absolutely sure that there is not some self-selection mechanism operating here that inclines those who are more information oriented to have more friends who share this orientation. Nonetheless, the results are quite clear and are consistent with the classic findings in communication research about the ultimately greater power of interpersonal communication. Indeed, we would contend that to a large extent information does not sink in (or become "deep processed") until it has been tested and evaluated against the norms and attitudes of one's peers and colleagues. Although it may be the case that people have less time or fewer opportunities for such social interaction now than when the original two-step flow model was proposed, word of mouth remains the easiest and most powerful way for information to make its way into public consciousness. Indeed, one might even conclude that until news is put to such communicative use, it is of minimal societal consequence.

Further, there is an even larger and simpler principle linking each of the items above. We suggested at the outset of this book and wish to reiterate it here:

(4) No one news medium should be viewed as "most" predominant. The public employs a variety of information sources and search strategies to keep informed about what is happening. Looking for the "Number 1" medium is a pointless exercise, because people use so many media and combinations of media for different purposes (e.g., TV for awareness, newspapers for explanation, or vice versa depending on the story involved). The more relevant question, then, is how might all the news media—and especially TV—be improved to take advantage of these media interdependencies.

This leads to our final conclusion:

(5) The news media can do a more effective job of informing the public. The main obstacles lie not in the potential costs and risks of making news more comprehensible but in the absence of organizational commitments to audience comprehension as an attainable goal.

We have made several initial suggestions to that end in Chapter 9. Our experiences with working journalists suggest they would have many more suggestions that offer as much promise. The problem lies in getting news organizations to examine how well their stories are getting through to the audience. Present news research perhaps has oversensitized newsworkers to the way audiences can be "sold"—and we share the journalist's distaste for seeing the audience solely from this marketing perspective. But the same research techniques can be used to allow journalists to open up a more human dialogue with their audiences. It is hard not to believe that such a "conversation" will lead to more effective and rewarding journalism.

It must also be reemphasized that the surveys we conducted and reviewed dealt almost exclusively with generic news and its comprehension. These studies were not geared, for example, to detecting those larger and very subtle differences in the way the print and broadcast media cover the news.[1] Indeed, it would take extremely precise research designs and elaborate sampling plans to isolate such differential effects on audiences in a naturalistic field setting. Until research of such subtlety is conducted, therefore, our present findings may represent the closest approximation of what does get through to the news audience.

There are still broader implications of our research findings, implications that are suggested by the subtitle of this chapter ("beyond comprehension"). We must again stress that most of the research presented was predicated on an "efficiency of transmission" or "transportation" model of mass communication (Carey, 1976, 1977). In that sense, we have dealt with only one kind of comprehension—namely, whether the messages sent by communicators were received and "understood" by the audience.

There is, however, another kind of learning from the media, a kind of learning that goes *beyond* the *comprehension* implied in the "efficiency" model. Indeed, this more subtle form of understanding is the central issue in the discussion of "information" versus "meaning" in Chapter 7. Although that chapter amply illustrates the conceptual and empirical difficulties of addressing this problem, the questions it raises represent a frontier area for mass communication research; these frontiers must be explored if the continuing debate over the media's effects on society is to move forward.

THE "HOW" FACTOR

Part of any examination of the metamessage phenomenon outlined in Chapter 7 is the study of what we will call the "how" factor. *How* do the media cover the story? That is, from what "angles," with what "spin," using what frames (Tuchman, 1978) do they choose to tell their stories? Do journalists, for example, convey the news in terms of familiar themes (e.g., "Public officials have the situation under control," or "This is an unpredictable turn of events")? Considerable insight into the relationship of this "how" factor and possible media effects can be found in works of Lang and Lang (1968, 1983); and a more structural approach to the "how" issue can be found in Schulz's (1982) pioneering content analyses of how audience political images are shaped by the way the news stories are structured.

One especially dramatic example of the "how" factor's effect on news awareness and comprehension can be found in William Greider's 1981 *Atlantic* magazine article on David Stockman. Reflecting on his story, Greider (1983) notes that even though there was little *new* information in his article, it nevertheless effectively embarrassed Stockman, budget director at the time, as well as the Reagan administration. Most of his allegations, says Greider, and many of his quotes had already appeared in the *Washington Post, New York Times,* and other news outlets as well. Greider (1983:2) admits he "assumed incorrectly ... that most people would not be surprised by his fundamental points, since these points had already been made in public print."

In hindsight, Greider's "surprise" over the special power of his "old" news story could have been anticipated by considering the "how" factor. What his article did was integrate earlier fragmented information about administration policies into a single message (the administration is "faking" its economic policy); it personalized the story around a single individual (Stockman) whose earlier newspaper quotes were "off the record" or unattributed; it highlighted the conflict within the Reagan administration; and it told the story in direct and human terms. *How* the story was told made all the difference between a dry account understandable only to a small elite who could "read between the lines" and front-page news that precipitated Stockman's "trip to the woodshed" and crippled his power in Washington.

Similar examples undoubtedly exist. Most good journalists probably know some even better ones. Indeed, they probably exchange them on a routine basis with fellow journalists around the water cooler or at other watering holes. The problem journalists face is getting enough information to give their story the proper "how" emphasis or slant, one that will allow them to tell that story according to the norms and constraints of proper journalism. If that were done, and it is not an easy task by any means, then it is possible that even news of official Washington might become interesting and comprehensible "outside the Beltway."

KNOWLEDGE GAPS AND
THE "INFORMATION POOR"

There has been much discussion in recent years about the state of public information levels. Concern is often raised about the needs of the "information poor" and of (easing) access to whatever information they need. Even information programs specifically designed to close the gap between the information rich and the information poor, such as *Sesame Street,* seem to end up contributing to that gap. Our research too reaffirms the existence and inevitability of the gap, at least under present media circumstances. But our research has introduced two new wrinkles: First, we have identified (prior) information as a factor contributing to the widening gap more important than formal education. Second, we have uncovered evidence that television news increases information levels more among less-educated respondents than among better-educated respondents (for a similar finding in a Third World context, see Shingi et al., 1982).

Both "wrinkles" could, of course, be used to provide support for a laissez-faire approach to the information-gap issue. Our first finding suggests it is an individual level variable (information), and not the aggregate level variable of (formal) education, that is mainly responsible for information accrual.[2] The second suggests that there is a simple and free news medium—television—that can help the information poor acquire the news and information their better-informed and more affluent counterparts absorb from the print media. In brief, both results suggest that where there is a will to be informed, there is a way.

Support for the laissez-faire position also comes from another unrelated argument, which questions the ultimate personal utility of news information and whether our investment of time and attention to the news has any long-term payoff. Given the dominance of emotional and aggressive information in the news content, Schulz (1982: 149) concludes that "these results seem to justify some doubts as to whether knowledge gain from the news media is necessarily beneficial to the citizen."

Schulz's gloomy conclusion comes to mind whenever one is outside the mainstream of news for an extended period—on an overseas trip, for example, or on vacation in a location remote from media. Whatever news hunger that builds up over that time can be satiated relatively rapidly, on return, from a few brief conversations or media accounts. Even as we look back at all the arduous and fascinating coverage of the Watergate scandal a decade ago, we wonder what we as individuals (or as a country) learned as a consequence. What are the real long-term cognitive rewards, then, from our attention to the news? Could not our time and energy be more wisely spent in reading the great works of literature, in learning how to make and repair technology, or in socializing with friends and family?

Ultimately, of course, the way one answers these questions depends on personal and societal values. For us, the choice is clear. If nearly everyone turned off the news, decision making in our democracy would fall even more firmly into the hands of uncaring bureaucrats and power-hungry politicians. As it stands now, only the *threat* of media exposure and the accompanying outcry from an attentive and informal public keeps political decision makers under any control. Recall the sentiments of Westmoreland juror Roth. She seemed happy enough in her ignorance of the way government policy was made—and *somewhere* in the media she probably could have found out what she later learned from serving on that jury. But Mrs. Roth was far from happy once she became aware of what had been going on. Although it is possible to argue that Mrs. Roth was better off in her ignorance, we believe that she and the rest of the country are always better off knowing.

THE NEWS MEDIA AS
SOCIAL LOOKING GLASS

Moving ever farther beyond "routine" comprehension, we now want to consider another "cognitive effect" of the news—its general role in "socializing" the public into various modes and interpretations of American political life. Media stories present a virtually continuous parade of groups and individuals who, for various reasons including injustice and maltreatment, are considered newsworthy. In this sense, the media function as a continual looking glass or barometer of one's personal well-being in society, a way of comparing how "I" am doing with the fortunes of others very much like or very dissimilar to oneself.

People have multiple group loyalties and affiliations, and they judge whether or not those loyalties and affiliations are receiving equitable political treatment in part by their coverage in the news media. If, for example, business groups are being singled out for criticism for costly business lunches or unfair tax breaks, and one is a businessman, that could lead one to feel "under attack."

Thus, the media can serve to alert, mobilize, and activate predispositions that existed prior to actual news reports. These media accounts may not create the divisions of public opinion that result; indeed, the media accounts may be simple reports of trends in public opinion that have already developed. What the media do in their framing of the issues, however, is to accelerate the process by which the public becomes aware of its own developing and differing points of view.[3] With the addition of television to the news environment, the members of the public may become much more rapidly and dramatically aware of how their views are similar to or different from those of others.

Civil rights groups and college activists in the 1960s perhaps were the first groups to recognize this mobilization potential of a television news environment. But the use of television as a forum has also allowed several other groups to go public in the 1970s and 1980s—homosexuals, feminists, antiabortion groups, "Yuppies," neopatriots, parents with missing children, victims of wife beating, and the like. It is not that these groups would not eventually have had their say, but rather that they have had their say much more quickly.

This looking-glass process, by which individuals become increasingly aware of how mainstream—or deviant—their points of view are, is not without its important political ramifications. Institutions now find themselves adapting not only to the long-term formal lobbying efforts of the pretelevision era, but to the sudden surges of special interest groups that have been able to make their case current in a television-dominated media environment. These new groups realize that their political power is fleeting, depending on media attention; they must mobilize while the media "iron" is hot. This results in a more rapidly changing and perhaps superficial political system, one that responds more to short-term disturbances that gain media attention rather than to longer-term problems.

The looking-glass culture has implications as well for the socialization of young people in society. Prior to television, the major source of political information was the newspaper. Interpretation of political stories in the newspaper is not an easy exercise for most young people; it usually requires the help of older readers and interpreters such as parents, teachers, or community "opinion leaders." However, with the advent of television young people had more direct access to the news events, with television reporters (rather than parents or teachers) acting as immediate interpreters of news events. All of us, in fact, now find ourselves less dependent on traditional elders and elites for news interpretations. Given the proper circumstances, we are directly and persuasively "reached" by the way journalists report and frame the news. Such effects may be greatest on those individuals who are most TV dependent—namely, those least open to counter information from their own experiences, from alternative media, or from interpersonal conversations.

Young people may compose the group at greatest risk. Thus, it would not be surprising to find young people most affected by TV news content; they are, after all, the group least committed to traditional political arrangements and most open to newer, shorter-run points of view. In the late 1970s, it is possible that the young were the group most directly affected by images of an America dominated by Middle Eastern oil sheiks, of Iranian religious zealots, and of an America powerless to stop Soviet "invasions" into Afghanistan and Poland. On the domestic scene, young people watched and "experienced" the ill effects of inflation and limited economic opportunities—and, if young and white, of laws favoring minorities for these opportunities. It is not inconceivable that what young people saw in the media looking glass precipitated their turn to the right in the late 1970s and early 1980s, just as it triggered youth's move to the left a decade and a half earlier.

In short, one major cognitive impact of the media is, then, to create a feeling that it is safe to "come out of the closet" regarding one's point of view. That is not to say that other individuals, particularly those expressing minority points of view, will not conceal their nonpopular views or pretend to go along with the publicized majority as the spiral-of-silence model would suggest. It is to say that for other individuals the end result is to make them think about how their own life chances and attitudes compare with the prevalent views as articulated by the media. What then, we ask, do we see reflected in the media looking glass?

Ultimately, what we see and know has powerful implications for modern life. As individuals, each of us will arrive at our own pictures of reality; as scholars, however, we have an obligation to help structure and inform that search. Future studies should be directed at understanding the consequences of short-run *and* long-run public understanding—looking-glass reflections, if you will—for the information of public opinion and the conduct of government. Perhaps, however, the most useful research that we could do would be with—and for—working journalists, particularly if they expressed a commitment to alter news practices in line with research findings. Such research holds out the very real prospect of increased theoretical and practical knowledge. We are ready for more. There is, after all, no good reasons why the news, particularly TV news, should remain beyond comprehension.

NOTES

1. In his content analysis of network news and newspaper coverage of news between 1967 and 1975, Rubin (1981: 163) noted a "tendency for television news not only to be more planned, more nationally oriented, more thematic, and more political than newspaper coverage." (Similar depictions of television's news coverage can be found in Robinson and Sheehan, 1983). Rubin also noted that news stresses "broad themes and linkages rather than detailed information, and personalizing and politicizing the news stories themselves" (p. 158).

2. It should be noted that this conclusion does not apply solely to comprehension of television news but to a wider range of audience phenomena as well. For example, we have found in our studies of public appreciation of classical music (e.g., Robinson and Fink, 1984) that information about music (in general) is a far more powerful predictor than education.

3. This "looking-glass" process of cognitive media effect is of course similar to the "spiral-of-silence" model of media effects developed by Professor Noelle-Neumann (1974) in West Germany. The difference between her model and this one lies in its portrayal of the dynamics of public opinion. In the spiral-of-silence model people develop opinions that conform to what is perceived as the prevailing group norm; no interaction or only imagined interaction takes place. In the present model, we see the public as having developed certain tendencies (predispositions) in their attitudes and viewpoints, which the media affect and mobilize through a process of articulation and definition. Viewers, particularly younger ones with less information and fewer experiences to resist media messages, use these media articulations and definitions as a way of defining points of view that diverge from the accepted positions of their elders.

Appendix A:
Psychological Measures
Related to News Comprehension

The six measures in this appendix come from the Flint-Toledo mass media study described in Chapter 3. The measures were developed to illuminate some of the behavioral processes and internal mechanisms by which people could become better informed. It was hoped that they might also serve the operational function of significantly explaining the degree to which education per se predicted information levels. Although they did not do well in this latter capacity, Table 3.3 in Chapter 3 shows that they were still able to predict information levels in their own right. They demonstrated satisfactory internal consistency as well, with items in each of the scales being significantly correlated with each other. As can be seen in columns 2 through 4 in Table 3.3 of Chapter 3, the scales were also quite useful as predictors of information about entertainers, certain cultural matters, and Watergate.

These scales therefore could be useful in future studies of information flow designed to separate the static effects of the education variable from the more dynamic psychological processes that may predispose an individual to absorb information. Scale items are mostly cast in forced-choice rather than agree-disagree format to reduce the influence of acquiescence or agreement response set. Actual wording of the scale items, along with frequency distributions for item responses and scale means based on the Flint-Toledo study, will now be presented. Item responses marked with an "X" are scored "1" and summed for all scale items into a single score.

NEWS-SEEKING SCALE
(Average = 2.24 out of 4.00)

Are you more the type of person:

X1.	Who talks quite a bit to other people about what's new and happening, or	56%
2.	Who doesn't have much occasion to talk to other people about what's new and happening.	44%
		100%

Are you more the type of person:
  X1. Who feels left out and a little anxious if you don't know what's going on, or 39%
  2. Who figures if anything important happens you'll find out eventually? 61%

                                                                           100%

Are you more the type of person?
  X1. Who tries new and different things to do, or 47%
  2. Who sticks pretty much to familiar things you've learned to like? 53%

                                                                           100%

Are you more the type of person:
  X1. Who, if you had to choose, would prefer to learn or understand something new, or 82%
  2. Who would choose to have fun and a good time? 18%

                                                                           100%

FREEDOM FROM DISTRACTION SCALE
(Average = 1.81 out of 4.00)

Some people daydream a lot of the time, thinking about how their life could be better or different. Is this very true for you, somewhat true for you, or not true for you?

5. VERY TRUE FOR YOU	3. SOMEWHAT TRUE FOR YOU	X1. NOT TRUE FOR YOU	8. DK
16%	43%	41%	

People we talk to would like to know more about things in the news but can't for various reasons:
  Some people can't because they are so busy with their work or other activities. Is this true for you, somewhat true for you, or not true for you?

5. VERY TRUE FOR YOU	3. SOMEWHAT TRUE FOR YOU	X1. NOT TRUE FOR YOU	8. DK
15%	43%	43%	

For some people their own worries and troubles seem to take up all their time and attention. Is this very true for you, somewhat true for you, or not true for you?

5. VERY TRUE FOR YOU	3. SOMEWHAT TRUE FOR YOU	X1. NOT TRUE FOR YOU	8. DK
9%	33%	57%	

Some people's only interest is in things close to home, like family, friends, and neighborhood. Is that very true for you, somewhat true for you, or not true for you?

5. VERY TRUE FOR YOU 20%	3. SOMEWHAT TRUE FOR YOU 40%	X1. NOT TRUE FOR YOU 40%	8. DK

PREFERENCE FOR REALISTIC
TV ENTERTAINMENT
(Average = 1.78 out of 3.00)

When you choose entertainment programs on TV
Are you more the type of person:
1. Who enjoys TV stories that let you relax, or   69%
X5. Who enjoys TV stories that get you worked up and involved?   31%
                                                        100%

Are you more the type of person:
X1. Who likes TV stories where things work out just like they do
    in real life, or   62%
5. Who likes TV stories where things work out better then they
    usually do in real life?   38%
                                                        100%

Are you more the type of person:
1. Who prefers TV stories where you know easily what is going
    on and how things will turn out, or   15%
X5. Who prefers TV stories that make you think and try to figure
    things out?   85%
                                                        100%

COSMOPOLITAN SCALE
(Average = 1.42 out of 4.00)

People pay attention to different kinds of news. We would like to ask the types
of government and public affairs that you follow.
    Let's start with local and city affairs, things going on in the (Toledo/Flint)
    area—do you pay a great deal, some, or not much attention to local
    affairs?

1. GREAT DEAL 41%	3. SOME 30%	X5. NOT MUCH 29%	8. DK

And how about state affairs, things going on in (Ohio, Michigan)—do you
pay a great deal, some, or not much attention to state affairs?

1. GREAT DEAL 30%	3. SOME 39%	X5. NOT MUCH 31%	8. DK

What about national affairs, things happening in Washington and around the
rest of the country—do you pay a great deal, some, or not much attention to
national affairs?

X1. GREAT DEAL	3. SOME	5. NOT MUCH	8. DK
48%	40%	12%	

Finally, how about international and world affairs—do you pay a great deal of attention, some attention, or not much attention to international affairs?

X1. GREAT DEAL	3. SOME	5. NOT MUCH	8. DK
34%	50%	16%	

ASSERTIVENESS SCALE
(Average = 0.86 out of 3.00)

When you meet with your friends or relatives or other people, are you more likely to talk or to listen?

X1. TALK	5. LISTEN	3. BOTH
27%	43%	30%

Are you more likely to give your opinions or to ask other people for their opinions?

X1. GIVE	5. ASK	3. BOTH
36%	34%	31%

When you talk with other people, are you more likely to see the value of what the other people have to say or to defend your own point of view?

5. SEE VALUE OF WHAT OTHER PEOPLE HAVE TO SAY	X1. DEFEND OWN POINT OF VIEW	3. BOTH	8. DK
59%	23%	17%	

NEWS COMPLAINT SCORE
(One point for each mention)

Is there any kind of news, either in newspapers or on TV, that you feel should be reported more than it is?

    1. YES   0. NO————GO TO NEXT QUESTION
    ↓

What kind of news is that?_____

_____

Is there any kind of news, either in newspapers or on TV, that you feel should be reported less than it is?

    1. YES   0. NO————SKIP TO "SOCIAL NETWORK SCALE"
    ↓

What kind of news is that?_____

_____

SOCIAL NETWORK SCALE
(Average = 1.32 out of 4.00)

Do you know and talk to someone who seems to know the inside story about things that happen in the (Toledo/Flint) area?

X1. YES   0. NO   GO TO NEXT QUESTION
30%   70%

What does that person do?_____

_____

Do you know and talk to someone who seems to know the inside story about things that happen in the (Toledo/Flint) area?

X1. YES   0. NO
30%   70%

Do you know and talk to anyone who knows a lot about national politics and foreign affairs?

X1. YES   0. NO
23%   77%

Do you know and talk to someone who tells you a lot of things you don't know about?

X1. YES   0. NO
49%   51%

Appendix B:
Review of British
Focus-Group Studies

In order to supplement the survey studies conducted at the BBC, and to enhance our understanding of how viewers actually process television news, we conducted seven focus-group sessions in the London and Leeds areas in February and March 1978.

Participants in these groups represented different social categories—working class and middle class, suburban and urban, old and young, and male and female. The groups ranged in size from six to ten, and those who were invited met in one person's house. The people involved usually did not know each other, even though they did live in the same general neighborhood.

The groups lasted about three hours. We first asked the participants to fill out a brief questionnaire that contained items similar to those in our earlier national survey (their answers matched rather closely). The groups then discussed the features of BBC and ITN news coverage they liked and disliked, describing particular examples of each when possible.

At nine o'clock, the group watched that evening's BBC newscast. While the newscast was on the air, we developed questions related to the news items to gauge the group's understanding of them; the gist of some of these questions had already been suggested from our discussions with news editors earlier that afternoon, as the newscast was being prepared.

We also obtained a very direct assessment of viewer attention to the newscast by switching off the set three or four times during the program and asking participants what they were thinking about at the exact moment the set was turned off. Although this was a group-viewing situation dealing with the news they were about to discuss, less than half of reported attention pertained to the more routine impersonal news (e.g., political negotiations, economic reports, and foreign affairs); rather it was on items with some "human interest" feature (e.g., Peter Townsend's new book, Anwar Sadat's latest actions, a laser rifle stolen from a museum, the costs of cleanup after the storm, how an oil rig was refloated, or Howard Hughes's "Spruce Goose").

Although some of our group members were thinking about something unrelated to the program (such as personal problems or situations), many viewers were mulling over other items on the newscast, mainly prior reports but also upcoming stories. In general, however, we felt our group members were asking themselves plausible and intelligent questions about those other stories: What would have been the outcome if Townsend had married Princess Margaret, or is he writing this book just for the money? Will the rabies plan actually work in practice? Do the White Paper statistics on defense include potential French or American military assistance? How much did it really cost to refloat the oil rig, or is it worth it? How would British workers fare in a Japanese plant? Why didn't the Science Museum put up a model of the gun rather than the genuine item that was stolen; why did it take three days to find out it was missing?

This exercise, then, was quite instructive about the irregularity of viewer attention and its relation to comprehending a TV news story. If viewers' attention wandered this much in a focused group setting, inattention might be much greater in the unfocused confusion of the home viewing environment.

When the newscast was over, the group participants were asked paper-and-pencil questions about some of the main items on the newscast. These were both of the closed and open-ended variety: for example, "Did the government figures show unemployment was *going up, going down,* or *staying the same*?" or "Why did the union leaders say the figures were going this way?" Given the dismal findings of earlier research on the comprehension of news items, we were generally quite surprised by the participants' ability to answer these questions correctly. To be sure, some of these questions dealt with the news items they were already familiar with. But it was clearly not the case that news stories were beyond the grasp of these viewers, and that became even more obvious in the group discussions that followed. Audience members, then, can grasp the gist of news stories, although often this understanding is filtered through their own idiosyncratic mental models of how the world operates.

Some exceptions to this pattern also emerged, particularly with regard to more complex or highly technical stories. Less than half of the respondents revealed an understanding of information in the newscast in their answers to such questions as these: What was the event that led to agreement on the green pound? What is the main issue in the Ilford by-election? What were the MPs arguing about today? What is the significance of the insurance settlement? Why is Dr. Owen optimistic about the Middle East? What type of agreement was being sought on imports of Japanese cars? Who is on strike at the *Times?* How many people died or survived in the Los Angeles plane crash? What were the conclusions of the Waterways Report?

At the same time, however, we found that more than half of these viewers were able to comprehend information that was briefly mentioned or involved fairly subtle cues: how the Scottish driver was able to survive being buried for days in a snowdrift; how long the Soviet cosmonauts had been in space; why the woman doctor was involved in the LSD ring; what the demonstrations regarding the animal farm were about; why people in Hong Kong objected to the deportation of the Hong Kong girl from Britain; and what the soccer official's reaction was to the report on soccer hooliganism. It is premature then, simply to characterize the audience as incapable of grasping subtle or complicated pieces of information that appear in newscasts. High levels of comprehension can be achieved particularly if viewers find the story or its presentation interesting or visually appealing.

Likewise, certain failures at comprehension seemed related to a lack of matchup between the story and the visual material that accompanied it: for example, a news item on a speedup in immigration accompanied by a filmed segment describing steps taken to ensure that immigrants did not enter illegally; a story on how a gasoline strike could force the schools to close by making it impossible for snow ploughs to clear the roads, accompanied by pictures of snowploughs *in operation;* or combat footage from the Ogaden that failed to identify clearly which side of the fighting was being shown or how the rival groups were linked to Western or Eastern bloc countries.

Perhaps the most intriguing insights from these group sessions, however, came when participants then watched the ITN ten o'clock version of the news. This allowed side-by-side comparison of those aspects of the BBC and ITN newscasts that were most appealing and that made the stories more understandable. This comparision seemed to work to the disadvantage of the BBC newscast, perhaps because as it was seen first, viewers were more likely to find fault with it. The subsequent ITN presentation was perceived as more informative either because it mentioned things that were missed or presented inadequately in the first (BBC) program or because the ITN newscast by and large repeated news heard earlier. On the other hand, there are plausible reasons why a first presentation might have worked to the advantage of the BBC version: A second viewing might have been considered to be a stale rehash of what viewers already knew—or group participants at that point might have been quite fatigued after two hours of meeting. Moreover, they could have continued to be courteous to us because of affiliation with the BBC and their previously mentioned preference for BBC news.

Not all aspects of ITN coverage were rated positively, however. On more than one news story, ITN coverage contained overly lengthy and rambling interviews with politicians, or inappropriate items. It was also felt that ITN treated some stories too casually or made inferences about news stories that were unwarranted given the information provided. Moreover, certain preferred story features noted by our respondents were fairly consistent across groups and newscasts. First, viewers preferred accounts that "brought the story home to them" in human "eyewitness" terms: for example, a *doctor's* account of how the Scottish driver was able to survive being buried alive in the snow; interviews with the *drivers* in gas lines about their motives for buying; the dangers of the oil rig going aground as retold not by the ship's officers or company officials but by *sailors in the pub*; the pictures of what the snow accumulation in the West looked like on the ground in terms of day-to-day problems *people* had to cope with; interviews with *train riders* affected by the rail strike; tips on how *all drivers* can save gas, which are incorporated into a story on new car gas consumption; and what the latest long-range weather forecast says next month's weather would be like. In each case, the personal utility, relevance, or consequences were brought home explicitly to the viewer, rather than being presented from a more abstract perspective.

Second, viewers sometimes enjoyed having specific stories described to them in considerable detail; that is, not just that Callaghan and Thatcher had a row, but the actual content of their disagreement; not just that people were shot in Northern Ireland, but that a new machine gun (shown previously in the news) was used in the shootings; and not just that a plane crashed and that 2 people died, but that 195 passengers survived.

Our group participants also generally appreciated diagrams and mock-ups used to embellish a story, however crude (and ITN's were extremely primitive in a couple of instances). Some group members also commented favorably when pictures of newspaper front pages were shown to suggest the importance of a given story. That favorable attitude did not carry over to printed excerpts from official reports, although viewers did appreciate identifications ("supers") of individuals being interviewed. Moreover, group members uniformly expressed a desire to keep statistical and quantitative information to a minimum. For example, in a report on gas consumption, they preferred mileage figures for three cars to be compared rather than for five or ten, dismissing data for the Rolls Royce as irrelevant. Further, statistics were often greeted with some skepticism: Different politicians were seen to use the same figures to defend different policies and the relevance of inflation and balance-of-payments for one's own grocery bills was often unclear. Indeed, very low comprehension was found for questions we asked on statistical or quantitative information, no matter how centrally it was stressed in the story. Possibly, the implications of this information eventually come through in some way, but it appears that few stories can be told well relying on statistics alone. Some people simply "block" on numbers; whereas for others, the numbers have low credibility. One of our groups made the explicit suggestion that TV news hire its own staff to assemble and interpret official statistics to avoid some of these problems. Finally, an almost virtually unanimous response occurred for the greater use of maps. A recurring question during a newscast is, "Where is *this* story taking place, either at home (e.g., the rabies story, the snow in Newcastle) or abroad (e.g., Somalia, India)?" Even those whose admitted geographical knowledge was essentially inadequate wanted to be at least reminded of the continent on which the story was taking place.

Overall, then, although the reactions from these few focus groups are not generalizable enough to provide a basis for firm conclusions or recommendations, they do illustrate some of the ways viewers process TV news content. It is instructive to find that viewers who enter these discussions with more positive views about BBC News find more features of ITN coverage they prefer, given that most social psychological studies find people reluctant to change their attitudes (and particularly to admit it in a group situation). Such discomfort may have motivated BBC partisans in some groups to explain this discrepancy in terms of BBC "having a bad night" or "Angela [a popular news presenter] wasn't there" or "BBC promoting their good correspondents to managerial positions." In general, our group members appreciated, where it was possible and within the bounds of accuracy, having explanations or other "hooks" upon which to interpret the "why" component of the news.

Appendix C:
News Awareness and
Comprehension Questions
(U.S. Regional and National Samples)

REGIONAL SURVEY

Central America

1. Have you heard anything about the Reagan administration's policy in Nicaragua and Central America?

2. Do you think the Reagan administration is trying to help the government in Nicaragua, trying to work against the government in Nicaragua, or is the U.S. government taking a neutral stand on Nicaragua?

3. What are the reasons the Reagan administration gives for working against the Nicaraguan government?

4. What possibly illegal activities of the Reagan administration in Nicaragua are American members of Congress worried about?

5. Did you happen to hear about votes in congressional intelligence committees this week on what the Reagan administration is doing in Nicaragua? Did the votes support Reagan administration policy, conflict with Reagan policies, or something else? In what way did they conflict?

6. And what about the government of El Salvador? Is the Reagan administration trying to help the government of El Salvador, work against the government of El Salvador, or is the U.S. government taking a neutral stance on El Salvador?

Middle East

7. Did you happen to hear anything about high-level negotiations in the Middle East about Lebanon? What are the negotiations about?

8. Are the negotiations about increasing the number of Israeli soldiers in Lebanon, withdrawing Israeli soldiers, or keeping them at the same level?

9. Did you hear anything about a bombing in Beirut?

Congress

10. Do you think most members of Congress want to spend more money on domestic social programs than President Reagan, less money on domestic

social programs than President Reagan, or almost the same amount? How about military aid to the government of El Salvador? Military and to the government of Nicaraugua? Military and defense spending?

11. In getting support for his military and defense program in the past few weeks, has President Reagan had more problems with Democratic senators, more problems with Republican senators, or both about equally?

12. Have you heard anything about the debate over the MX missile?

13. Did you happen to hear anything about a resolution passed by the House of Representatives about nuclear arms control? Did the resolution support Reagan administration policy, conflict with the Reagan administration policy, or something else?

Miscellaneous

14. Did you hear anything about a pastoral letter that the American Catholic bishops approved about nuclear weapons and war? Did the letter support the Reagan administration policies on nuclear weapons, conflict with the Reagan administration policies, or something else? In what way did the Bishop's letter support/conflict?

15. Did you happen to hear anything about an earthquake in California? How many people were killed in the earthquake: Was it none, one or two, between three and twenty, between twenty and one hundred, more than one hundred?

16. Did you happen to hear anything about an artist doing something to some islands in Florida? What did the artist do?

17. Did you hear anything about the mayor's race in Chicago? What was historic about this particular election? Was the man who lost the election, Bernard Epton, a Democrat, a Republican, or Independent?

Names in the News

("Here are some names that appeared in the news in the last few weeks. Can you tell me who they are? Why were they in the news?")

18. John Glenn
19. James Watt
20. Lech Walesa
21. Yuri Andropov
22. George Schultz
23. Ralph Nader

NATIONAL SURVEY

Central America

1. Have you heard or read anything about the Reagan administration's policy in Nicaragua and Central America?

2. Do you think the Reagan administration is trying to help the government of Nicaragua, trying to work against the government in Nicaragua, or is the U.S. government taking a neutral stand on Nicaragua?

3. Do you know of anything the Nicaraguan government is doing in other Central American countries that the Reagan administration wants to stop? What is that?

4. And what about the government of El Salvador? Is the Reagan administration trying to help the government of El Salvador, work against the government of El Salvador, or is the U.S. government taking a neutral stand on El Salvador?

5. In the last week, did you hear of any changes the Reagan administration made in the people who deal with the situation in El Salvador and Central America? What changes were made?

6. Did you hear anything about an American who was killed last week in El Salvador? What was that person doing in El Salvador? Was he shot by El Salvador government forces, by antigovernment forces, or by some other group?

7. Did you hear anything about two Americans killed in Central America last week? Were these Americans: diplomats, military advisors, journalists, or something else?

8. In the last week, did you hear anything that happened to American ambassadors to Nicaragua, or to Nicaraguan ambassadors to the U.S.? What happened to the American ambassadors? What reason did the Nicaraguan government give for doing this? What happened to the Nicaraguan ambassadors? What reasons did the American government give for doing this?

International News

9. Did you hear anything about the elections in Great Britain? Was there anything particularly different about this election compared to previous British elections?

10. Do you happen to know what country Pope John Paul is visiting this week? What do you think the purpose of the Pope's visit was? In his speeches was the Pope very critical, slightly critical, or not critical of the government in Poland?

11. Did you hear anything about the economic summit in Williamsburg, Virginia? Did the summit conference include only American leaders, leaders from America and other industrial countries, or leaders from both industrial and less-developed countries?

12. Did you hear anything about a new approach the Reagan administration is taking toward the arms control talks in Geneva with the Soviet Union? Did the Reagan administration say they are taking a tougher line, a more flexible approach, or something else?

Domestic News

13. Have you heard anything about floods in Utah and Nevada? What is the main cause of those floods—is it heavy rains or something else? (If "something else"): What is that?

14. Did you hear anything about a mysterious new disease called AIDS? Do you know any particular group of people who have been affected more than others?

15. In the last week, did you hear any statements about education in America by President Reagan or by Walter Mondale? What did Reagan/Mondale say? Does President Reagan want to raise the salaries of all teachers, some teachers, or no teachers? Which teachers in particular?

16. Did you hear or read about a Supreme Court ruling on legislative vetoes in Congress? Did the Court's ruling give more power to Congress, more power to the President, or did it not change the power of Congress or the President?

17. Did you hear or read about a Supreme Court ruling on abortion? Did the Court's ruling make it easier to get an abortion, harder to get an abortion, or not change how easy or hard it is to get an abortion?

18. Did you hear about American astronauts on a space shuttle mission? Did the astronauts' mission go perfectly from takeoff to landing or did something have to be changed? What had to be changed?

19. Did you hear or read anything about Congress trying to put a cap or limit on the July 1 tax cut? Why did Congress want to limit the tax cut?

20. Did you happen to hear or read about a high school student who criticized President Reagan while attending a ceremony at the White House? What did the student criticize Reagan about?

21. Have you heard any new information about the 1980 debate between Ronald Reagan and Jimmy Carter? What did you hear?

22. Have you heard anything about a Los Angeles lawyer who claims to have a videotape? What appears on the tapes?

Names in the News

("Here are some names that appeared in the news in the last few weeks. Can you tell me who they are? Why were they in the news?")

23. Henry Kissinger
24. Dan Rather
25. Margaret Thatcher
26. Yuri Andropov
27. Paul Volcker
28. Lech Walesa
29. Sally Ride
30. Sirhan Sirhan
31. Jesse Jackson

References

ABEL, E. (1981) What's News: The Media in American Society. San Francisco: Institute for Contemporary Studies.

ADAMS, R. (1981) "Newspapers and television as news information media." Journalism Quarterly 58: 627-629.

ADAMS, W. (1978) "Local public affairs content of TV news." Journalism Quarterly 55: 690-695.

ADONI, H. and A. COHEN (1978) "Television economic news and the social construction of economic reality." Journal of Communication 28, 4: 61-70.

———and S. MANE (1984) "Social reality and television news: perceptual dimensions of social conflicts in selected life areas." Journal of Broadcasting 28: 33-49.

ADONI, H. and S. MANE (1984) "Media and the social construction of reality: toward an integration of theory and research." Communication Research 11: 323-340.

ALLPORT, G. and L. POSTMAN (1945) "The basic psychology of rumor." Transactions of the New York Academy of Sciences 8 (Series 2): 61-81.

ALTHEIDE, D. (1976) Creating Reality. Beverly Hills, CA: Sage.

———and J. JOHNSON (1980) Bureaucratic Propaganda. Boston: Allyn & Bacon.

ANDERSON, J. (1980) Cognitive Psychology and Its Implications. San Francisco: Freeman.

———(1981) Cognitive Skills and Their Acquisition. Hillsdale, NJ: Lawrence Erlbaum.

ANDREWS, F., J. MORGAN, J. SONQUIST, and L. KLEM (1973) Multiple Classification Analysis. Ann Arbor: Institute for Social Research, University of Michigan.

ATKIN, C., J. GALLOWAY, and O. NAYMAN (1976) "News media exposure, political knowledge and campaign interest." Journalism Quarterly 53: 231-237.

AXELROD, R. (1973) "Schema theory: an information processing model of perception and cognition." American Political Science Review 67: 1248-1266.

BAGDIKIAN, B. (1971) The Information Machines. New York: Harper & Row.

BARBER, J. (1979) "Not the New York Times: what network news should be." Washington Monthly (September): 14-21.

BECKER, L., M. McCOMBS, and J. McLEOD (1975) "The development of political cognitions," in S. Chaffee (ed.) Political Communication: Issues and Strategies for Research. Beverly Hills, CA: Sage.

BECKER, L. and D. C. WHITNEY (1980) "Effects of media dependencies." Communication Research 7: 95-120.

BENNETT, W. L. (1983) News: The Politics of Illusion. New York: Longman.

256

BERELSON, B., P. LAZARSFELD, and W. McPHEE (1954) Voting: A Study of Opinion Formation in a Presidential Campaign. Chicago: University of Chicago Press.

BERGER, P. and T. LUCKMANN (1966) The Social Construction of Reality. Garden City, NY: Doubleday.

BERNSTEIN, B. (1971) Class, Codes, and Control, Vol. 1. London: Routledge.

BERRY, C. (1983) "Learning from television news: a critique of the research." Journal of Broadcasting 27: 359-370.

———B. GUNTER, and B. CLIFFORD (1982) "Research on television news." Bulletin of the British Psychological Society 35: 301-304.

BIRT, J. and P. JAY (1975) "Bias against understanding." London Times (February 28, September 30, October 1).

BLAKE, M. (1967) "Time of day effects on performance in a range of tasks." Psychonomic Science 9: 349-350.

BLUMLER, J. (1983) "Communication and democracy: the crisis beyond and the ferment within." Journal of Communication 33: 604-610.

———and D. McQUAIL (1969) Television in Politics: Its Uses and Influence. Chicago: University of Chicago Press.

BLUMLER, J. and E. KATZ [eds.] (1974) The Uses of Mass Communications: Current Perspectives on Gratifications Research. Beverly Hills, CA: Sage.

BLUMLER, J. and J. McLEOD (1974) "Communication and voter turnout in Britain," in T. Leggatt (ed.) Sociological Theory and Survey Research: Institutional Change and Social Policy. Beverly Hills, CA: Sage.

BOOTH, A. (1970) "The recall of news items." Public Opinion Quarterly 36: 604-610.

Broadcasting (1979) "The Arledge differential at ABC News." December 10: 70-80.

———(1985) "NBC affiliates bask in ratings glory." May 20: 88-92.

BROWNELL, B. (1983) "Interpretations of twentieth-century urban progressive reform," in D. Colburn and G. Pozzetta (eds.) Reform and Reformers in the Progressive Era. Westport, CT: Greenwood.

BUDD, R., M. MacLEAN, Jr., and A. BARNES (1966) "Regularities in the diffusion of two news events." Journalism Quarterly 43: 221-230.

BURNS, T. (1969) "Public service and private world." Sociological Review Monograph 13: 53-73.

CANTOR, M. (1980) Prime Time Television: Content and Control. Beverly Hills, CA: Sage.

CAREY, J. (1976) "A cultural approach to communication." Communication 2: 1-22.

———(1977) "Mass communication research and cultural studies: an American view," in J. Curran, M. Gurevitch, and J. Woollacott (eds.) Mass Communication and Society. Beverly Hills, CA: Sage.

CARLSTON, D. (1980) "Events, inferences and impression formation," in R. Hastie et al. (eds.) Person Memory: The Cognitive Basis of Social Perception. Hillsdale, NJ: Lawrence Erlbaum.

CARTER, R. and B. GREENBERG (1965) "Newspapers or television: which do you believe?" Journalism Quarterly 42: 29-34.

CHAFFEE, S. (1975) "The diffusion of political information," in S. Chaffee (ed.) Political Communication. Beverly Hills, CA: Sage.

CLARKE, P. and E. FREDIN (1978) "Newspapers, television and political reasoning." Public Opinion Quarterly 42: 143-160.

CLARKE, P. and L. RUGGELS (1970) "Preferences among news media for coverage of public affairs." Journalism Quarterly 47: 464-471.

COHEN, S. and J. YOUNG [eds.] (1973) The Manufacture of News. London: Constable.

COLLINS, A. and E. LOFTUS (1975) "A spreading-activation theory of semantic processing." Psychological Review 82: 407-428.

COLLINS, W. (1982) "Social scripts and developmental patterns in comprehension of televised narratives." Communication Research 9: 380-398.

CORNER, J. and J. HAWTHORN [eds.] (1983) Communication Studies. London: Edward Arnold.

CRAIK, F. and K. BLANKSTEIN (1975) "Psychophysiology and human memory," in P. Venables and M. Christie (eds.) Research in Psychophysiology. London: John Wiley.

CRAIK, F. and R. LOCKHART (1972) "Levels of processing: a framework for memory research." Journal of Verbal Learning and Verbal Behavior 11: 671-684.

CROUSE, T. (1973) The Boys on the Bus. New York: Random House.

CURRAN, J., M. GUREVITCH, and J. WOOLLACOTT (1982) "The study of the media: theoretical approaches," in M. Gurevitch et al., (eds.) Culture, Society, and the Media. New York: Methuen.

DAHLGREN, P. (1983) Making Sense of TV News: An Ethnographic Perspective. Graduate Program in Communication Working Paper Series. Montreal: McGill University.

DAVIS, D. and S. BARAN (1981) Mass Communication and Everyday Life: A Perspective on Theory and Effects. Belmont, CA: Wadsworth.

DeFLEUR, M. and O. LARSEN (1958) The Flow of Information. New York: Harper & Brothers.

DEUTSCHMANN, P. and W. DANIELSON (1960) "Diffusion of knowledge of the major news story." Journalism Quarterly 37: 345-355.

DOMINICK, J., A. WURTZEL, and G. LOMETTI (1975) "Television journalism vs. show business: a content analysis of eyewitness news." Journalism Quarterly 52: 213-218.

DREW, D. and B. REEVES (1980) "Learning from a television news story." Communication Research 7: 121-135.

DYER, N. and J. ROBINSON (1980) "News comprehension research in Great Britain." Presented at the annual meeting of the International Communication Association, Acapulco, Mexico.

EASTON, D. (1965) A Systems Analysis of Political Life. New York: John Wiley.

ECO, U. (1983) "Towards a semiotic inquiry into the television message," in J. Corner and J. Hawthorne (eds.) Communication Studies. London: Edward Arnold.

EDELMAN, M (1964) The Symbolic Uses of Politics. Chicago: University of Illinois Press.

———(1971) Politics as Symbolic Action. Chicago: Markham.

EDELSTEIN, A. (1973) "Decision-making and mass communication: a conceptual and methodological approach to public opinion," in P. Clarke (ed.) New Models for Communication Research. Beverly Hills, CA: Sage.

———(1974) The Uses of Communication in Decision-Making. New York: Praeger.

————(1985) "Comparative public opinion: working within a tradition." Presented at the annual meeting of the International Communcation Association, Honolulu.

Editor & Publisher (1983) "For the big story, TV outstrips newspapers." May 14: 13.

EDWARDSON, M., P. GROOMS, and P. PRINGLE (1976) "Visualization and TV news information gain." Journal of Broadcasting 20: 373-380.

EDWARDSON, M., P. GROOMS, and S. PROUDLOVE (1981) "Television news information gain from interesting video vs. talking heads." Journal of Broadcasting 25: 15-24.

ELDER, C. and R. COBB (1983) The Political Uses of Symbols. New York: Longman.

ELKIN, L. (1985) "Juror in Westmoreland-CBS case penned it one day at a time." Washington Post (February 24): A4.

ELLIOTT, P. (1974) "Uses and gratifications research: a critique and a sociological alternative," in J. Blumler and E. Katz (eds.) The Uses of Mass Communications: Current Perspectives on Gratifications Research. Beverly Hills, CA: Sage.

EPSTEIN, E. (1973) News from Nowhere: Television and the News. New York: Vintage.

————(1975) Between Fact and Fiction: The Problems of Journalism. New York: Vintage.

ERBRING, L., E. GOLDENBERG, and A. MILLER (1980) "Front-page news and real-world cues: a new look at agenda setting by the media." American Journal of Political Science 24: 16-49.

FEJES, F. (1984) "Critical communication research and media effects: the problem of the the disappearing audience." Media, Culture, and Society 6: 219-232.

FINDAHL, O. (1971) The Effect of Visual Illustrations on Perception and Retention of News Programmes. Stockholm: Sveriges Radio/PUB.

————and B. HÖIJER (1972) Man as a Receiver of Information: Repetitions and Reformulations in a News Program. Stockholm: Sveriges Radio/PUB.

————(1973) An Analysis of Errors in the Recollection of a News Program. Stockholm: Sveriges Radio/PUB.

————(1974) On Knowledge, Social Privilege and the News. Stockholm: Sveriges Radio/PUB.

————(1975) "Effects of additional verbal information on retention of a radio news program." Journalism Quarterly 52: 493-498.

————(1976) Fragments of Reality: An Experiment with News and TV Visuals. Stockholm: Sveriges Radio/PUB.

————(1979) What Does the News Tell Us? Part 1. The Crisis in Swedish Industry. Stockholm: Sveriges Radio/PUB.

————(1981a) "Studies of news from the perspective of human comprehension," in C. Wilhoit and H. de Bock (eds.) Mass Communication Review Yearbook, Vol. 2. Beverly Hills, CA: Sage.

————(1981b) "Media content and human comprehension," in K. E. Rosengren (ed.) Advances in Content Analysis. Beverly Hills, CA: Sage.

FISHMAN, M. (1980) Manufacturing the News. Austin: University of Texas Press.

FISKE, J. and J. HARTLEY (1978) Reading Television. London: Methuen.

FORD, G. and G. YALCH (1982) "Viewer miscomprehension of televised communication: a comment." Journal of Marketing 46, 4: 27-31.

FRANK, R. (1973) Message Dimensions of Television News. Lexington, MA: Lexington Books.

FUNKHOUSER, G. (1973) "Trends in media coverage of the issues of the '60s." Journalism Quarterly 50: 533-538.

———and M. McCOMBS (1971) "The rise and fall of news diffusion." Public Opinion Quarterly 35: 107-113.

GANS, H. (1979) Deciding What's News. New York: Pantheon.

———(1980) "The audience for television—and in television," in S. Withey and R. Abeles (eds.) Television and Social Behavior: Beyond Violence and Children. Hillsdale, NJ: Lawrence Erlbaum.

GANTZ, W. (1978) "How uses and gratifications affect recall of television news." Journalism Quarterly 55: 664-672, 681.

GAZIANO, C. (1983) "The knowledge gap hypothesis: an analytical review of effects." Communication Research 10: 447-486.

GERBNER, G., L. GROSS, and S. SIGNORIELLI (1979) "The demonstration of power: violence profile no. 10." Journal of Communication 29: 177-196.

GIEBER, W. (1964) "News is what newspapermen make it," in L. A. Dexter and D. M. White (eds.) People, Society and Mass Communications. New York: Free Press.

GITLIN, T. (1980) The Whole World Is Watching. Berkeley: University of California Press.

Glasgow University Media Group (1976) Bad News. London: Routledge & Kegan Paul.

———(1980) More Bad News. London: Routledge & Kegan Paul.

———(1982) Really Bad news. London: Writers & Readers Publishing Cooperative.

GOLDING, P. (1981) "The missing dimensions: news media and the management of social change," in E. Katz and T. Szecsko (eds.) Mass Media and Social Change. London: Sage.

———and P. ELLIOTT (1979) Making the News. London: Longman.

GOLDING, P. and G. MURDOCH (1978) "Theories of communication and theories of society." Communication Research 5: 339-356.

GOODHARDT, G., A. EHRENBERG, and M. COLLINS (1975) The Television Audience: Patterns of Viewing. London: Saxon House.

GRABER, D. (1984) Processing the News. New York: Longman.

———and Y. KIM (1978) "Why John Q. Voter did not learn much from the 1976 presidential debates," in B. Ruben (ed.) Communication Yearbook 2. New Brunswick, NJ: Transaction Books.

GREENBERG, B. (1964a) "Diffusion of news of the Kennedy assassination." Public Opinion Quarterly 28: 225-232.

———(1964b) "Person to person communication in the diffusion of news events." Journalism Quarterly 41: 489-494.

———(1974) "Gratifications of television viewing and their correlates for British children," in J. Blumler and E. Katz (eds.) The Uses of Mass Communications: Current Perspectives on Gratifications Research. Beverly Hills, CA: Sage.

———and E. PARKER (1965) The Kennedy Assassination and the American Public: Social Communication in Crisis. Stanford, CA: Stanford University Press.

GRIEDER, W. (1981) The Education of David Stockman and Other Americans. New York: E. P. Dutton.

————(1983) "Opening statement," in Making Sense of the News. St. Petersburg, FL: Modern Media Institute.

GUNTER, B. (1979) "Recall of brief television news items: effects of presentation mode, picture content and serial position." Journal of Educational Television 5: 57-61.

————(1980a) "Remembering televised news: effects of visual format on information gain." Journal of Education Television 6: 8-11.

————(1980b) "Remembering television news: effects of picture content." Journal of General Psychology 102: 127-133.

————(1983) "Forgetting the news," in E. Wartella and D. C. Whitney (eds.) Mass Communication Review Yearbook, Vol. 4. Beverly Hills, CA: Sage.

————(1984) "News awareness: a British survey." London: Independent Broadcasting Authority Research Department. (mimeo)

————C. BERRY and B. CLIFFORD (1981) "Proactive interference effects with television news items: further evidence." Journal of Experimental Psychology: Human Learning and Memory 7: 480-487.

————(1982) "Remembering broadcast news: the implications of experimental research for production techniques." Human Learning: A Journal of Practical Research and Application 1: 13-29.

GUNTER, B., B. CLIFFORD, and C. BERRY (1980) "Release from proactive interference with television news items: evidence for encoding within televised news." Journal of Experimental Psychology: Human Learning and Memory 6: 216-223.

GUNTER, B., A. FURNHAM, and J. JARRETT (1984) "Personality, time of day and delayed memory for television news." Personality and Individual Differences 5: 35-39.

GUNTER, B., J. JARRETT, and A. FURNHAM (1983) "Time of day effects on immediate memory for television news." Human Learning 2: 1-7.

GUSFIELD, J. (1981) The Culture of Public Problems. Chicago: University of Chicago Press.

HALL, S. (1980) "Encoding and decoding," in S. Hall et al. (eds.) Culture, Media, and Language. London: Hutchinson.

————(1982) "The rediscovery of 'ideology,'" in M. Gurevitch et al. (eds.) Culture, Society and the Media. New York: Methuen.

HALLORAN, J. (1970) The Effects of Television. London: Panther Books.

HASTIE, R., T. OSTROM, E. EBBESEN, R. WYER, D. HAMILTON, and D. CARLSTON [eds.] (1980) Person Memory: The Cognitive Basis of Social Perception. Hillsdale, NJ: Lawrence Erlbaum.

HIGGINS, E., C. HERMAN, and M. ZANNA [eds.] (1981) Social Cognition: The Ontario Symposium, Vol. 1. Hillsdale, NJ: Lawrence Erlbaum.

HILL, R. and C. BONJEAN (1964) "News diffusion: a test of the regularity hypothesis." Journalism Quarterly 41: 336-342.

HOFFER, T. and J. WOLF (1985) "Hypotheses about the causes of the SAT test score decline." Presented at the annual meeting of the American Association for Public Opinion Research, McAfee, NJ.

HOFSTETTER, C., C. ZUKIN, and T. BUSS (1978) "Political imagery and information in an age of television." Journalism Quarterly 55: 562-569.

HYMAN, H., C. WRIGHT, and J. REED (1975) The Enduring Effects of Education. Chicago: University of Chicago Press.

IYENGAR, S., M. PETERS, and D. KINDER (1982) "Experimental demonstrations of the 'not-so-minimal' consequences of television news programs." American Political Science Review 76: 848-858.

JACOBY, J. and W. HOYER (1982) "Viewer miscomprehension of televised communication: selected findings." Journal of Marketing 46: 12-26.

JOHNSTONE, J., E. SLAWSKI, and W. BOWMAN (1976) The News People: A Sociological Portrait of American Journalists and Their Work. Urbana: University of Illinois Press.

KAHNEMAN, D. and A. TVERSKY (1971) "Subjective probability: a judgment of representativeness." Cognitive Psychology 3: 430-454.

KAISER, R. (1984) "What's happened to serious TV." Washington Post (July 15): B1.

KATZ, E. (1957) "The two-step flow of mass communication." Public Opinion Quarterly 21: 61-78.

———(1975) "The mass communication of knowledge," in Getting the Message Across. Paris: UNESCO.

———(1977) Social Research on Broadcasting: Proposals for Further Development. London: BBC.

———and P. LAZARSFELD (1955) Personal Influence. New York: Free Press.

KATZ, E., H. ADONI, and P. PARNESS (1977) "Remembering the news: what the picture adds to recall." Journalism Quarterly 54: 231-239.

KATZ, E., J. BLUMLER, and M. GUREVITCH (1974) "Utilization of mass communication by the individual," in J. Blumler and E. Katz (eds.) The Uses of Mass Communications: Current Perspectives on Gratifications Research. Beverly Hills, CA: Sage.

KATZ, E., M. GUREVITCH, and H. HAAS (1973) "On the use of mass media for important things." American Sociological Review 38: 164-181.

KENNAMER, J. (1983) "A comparison of media use measures: the relationship of four measures of media use to economic knowledge and discussion." Presented at the annual conference of AAPOR, Buck Hill Falls, PA, May.

KINDER, D. and D. SEARS (1985) "Public opinion and political action," in G. Lindzey and E. Aronson (eds.) The Handbook of Social Psychology. New York: Random House.

KINTSCH, W. (1979) "On modeling comprehension." Educational Psychologist 14: 3-14.

KIPPAX, S. and J. MURRAY (1980) "Using the mass media: need gratification and perceived utility." Communication Research 7: 335-360.

KLAPPER, J. (1960) The Effects of Mass Communication. New York: Free Press.

KLEIN, A. (1978) "How telecast's organization affects viewer retention." Journalism Quarterly 55: 231-239.

KRAUS, S. and D. DAVIS (1976) The Effects of Mass Communication on Political Behavior. University Park: Pennsylvania State University Press.

LANG, K. and G. LANG (1968) Politics and Television. New York: Quadrangle.

———(1983) The Battle for Public Opinion: The President, the Press, and the Polls during Watergate. New York: Columbia University Press.

LARSEN, O. and R. HILL (1954) "Mass media and interpersonal communication in the diffusion of a news event." American Sociological Review 19: 426-433.

LASSWELL, H. (1948) "The structure and function of communications in society," in L. Bryson (ed.) Communication of Ideas. New York: Harper & Brothers.

LAZARSFELD, P. and R. MERTON (1948) "Mass communication, popular taste, and organized social action," in L. Bryson (ed.) Communication of Ideas. New York: Harper & Brothers.

LAZARSFELD, P., B. BERELSON, and H. GAUDET (1944) The People's Choice. New York: Duell, Sloan & Pearce.

LEMERT, J. (1970) "News media competition under conditions favorable to newspapers." Journalism Quarterly 47: 272-280.

———(1981) Does Mass Communication Change Public Opinion After All? A New Approach to Effects Analysis. Chicago: Nelson-Hall.

LEONARD, W. (1978) "The history of electronic journalism is now in chapter one." U.S. News & World Report (November 20).

LEVY, M. (1978a) The Audience Experience with Television News. Journalism Monographs 55 (April).

———(1978b) "Television news uses: a cross-national comparison." Journalism Quarterly 53: 334-337.

———and S. WINDAHL (1985) "The concept of audience activity," in K. E. Rosengren et al. (eds.) Media Gratifications Research: Current Perspectives. Beverly Hills, CA: Sage.

LICHTY, L. (1982) "Video vs. print." The Wilson Quarterly 6 (Special Issue).

LIPPMANN, W. (1922) Public Opinion. New York: Harcourt Brace.

LOUNSBURY, J., E. SUNDSTROM, and R. DeVAULT (1979) "Moderating effects of respondent knowledge in public opinion research." Journal of Applied Psychology 64: 558-563.

MacKUEN, M. and S. COOMBS (1981) More than News: Media Power in Public Affairs. Beverly Hills, CA: Sage.

MANHEIM, J. (1976) "Can democracy survive television?" Journal of Communication 26: 84-90.

MANN, T. (1978) Unsafe at Any Margin: Interpreting Congressional Elections. Washington, DC: American Enterprise Institute.

McCLURE, R. and T. PATTERSON (1976) "Print vs. network news." Journal of Communication 26: 23-28.

McCOMBS, M. (1981) "The agenda-setting approach," in D. Nimmo and K. Sanders (eds.) Handbook of Political Communication. Beverly Hills, CA: Sage.

———and D. SHAW (1972) "The agenda-setting function of mass media." Public Opinion Quarterly 36: 176-187.

———(1976) "Structuring the 'unseen environment.'" Journal of Communication 26: 18-22.

McQUAIL, D. (1983) Mass Communication Theory: An Introduction. Beverly Hills, CA: Sage.

McQUAIL, D., J. BLUMLER, and J. BROWN (1972) "The television audience: a revised perspective," in D. McQuail (ed.) Sociology of Mass Communications. Harmondsworth: Penguin.

Modern Media Institute (1983) Making Sense of the News. Modern Media Institute Center Seminar, St. Petersburg, FL.

MOGAVERO, D. (1982) "The American press ombudsman." Journalism Quarterly 59 (Winter): 548-553.

MORELY, D. (1980) The "Nationwide" Audience. London: British Film Institute.

NAGEL, E. (1952) "Wholes, sums and organic unities." Philosophical Studies 3: 17-32.

NEUMAN, W. R. (1976) "Patterns of recall among television viewers." Public Opinion Quarterly 40: 115-123.

NEWCOMB, H. (1984) "On the dialogic aspects of mass communication." Critical Studies in Mass Communication 1: 34-50.

———and P. HIRSCH (1983) "Television as a cultural forum: implications for research." Quarterly Review of Film Studies 8, 2: 45-55.

Newsweek (1980) "Sex and the anchor person." December 15: 65-66.

NIE, N., S. VERBA, and J. PETROCIK (1976) The Changing American Voter. Cambridge, MA: Harvard University Press.

NIMMO, D. and K. SANDERS [eds.] (1981) Handbook of Political Communication. Beverly Hills, CA: Sage.

NISBETT, R. and L. ROSS (1980) Human Inference: Strategies and Shortcomings of Social Judgment. Englewood Cliffs, NJ: Prentice-Hall.

NOELLE-NEUMANN, E. (1974) "The spiral of silence: a theory of public opinion." Journal of Communication 24: 43-51.

NORDENSTRENG, K. (1972) "Policy for news transmission," in D. McQuail (ed.) Sociology of Mass Communications. Harmondsworth: Penguin.

———(1973) "Extension of the senses: an audience point of view," in K. Nordenstreng (ed.) Informational Mass Communication. Helsinki, Finland: Tammi.

NOWAK, K. (1977) "From information gaps to communication potential," in M. Berg et al. (eds.) Current Theories in Scandinavian Mass Communication Research. Grenaa, Denmark: GMT.

ORTONY, A. (1978) "Remembering, understanding, and representation." Cognitive Science 2: 53-69.

PAGE, B., R. SHAPIRO, and G. DEMPSEY (1985) "The mass media do affect policy preferences." Presented at the annual meeting of the American Association for Public Opinion Research, McAffee, NJ.

PAIVIO, A. (1971) Imagery and Verbal Processes. New York: Rinehart & Winston.

PALMGREEN, P., L. WENNER, and J. RAYBURN (1980) "Relations between gratifications sought and obtained: a study of television news." Communication Research 7: 161-192.

PATEMAN, C. (1980) "The civic culture: a philosophical critique," in G. Almond and S. Verba (eds.) The Civic Culture Revisited. Boston: Little, Brown.

PATTERSON, T. (1980) The Mass Media Election: How Americans Choose Their President. New York: Praeger.

———and R. McCLURE (1976) The Unseeing Eye: The Myth of Television Power in National Politics. New York: G. P. Putnam.

PERLOFF, R., E. WARTELLA, and L. BECKER (1982) "Increasing learning from TV news." Journalism Quarterly 59: 83-86.

PETTY, R. and J. CACIOPPO (1981) Attitudes and Persuasion: Classic and Contemporary Approaches. Dubuque, IA: W. C. Brown.

POOL, I. and I. SCHULMAN (1959) "Newsmen's fantasies, audiences and newswriting." Public Opinion Quarterly 23: 145-158.

POWERS, R. (1977a) "Eyewitless news." Columbia Journalism Review 20 (May): 17-23.

———(1977b) The Newscasters. New York: St. Martin's.

QUILLIAN, M. (1968) "Semantic memory," in M. Minsky (ed.) Semantic Information Processing. Cambridge: MIT.

ROBINSON, J. (1967) "World affairs information and mass media exposure." Journalism Quarterly 44: 23-30.

———(1971) "The audience for national TV news programs." Public Opinion Quarterly 35: 403-405.

———(1972a) "Mass communication and information diffusion," in F. Kline and P. Tichenor (eds.) Current Perspectives in Mass Communication Research. Beverly Hills, CA: Sage.

———(1972b) "Toward defining the functions of television," in E. Rubinstein et al. (eds.) Television and Social Behavior, Vol. 4. Washington, DC: Government Printing Office.

———(1974) "Public opinion during the Watergate crisis." Communication Research 1: 391-405.

———(1976) "Interpersonal influences in election campaigns: two-step flow hypotheses." Public Opinion Quarterly 40: 304-319.

———(1977) How Americans Use Time. New York: Praeger.

———(1978) "Daily news habits of the American public." ANPA News Research Report No. 15. Washington, DC: American Newspaper Publishers Association.

———and E. FINK (1984) "Music preferences and information in the American public." Presented at the 79th Annual Meeting of the American Sociological Association, San Antonio, TX.

ROBINSON, J. and P. HIRSCH (1969) "It's the sound that does it." Psychology Today (October): 42-95.

———(1980) "Rock music: political lightning rod and cultural indicator." Lo Spettacolo 30, 4: 275-288.

ROBINSON, J. and R. MEADOW (1982) Polls Apart. Washington, DC: Seven Locks Press.

ROBINSON, J. and H. SAHIN (1984) Audience Comprehension of Television News: Results from Some Exploratory Research. London: BBC Broadcasting Research Department.

ROBINSON, J., H. SAHIN, and D. DAVIS (1982) "Television journalists and their audiences," in J. Ettema and D. Whitney (eds.) Individuals in Mass Media Organizations: Creativity and Constraints. Beverly Hills, CA: Sage.

ROBINSON, M. (1976) "Public affairs television and the growth of political malaise: the case of the 'Selling of the Pentagon.'" American Political Science Review 70: 409-432

———and M. CLANCEY (1984) "Teflon politics." Public Opinion 7: 14-18.

ROBINSON, M. and M. SHEEHAN (1983) Over the Wire and on TV. New York: Russell Sage Foundation.

Roper Organization (1984) Public Perceptions of Television and Other Mass Media. New York: Television Information Office.

————(1985) Public Attitudes Toward Television and Other Media in a Time of Change. New York: Television Information Office.

ROSCHO, B. (1975) Newsmaking. Chicago: University of Chicago Press.

RUBENS, W. (1980) "Some rough notes on news vs. research." New York: NBC Audience Research Department. (mimeo)

RUBIN, R. (1981) Press, Party and Presidency. New York: Norton.

RUBINSTEIN, E., G. COMSTOCK, and J. MURRAY [eds.] (1972) Television and Social Behavior, Vol. 4: Television in Day-to-Day Life. Washington, DC: Government Printing Office.

SAHIN, H. and J. ROBINSON (1980) "Is there light at the end of the flow?" Presented at the World Communications Conference, Philadelphia.

SAHIN, H., D. DAVIS, and J. ROBINSON (1981) "Improving the TV news." Irish Broadcasting Review 11, Summer: 50-55.

SALANT, R. (1980) Memorandum to William Rubens. New York: NBC Audience Research Department. (mimeo)

SALOMON, G. (1979) Interaction of Media, Cognition and Learning. San Francisco: Jossey-Bass.

SCHANK, R. and R. ABELSON (1977) Scripts, Plans, Goals and Understanding: An Inquiry into Human Knowledge Structures. Hillsdale, NJ: Lawrence Erlbaum.

SCHILLER, D. (1981) Objectivity and the News: The Public and the Rise of Commercial Journalism. Philadelphia: University of Pennsylvania Press.

SCHLESINGER, P. (1978) Putting "Reality" Together: BBC News. London: Constable.

SCHUDSON, M. (1978) Discovering the News: A Social History of American Newspapers. New York: Basic Books.

SCHULZ, W. (1976) Die Konstruktion von Realität in den Nachrichtenmedien: Analyse der acktuellen Berichterstattung. Freiburg: Karl Alber.

————(1982) "News structure and people's awareness of political events." Gazette 30: 139-153.

SCHUTZ, A. (1967) The Phenomenology of the Social World. Evanston, IL: Northwestern University Press.

SHANNON, C. and W. WEAVER (1949) The Mathematical Theory of Communication. Urbana: University of Illinois Press.

SHAWCROSS, W. (1984) The Quality of Mercy: Cambodia, Holocaust, and Modern Conscience. New York: Simon & Schuster.

SHIBUTANI, T. (1966) Improvised News: A Sociological Study of Rumor. New York: Bobbs-Merrill.

SHINGI, P., G. KAUR, and R. PRAKASH (1982) "Television and knowledge-gap hypothesis." CMA Monograph No. 82. Ahmedabad, India: Centre for Management in Agriculture, Indian Institute of Management.

SIEBERT, F., T. PETERSON, and W. SCHRAMM (1956) Four Theories of the Press. Urbana: University of Illinois Press.

SMITH, A. (1973) The Shadow in the Cave: A Study of the Relationship between the Broadcaster, His Audience, and the State. London: George Allen & Unwin.

STAUFFER, J., R. FROST, and W. RYBOLT (1978) "Literacy, illiteracy and learning from television news." Communication Research 5: 211-232.

————(1983) "The attention factor in recalling network television news." Journal of Communication 33: 29-37.

STEMPEL, G. III (1973) Effects on Performance of a Cross-Media Monopoly. Journalism Monographs No. 29.

STEVENSON, R. and K. WHITE (1980) "The cumulative audience of network television news." Journalism Quarterly 57: 477-481.

STONE, V. (1969-1970) "Sources of most news: evidence and influence." Journal of Broadcasting 14: 1-4.

TAN, A. and P. VAUGHN (1976) "Mass media exposure, public affairs knowledge, and black militancy." Journalism Quarterly 53: 271-279.

TANNENBAUM, P. (1954) "Effect of serial position on recall of radio news stories." Journalism Quarterly 31: 319-323.

THORNDYKE, P. and B. HAYES-ROTH (1979) "The use of schemata in the acquisition and transfer of knowledge." Cognitive Psychology 11: 82-106.

TICHENOR, P., G. DONOHUE, and C. OLIEN (1970) "Mass media flow and differential growth in knowledge." Public Opinion Quarterly 34: 159-170.

————(1980) Community Conflict and the Press. Beverly Hills, CA: Sage.

Time (1965) "Newscasting: editing for viewers." February 26: 52.

TRENAMAN, J. (1967) Communication and Comprehension. London: Longman.

TROLDAHL, V. and R. VAN DAM (1965) "Face-to-face communication about major topics in the news." Public Opinion Quarterly 29: 626-634.

TUCHMAN, G. (1978) Making news: A Study in the Construction of Reality. New York: Free Press.

TULVING, E. and D. THOMSON (1973) "Encoding specificity and retrieval processes in episodic memory." Psychological Review 80: 353-373.

TUNSTALL, J. (1971) Journalists at Work. London: Constable.

————(1983) The Media in Britain. New York: Columbia University Press.

TURNER, R. and D. PAZ (1984) "The mass media and earthquake warnings: research in southern California." Presented at the 79th Annual Meeting of the American Sociological Association, San Antonio, TX.

TUROW, J. (1983) "Local television: producing soft news." Journal of Communication 33: 111-123.

TVERSKY, A. and D. KAHNEMAN (1973) "Availability: a heuristic for judging frequency and probability." Cognitive Psychology 5: 207-232.

VAN DIJK, T. (1983) "Discourse analysis: its development and application to the structure of news." Journal of Communication 33: 20-43.

WADE, S. and W. SCHRAMM (1969) "The mass media as sources of public affairs, science, and health knowledge." Public Opinion Quarterly 33: 197-209.

WATKINS, W. and E. TULVING (1975) "Episodic memory: when recognition fails." Journal of Experimental Psychology 104: 5-29.

WEISS, W. (1969) "Effects of the mass media of communication," in G. Lindzey and E. Aronson (eds.) The Handbook of Social Psychology, Vol. 5. Reading, MA: Addison-Wesley.

WESTIN, A. (1982) Newswatch: How TV Decides the News. New York: Simon & Schuster.

WICKENS, D. (1970) "Encoding categories of words: an empirical approach to memory." Psychological Review 77: 1-15.

————(1972) "Characteristics of word encoding," in A. Melton and E. Martin (eds.) Coding Processes in Human Memory. New York: John Wiley.

WILLIAMS, R. (1974) Television: Technology and Cultural Form. London: Fontana/ Collins.

WOODALL, W. G. (1984) "Attitude and comprehension processes: some un-examined and re-examined relations." Presented at the annual meeting of the International Communication Association, San Francisco, May.

————D. DAVIS, and H. SAHIN (1983) "From the boob tube to the black box: television news from an information processing perspective." Journal of Broadcasting 27: 1-23.

WRIGHT, C. (1975) Mass Communication: A Sociological Perspective. New York: Random House.

ZUCKER, H. (1978) "The variable nature of news media influence," in B. Ruben (ed.) Communication Yearbook 2. New Brunswick, NJ: Transaction Books.

ZUKIN, C. (1981) "Mass communication and public opinion," in D. Nimmo and K. Sanders (eds.) Handbook of Political Communication. Beverly Hills, CA: Sage.

Index

About the Authors

JOHN P. ROBINSON is Professor of Sociology and Director of the Survey Research Center at the University of Maryland. He is the author of *How Americans Use Time,* and the first author of *Polls Apart* and *Measures of Social Psychological Attitudes.* He has acted as a research coordinator for the U.S. Surgeon General's study of television and social behavior, and as research consultant for the British Broadcasting Corporation. His continuing research interests include the social uses of time, mass media audiences, new communication technologies, popular culture, and social science methodology.

MARK R. LEVY is Associate Professor of Journalism and a Research Associate of the Center for Research in Public Communication at the University of Maryland. Formerly a journalist with NBC News and *Newsweek,* he has written extensively on the news audience, uses and gratifications theory, and home communication technologies. He is the author of *The Audience Experience with Television News* and coeditor of the *Mass Communication Review Yearbook*, Volumes 5 and 6.

DENNIS K. DAVIS is Professor in the Department of Speech Communication at Southern Illinois University, Carbondale. He is coauthor of *The Effects of Mass Communication on Political Behavior* and *Mass Communication and Everyday Life: A Perspective on Theory and Effects.* His current research interests center on experimental studies of news comprehension.

W. GILL WOODALL is Associate Professor of Speech Communication at the University of New Mexico. He has published in major communication journals, including *Communication Monographs* and *Communication Yearbook 6.* His continuing research focuses on information-processing theory, news comprehension, and processes of nonverbal communication.

MICHAEL GUREVITCH is Professor of Journalism and Director of the Center for Research in Public Communication at the University of Maryland. He is coauthor of *The Secularization of Leisure* and *The Challenge of Election Broadcasting,* and coeditor of the *Mass Communication Review Yearbook,* Volumes 5 and 6. His ongoing research interests include media-source relations and media portrayals of public issues.